# Spurgeon's Commentary
## on the Bible

# Spurgeon's Commentary on the Bible

## Compiled by Robert Backhouse

Hodder & Stoughton
LONDON SYDNEY AUCKLAND

Compilation Copyright © 1997 by Robert Backhouse
First published in Great Britain 1997

10 9 8 7 6 5 4 3 2 1

British Library Cataloguing in Publication Data
A record for this book is available from the British Library

ISBN 0 340 67902 6

Printed and bound in Great Britain by
Mackays of Chatham PLC, Chatham, Kent

Hodder and Stoughton Ltd
A Division of Hodder Headline PLC
338 Euston Road
London NW1 3BH

# Contents

# Contents

## Contents

# Introduction

'Charles Haddon Spurgeon (1834–1892), the greatest preacher of his time . . . was in truth a superb theologian of the older reformed sort,' writes J.I. Packer.[1] Spurgeon was instrumental in founding, financing (through the sales of his sermons) and supporting a pastors' college which trained 900 men for the Baptist ministry in his lifetime (and continues to this day as Spurgeon's College); a colportage association which supported 96 full-time workers distributing Christian literature (between 1866 and 1891 they made twelve million visits to families, distributing over a quarter of a million Bibles and portions of Bibles in one year); and an orphanage which looked after 1,600 boys and girls during his lifetime. His wife wrote:

> During the period that these various institutions were growing and flourishing, the Tabernacle Church, the foster-mother of them all, was prospering beyond all precedent. At the time of Mr Spurgeon's home-call, the number of members of the church roll was 5,311. There were 22 mission stations, and 27 Sunday and Ragged Schools, with 612 preachers, and 8,034 scholars. Comparing this great host with the little company of anxious but praying people to whom 'the boy-preacher' delivered his first discourse, in New Park Street Chapel, on that historic morning, in December 1853, one can only say, as he said, times without number, when speaking of the blessing which the Lord had graciously vouchsafed to his ministry – WHAT HATH GOD WROUGHT![2]

## Spurgeon's sermons

This book is a selection of Spurgeon's sermons. They are in the form of complete sermons, outline sermons and what

Spurgeon called 'skeletons'. There are forty-two from the Old Testament and sixty-three from the New Testament. In addition to this there are extracts from Spurgeon's commentary on the Psalms, *The Treasury of David*, featuring nine psalms.

When one reads that shortly after Spurgeon's death there were one hundred million copies of his sermons in circulation, one is inclined to think that this must be an exaggeration until one remembers that during his lifetime 2,241 of his weekly sermons were published individually under the title of *Penny Pulpit*. And also, in each year from 1855 to 1917 a year's worth of sermons were published in book form, sixty-two volumes of his sermons, appearing under the titles of *The New Park Street Pulpit* and *The Metropolitan Tabernacle Pulpit*, which gives a total of more than 3,400.

To make a uniform selection from so many sermons is hardly possible. For example, which of the 268 sermons which Spurgeon published from the book of Isaiah should be included? The Banner of Truth has published a 'Complete Textual Index to C.H. Spurgeon's Sermons' at the back of Spurgeon's *Commenting & Commentaries*.[3]

In addition to drawing on the volumes of Spurgeon's sermons in *The New Park Street Pulpit* and *The Metropolitan Tabernacle Pulpit* series of books, the present selection of sermons has been made with the assistance of selections of sermons which other people have made[4] and especially some of the selections of sermons which Spurgeon made himself.[5]

The extracts from Spurgeon's commentary on the Psalms are not taken from his sermons but from his most famous publication, *The Treasury of David*, which in its original form consists of some 5,000 pages in seven volumes.

## Spurgeon the preacher

Spurgeon was often written off as an ignorant country preacher. It is true that he had no smart degrees from Oxford or Cambridge. In fact, he had no formal theological education. Before he wrote his commentary on the Psalms he went to Dr Williams's library in London and read every commentary on the Psalms which he could lay his hands on. This was in addition to the commentaries on the Psalms he had among the 30,000 volumes in his own personal library.

The present volume was also compiled with the help of many borrowed volumes from Dr Williams's library. On an inside page of one volume, *The New Park Street Pulpit, containing sermons preached and revised by the Rev. C.H. Spurgeon, Minister of the Chapel, during the year 1855*, volume i, I thought I saw a familiar signature as I flicked through the opening pages.[6] I turned back to the opening page and was delighted to find the following inscription, written in blotchy black ink: 'This Volume & fifteen others presented to Dr Williams Library by C.H. Spurgeon with profound gratitude for help recd. from the valuable library. June 1870.'

However, Spurgeon did not parade his learning by padding out his sermons with erudite quotations, but passed on the spiritual truths that God had taught him from his own Bible study. Spurgeon endeavoured to keep his style simple and straightforward so that he could be easily understood by all his readers and listeners.

## Spurgeon and his conversion

Perhaps the best way to understand Spurgeon's passion for preaching is to read of his own conversion story. It explains why Spurgeon believed in the value of preaching, why his preaching always concentrated on explaining the Bible, and why his themes were so focused on the Lord Jesus Christ.

I sometimes think I might have been in darkness and despair until now had it not been for the goodness of God in sending a snowstorm, one Sunday morning, while I was going to a certain place of worship. When I could go no further, I turned down a side street, and came to a little Primitive Methodist Chapel. In that chapel there may have been a dozen or fifteen people. I had heard of the Primitive Methodists, how they sang so loudly that they made people's heads ache; but that did not matter to me. I wanted to know how I might be saved, and if they could tell me that, I did not care how much they made my head ache. The minister did not come that morning; he was snowed up, I suppose. At last, a very thin-looking man, a shoemaker, or tailor, or something of that sort, went up into the pulpit to preach. Now, it is well that preachers should be instructed, but this man was really stupid. He was obliged to stick to his text, for the simple reason that he had little else to say. The text was, 'Look unto me, and be ye saved, all the ends of the earth.'

He did not even pronounced the words rightly, but that did not matter. There was, I thought, a glimpse of hope for me in that text. The preacher began thus: 'My dear friends, this is a very simple text indeed. It says, "Look." Now lookin' don't take a deal of pain. It ain't liftin' your foot or your finger; it is just, "Look." You may be the biggest fool, and yet you can look. A man needn't be worth a thousand a year to be able to look. Anyone can look; even a child can look. But then the text says, "Look unto Me." Ay!' said he, in broad Essex, 'many on ye are lookin' to yourselves, but it's no use lookin' there. You'll never find any comfort in yourselves. Some on ye say, "We must wait for the Spirit's workin'." You have no business with that just now. Look to *Christ*. The text says, "Look unto *Me*."'

Then the good man followed up his text in this way: 'Look unto Me; I am sweatin' great drops of blood. Look unto Me; I am hangin' on the cross. Look unto Me, I am dead and buried. Look unto Me, I am sitting at the Father's right hand. O poor sinner, look unto Me! Look unto Me!'

When he had gone to about that length, and managed to spin out ten minutes or so, he was at the end of his tether. Then he looked at me under the gallery, and I dare say, with so few present, he knew me to be a stranger. Just fixing his eyes on me, as if he knew all my heart, he said, 'Young man, you look very miserable.' Well, I did, but I had not been accustomed to have remarks made from the pulpit on my personal appearance before. However, it was a good blow, and it struck right home. He continued, 'and you always will be miserable – miserable in life and miserable in death – if you don't obey my text; but if you obey now, this moment you will be saved.' Then lifting up his hands, he shouted, as only a Primitive Methodist could do, 'Young man, look to Jesus Christ. Look! Look! Look! You have nothing to do but to look and live.'

I saw at once the way of salvation. I knew not what else he said – I did not take much notice of it – I was so possessed with that one thought. Like as when the brazen serpent was lifted up, the people only looked and were healed, so it was with me. I had been waiting to do fifty things, but when I heard that word, 'Look!' what a charming word it seemed to me! Oh! I looked until I could almost have looked my eyes away. There and then the cloud was gone, the darkness had rolled away, and that moment I saw the sun; and I could have risen that instant, and sung with the most enthusiastic of them, of the precious blood of Christ, and the simple faith which looks alone to Him.

Oh, that somebody had told me this before, 'Trust Christ, and you shall be saved.' Yet it was, no doubt, all wisely ordered, and now I can say –

> Ere since by faith I saw the stream
> Thy flowing wounds supply,
> Redeeming love has been my theme,
> And shall be till I die.[7]

## Spurgeon and opposition

Spurgeon became pastor and village preacher of Waterbeach Baptist Church, Cambridgeshire, the year after his conversion. In 1854, aged nineteen, he moved to south London on being appointed pastor of New Park Street Baptist Church. Seven years later Spurgeon moved with his congregation to a purpose-built church, the Metropolitan Tabernacle.

Spurgeon's popularity – he regularly preached to a seated congregation of 3,600, with a further 2,000 people squeezed in around the building – did not prevent him from being harshly criticised and cruelly mocked. Glimpses of such opposition can be gleaned from the prefaces he wrote to his own collections of sermons. In 1856 he wrote, 'Little can be said in praise of these Sermons, and nothing can be said against them more bitter than has been already spoken. Happily the author has heard abuse exhaust itself; he has seen its vocabulary used up, and its utmost venom entirely spent.'[8]

Then in 1857, commenting on a pressure from a different source, he wrote,

> Our ministry is a testimony that no new theology is needed to stir the masses and save souls; we defy all the Negative Theologians in England to give such proof of their ministry as we can . . . We confess the truth of all that is uttered to our disparagement, for therein we do but magnify the grace of God, who worketh by the least of instruments the greatest acts of his love.[9]

Throughout his thirty-eight-year London ministry Spurgeon was the target of disparaging attacks from daily newspapers and leading churchmen alike.

## Spurgeon and depression

It may be that one reason why many of Spurgeon's sermons have such a warm, comforting, pastoral tone stems from the preacher's own personal experience of depression. Many of Spurgeon's sermons are evangelistic and others are strong on teaching doctrine. But this collection reflects another, and often forgotten, strand: his pastoral preaching. He knew how to preach comfort to the depressed, how to call back the backslidden and reach out to the anxious and frightened. As early as 1850 he records in his personal diary, 'when I become the prey of doubting thoughts . . .'

Spurgeon suffered one of his most serious bouts of depression after the catastrophe at the Music Hall of the Royal Surrey Gardens, where he was preaching to some 12,000 people; several people were trampled to death after others had maliciously started a panic by shouting 'Fire!' He records his own feelings about this tragedy as follows:

> On a night which time will never erase from my memory, large numbers of my congregation were scattered, many of

them wounded and some killed, by the malicious act of wicked men. Strong amid danger, I battled against the storm; nor did my spirit yield to the overwhelming pressure while my courage could reassure the wavering, or confirm the bold; but when, like a whirlwind, the destruction was overpast, when the whole of its devastation was visible to my eye, who can conceive the anguish of my sad spirit? I refused to be comforted; tears were my meat by day, and dreams my terror by night. I felt as I never felt before. My thoughts were all a case of knives, cutting my heart in pieces, until a kind of stupor of grief ministered a mournful medicine to me. I could have truly said, I am not mad, but surely I have had enough to madden me, if I should indulge in meditation on it. I sought and found a solitude which seemed congenial to me. I could tell my griefs to the flowers, and the dews could weep with me. Here my mind lay, like a wreck upon the sand, incapable of its usual motion. I was in a strange land, and a stranger in it. My Bible, once my daily food, was but a hand to lift the sluices of my woe. Prayer yielded no balm to me; in fact, my soul was like an infant's soul, and I could not rise to the dignity of supplication.[10]

## Spurgeon and the Holy Spirit

It is not without justification that Spurgeon became known as 'the prince of preachers'. Today's aspiring preachers would do well to model themselves on Spurgeon's preaching 'technique' as well as his spiritual power. This present collection of sermons and outlines gives ideas on how to preach on famous texts, such as John 3:16, how to preach about Christmas, Good Friday, the Ascension of Jesus, and what to say about the Holy Spirit's work in revival, as well as how to expound massive doctrinal topics such as election, justification, adoption, substitution and the day of atonement. These outlines and sermons are equally valuable as a springboard for personal Bible study. Even to read them in an abbreviated form, a hundred years after they were first delivered, is to be stirred and challenged.

But one thing above everything else was clear to Spurgeon. No work of God could take place through any preaching unless the Holy Spirit was active in the hearts of his hearers, not to mention in the heart of the preacher. As Spurgeon climbed the steps into his raised pulpit he could be heard to pray under his breath, 'I believe in the Holy Spirit. I believe in the Holy Spirit. I believe in the Holy Spirit.' He might have been the most popular preacher in England, but he never forgot that that was pointless unless God's Spirit blessed his every sermon.

On the title page of the first collection of outlines of his sermons, Spurgeon wrote under the printed words *Skeletons – I to LXXVII*, 'and only skeletons without the Holy Ghost'.

Spurgeon had a most disarming habit of praying in the middle of his sermons. He would ask that God's Spirit would make the next point clear in the hearts and minds of his hearers. During one of his last sermons Spurgeon pleaded with his congregation, to whom he had been preaching for thirty-three years, that both they and he should take action should they ever lose their first love of Jesus. Preaching on Revelation 2:4–7, he concluded with words which make a fitting summary of all his preaching: 'As a church we must love Jesus, or else we have lost our reason for existence.'

## Notes

1 C.H. Spurgeon, *Psalms*, volume i (Crossway Books, 1993), introduction pp. xi–xii.
2 *C.H. Spurgeon's Autobiography, compiled from his diary, letters and records*, volume iv, (Passmore & Alabaster, 1900), p. 278.
3 C.H. Spurgeon, *Commenting & Commentaries* (The Banner of Truth Trust, 1969), pp. 201–4.
4 *C.H. Spurgeon's Sermons for Special Occasions*, selected and edited by C.T. Cook, (Marshall, Morgan & Scott, 1958).
5 C.H. Spurgeon, *Messages to the Multitude, being ten representative sermons selected at Mentone, and two unpublished addresses delivered on memorable occasions* (Sampson Low, Marston, 1892).
6 C.H. Spurgeon, *The New Park Street Pulpit*, volume i (Alabaster & Passmore, 1856).
7 *C.H. Spurgeon's Autobiography*, volume i (Passmore & Alabaster), pp. 98–100.

8 C.H. Spurgeon, *The New Park Street Pulpit*, volume i (Alabaster & Passmore, 1856), p. vii.
9 C.H. Spurgeon, *The New Park Street Pulpit*, volume ii (Alabaster & Passmore, 1857), p. iv.
10 *The Autobiography of C.H. Spurgeon* (Hodder & Stoughton, 1993), p. 160.

# OLD TESTAMENT

# Abraham justified by faith

'And he believed in the LORD; and he counted it to him for righteousness' Genesis 15:6

## The fact

'He believed in the LORD.'
Leaving his country. Life in Canaan. Sodom.
Isaac's birth. Promises to him. Isaac's sacrifice.
Two sorts of faith:

(a)  Historical or dead faith
(b)  Living faith, producing deeds

## The result

'He counted it to him for righteousness.'

(a)  Sins forgiven
(b)  Righteousness imputed – by faith
By it, gained God's favour and love, heaven, and eternal life.
These bring:
| | |
|---|---|
| Peace | How easy lies the head that does not ill! |
| Love | When we are pure, we love God |
| Joy | The justified person has true joy |
| Comfort | All things work together for good |
| Security | None can condemn, nor destroy |

## As Abraham was saved, so must we be

(a)  Not by works, or Abraham would have been

(b) Not by ceremonies. Abraham believed before circumcision
(c) Reasons why sinners and Christians should believe God; exhortations to faith

# Omniscience

'Thou God seest me' Genesis 16:13

### Introduction

There are more eyes fixed on man than he is aware of: he sees not as he is seen. He thinks himself unobserved, but let him remember that a cloud of witnesses hold him in full view. Angels are spectators of your labours. But it is nothing that devils watch me, it is nothing that glorified spirits observe me, compared with the overwhelming truth, that you God at all times see me.

### The general doctrine

First comes the general doctrine, that God sees us.

*God's nature* This may be easily proved from God's nature. It would be hard to imagine a God who could not see his own creatures. God Almighty, from his very essence, must be an omniscient God. Strike out the thought that he sees me, and you extinguish deity in a single stroke. There would be no God if that God had no eyes, for a blind God would be no God at all.

*God is everywhere* Further, we are sure that God must see us, for we are taught in the Scriptures that *God is everywhere*, and if God is everywhere, what stops him from seeing all that is done in every part of his universe? God is here. I do not simply live near him, but '*in* him I live, and move, and have my being'. If God is everywhere he must see everything, and therefore it is true that 'Thou God seest me.'

*God's activity* In case anyone should think that God may be in a place, but asleep there, let me remind you that in every place to which you can travel there is, not simply God, but also *God's activity*. Wherever I go I will find, not a slumbering God, but a God busy about the affairs of the world.

*God can see something before it happens* I have one more proof to offer which I think is conclusive. God, we may be sure, sees us, when we remember that *he can see a thing before it happens*. If he sees an event before it happens, surely, reason dictates, he must see a thing that is happening now. Is not God a God of foreknowledge? Can he not see the things that are to come?

## The special doctrine

Now, I come, second, to the special doctrine: 'Thou God seest *me.*'

*God sees you* Take note, God sees *you*. Out of this whole congregation, God sees you, and he sees you *as if there was nobody else in the world for him to look at*. God sees you, with all his eyes, with the whole of his sight – you – you – you – you are the particular object of his attention at this very moment. God's eyes are looking down on you; remember that!

*God sees you entirely* In the next place God sees you *entirely*. He does not merely note your actions, he knows your every thought, every imagination, every thought, yes, every informed imagination. He sees it all, every particle, every atom of it. He knows you behind and before. 'Thou God seest me', you see me entirely.

*God sees you constantly* Note this, God sees you *constantly*. Remember, wherever you are, God sees you. If for Christ's sake I am in prison, one voice will say, 'Fear not; I will help

5

thee.' At all times, in all places, in all your thoughts, in all your acts, in all your privacy, in all your public activities, on every occasion, this is true, 'Thou God seest me.'

*God sees you supremely* Men see me better than I can see myself; but man cannot see me as God sees me. If you were chained, as Paul was, with a soldier at your arm; if he was with you night and day, sleeping with you, rising with you; if he could hear all your thoughts, he could not know you as God knows you, for God sees you superlatively and supremely.

It is said that when you heard the preacher Rowland Hill, if you were stuck in a window, or further away in a doorway, you always had the conviction that he was preaching at you. Try and think, then, 'Thou God seest me.'

## Different inferences

Now I come to different inferences for different people, to serve different purposes.

*The prayerful* First, to the prayerful. Prayerful men, prayerful women, here is consolation – God sees you. And if he can see you, surely he can hear you. Perhaps you cannot say a word when you pray. Never mind; God does not want to hear; he can tell what you mean just by looking at you. 'There,' says the Lord, 'is a child of mine in prayer. He says not a word; but do you see that tear rolling down his cheek? Do you hear that sigh?' Oh, mighty God, you can see both tear and sigh, you can read desire when desire has not clothed itself in words. There is comfort for you, you praying ones, that God sees you. That is enough. If you cannot speak he can see you.

'Oh, mighty God, you can see both tear and sigh, you can read desire when desire has not clothed itself in words.'

*The anxious* I have given a word for the prayerful, now a word for the anxious. Some people here are very full of care and doubts and anxieties and fears. 'Oh, sir,' you say, 'if you could come to my poor house, you would not wonder that I should feel anxious. I have had to part with much of my little furniture to provide myself with living; I am brought very low; I have not a friend in London; I am alone, alone in the wide world.' Stop, stop, sir! You are not alone in the world. There is at least one eye watching over you; there is one hand that is ready to help you. Don't give up in despair. Go on then, hope yet. In night's darkest hour, hope for a brighter tomorrow. God sees you, whatever you are doing.

*The slandered* And now a word to the slandered. There are some of us who come in for a very large share of slander. I am the subject of detraction, but I can point to hundreds of souls that have been saved on earth by my feeble instrumentality, and my reply to my enemies is this, 'You may find fault with the style or manner, but God saves souls.' Go straight on and you will live down your slanderers; and remember when you are most distressed, 'Thou God seest me.'

*The ungodly* Now, a sentence or two to some of you who are ungodly and know not Christ. What shall I say to you but this – how heinous are your sins when they are put in the light of this doctrine! Remember, sinner, whenever you sin, you sin in the teeth of God. It is bad enough to steal in darkness, but imagine a thief stealing in daylight. It is vile, it is fearfully vile to commit a sin which I desire to cover, but to do my sin when man is looking at me shows much hardness of heart. Ah, sinner, remember, you sin with God's eyes looking on you. How awful must be your sin. For you sin in the very face of justice when God's eye is fixed on you.

Lastly, you ask me what you must do to be saved? Paul told the jailer, 'Believe on the Lord Jesus Christ, and thou shalt be saved.' You must believe that Christ died and rose again; that by his death he bore the punishment for all believers; and that by his resurrection he wiped away all the faults of his children. If God gives you faith, you will believe that Christ died for you; and that you will be washed by his blood, and you will trust his mercy and his love to be your everlasting redemption when this world will end.

# Instability

'Unstable as water, thou shalt not excel' Genesis 49:4

## Introduction

Perfect stability has ceased from the world since the day when Adam fell.

## All Christians

First, then, to all Christians, permit me to address myself. Our father, Adam, spoilt us all; and, although the second Adam has renewed us, he has not yet removed from us the infirmities which the first Adam left us as a mournful legacy. None of us are as stable as we should be.

## Christians noted for glaring instability

I believe these people to be true Christians, but they are as unstable as water. They can easily be talked into anything or out of anything. They believe the last person they hear, and are easily led by him. They need to study God's will more and God's Word more. For an unstable Christian will never excel.

## The pretenders

These people are as unstable as water in the worst sense. They pretend to be true Christians. They have been baptised, they receive the Lord's Supper, they attend prayer meetings and other church meetings. As far as the externals of godliness are concerned there is nothing to be desired. But they are hypocrites. They find fault with everything in the church and commit all kinds of wickedness. As Paul wrote, they are 'enemies of the cross of Christ, for their God is their belly, and they glory in their shame'.

### The open sinners

These people make no pretension to religion whatever. I pray the Lord to work in you something that will be stable.

# Joseph attacked by archers

'The archers have sorely grieved him, and shot at him, and hated him; but his bow abode in strength, and the arms of his hands were made strong by the hands of the mighty God of Jacob; (from thence is the shepherd, the stone of Israel)' Genesis 49:23–4

### The cruel attack

   (a)  Joseph had to endure the archers of envy
   (b)  Joseph had to endure the archers of temptation
   (c)  Joseph had to endure the archers of malicious slander

### The shielded warrior

'His bow abode in strength.'

### Joseph's secret strength

'The arms of his hands were made strong by the mighty power of the God of Jacob.'

### The glorious parallel

The glorious parallel drawn between Joseph and Christ – 'from thence is the shepherd, the stone of Israel'.

# The Exodus

'And it came to pass at the end of the four hundred and thirty years, even the selfsame day it came to pass, that all the hosts of the LORD went out from the land of Egypt' Exodus 12:41

## Introduction

It is our firm conviction that the historical books of Scripture were intended to teach us through types and figures spiritual things. We believe that every part of Scripture history is not only a faithful transcript of what did actually happen, but also a shadow of what happens spiritually in the dealings of God with his people.

Egypt is a picture of the house of slavery into which all God's covenant people will, sooner or later, be brought because of their sin. Everyone whom God means to give an inheritance in Canaan is first taken down to Egypt. Taking this as a key, you will see that the deliverance out of Egypt is a beautiful picture of the deliverance of all God's people from the bondage of the law and the slavery of their sins.

## The mode of their going out

*They were forced out by the Egyptians* When the children of Israel went out of Egypt it is a remarkable thing that they were forced out by the Egyptians. Those Egyptians who had enriched themselves with their slavery said, 'Get ye hence, for we be all dead men.' They begged them to go.

Once our sins kept us from Christ, but now every sin drives us to him for pardon. I had not known Christ if I had not known sin; I had not known a deliverer, if I had not smarted under the Egyptians. The Holy Spirit drives us to Christ, just as the Egyptians drove the people out of Egypt.

*They were dressed in their best clothes* Then, the children of Israel went out of Egypt covered with jewels and dressed in their best clothes. On their feast days the Jews always wished to wear jewels and fine clothes. When they were too poor to possess them they borrowed them. So it was at this remarkable Passover. They had been so oppressed that they had kept no festival for many years, but now they were dressed in their best clothes, 'and the Lord gave them favour in the sight of the Egyptians, so that they lent unto them such things as they required. And they spoiled the Egyptians.' Every child of God, when he comes out of Egypt, is dressed in goodly apparel.

*They left in haste* There is one more thought about the way in which they came out. They left in haste. I never met a poor sinner under conviction of sin, who was not *in haste* to get his burden off his back. '*Today* if ye will hear his voice, harden not your heart,' says the Holy Spirit. He never says tomorrow; today is his constant cry, and every true-born Israelite will pant to get out of Egypt, whenever he has the opportunity.

## The magnitude of this deliverance

Did it never strike you what a wonderful exodus of the people of Israel this was? Do you know how many people left? According to the very lowest calculation there must have been two and a half million (see Exodus 12:37), all assembled together in one place, and all coming out of the country at one time. Oh, mighty God, how great is that deliverance which brought out a host of your elect, more numerous than the stars and more numerous than the sand on a thousand shores. All hail to your power that does all this!

*It was only one Passover that set them all free* I would have you, beloved, particularly remember one thing; and that is, that great as this emigration was, and enormous as were the multitudes that left Egypt, *it was only one Passover that set them all free*. They did not want two celebrations of the supper; they did not need two angels to fly through Egypt; it was not necessary to have two deliverances: but all in one night, all by the paschal lamb, all by the Passover supper, they were saved.

> 'One agonising sacrifice, one death on Calvary, one bloody sweat on Gethsemane, one shriek of "It is finished" consummated all the work of redemption.'

One agonising sacrifice, one death on Calvary, one bloody sweat on Gethsemane, one shriek of 'It is finished' consummated all the work of redemption. I love it when I think it saves one sinner; but oh! to think of the multitude of sinners that it saves!

## The completeness of their deliverance

This brings us to speak more fully of the completeness of their deliverance. Our text says, 'It came to pass at the end of the four hundred and thirty years, even the selfsame day it came to pass, that *all the hosts of the LORD* went out from the land of Egypt.' 'For there was not one feeble person in all their tribes' (Psalm 105:37). They all came out.

*They all had their cattle with them* But not only so; they all had their cattle with them. As Moses said, 'Not a hoof shall be left behind.' They were to have all their goods, as well as their persons. What does this teach us? Why, not only that all God's people will be saved, but that all that God's people ever had will be restored.

## The time the Israelites came out of Egypt

This brings us to note, fourth, the time the Israelites came out of Egypt. 'It came to pass at the end of the four hundred and thirty years, even the selfsame day it came to pass, that all the hosts of the LORD went out from the land of Egypt.' God had promised to Abraham that his people would be slaves for four hundred and thirty years, and they were in slavery for not a day more.

## Conclusion

But now, beloved, we must finish in a very solemn manner, by reminding you of the companions who came out of Egypt with the children of Israel (see Exodus 12:38). These were Egyptians. 'Ah,' says someone, 'but I thought if they had been in Egypt, especially if they came out, they must have been Christians.' But note how these people were in Egypt. They were never *in bondage* in Egypt.

O you members of Christian churches! There are many of you who have a feigned experience and a feigned religion. My dear hearers, do test yourselves, to see whether you are true Israelites. If Jesus Christ is not in you, you are reprobates. The Lord bring all his people out of Egypt, and deliver all his children from the house of bondage.


# The war of truth

'And Moses said unto Joshua, Choose us out men and go out, fight with Amalek; to morrow I will stand on the top of the hill with the rod of God in mine hand' Exodus 17:9

## The great warfare

    (a) The war is not with men, but with Satan and error
    (b) It is a righteous warfare
    (c) It is a war of the greatest importance
    (d) The fight is against powerful foes
    (e) The war is of perpetual duration

## The appointed means of warfare

    (a) There must be practical action
    (b) There must be prayer

**Stir up God's people for the warfare**

You are engaged in a hereditary warfare: it has been passed on to you.


# 'Who is on the LORD's side?'


'Then Moses stood in the gate of the camp, and said, Who is on the LORD's side? let him come unto me. And all the sons of Levi gathered themselves together unto him' Exodus 32:26

## Introduction

These idolatrous people seem to have been awestruck by the appearance of Moses in the midst. You can picture them gathered around Aaron, worshipping the golden calf. As soon as Moses marches into the camp the calf is hurled from its pedestal, burnt in the fire, ground to powder and mingled with the water that the idolaters drank. Then rings out the grand challenge of our text, 'Who is on the LORD's side? Let him come unto me.'

## A description of the conflict, to show which is 'the Lord's side'

This is not a very difficult task, and the conscience of each of you ought to help me to accomplish this. This is where 'the LORD's side' begins:

- (a) Belief in God against atheism and other forms of unbelief
- (b) Obedience to God's commands, or a determination to please ourselves
- (c) Christ and his righteousness, or your self-righteousness

(d) The gospel of the grace of God, or the superstitions and falsehoods of men
(e) The battle between Scripture and tradition

## Who the Lord's followers are, and what they must do to show that they are on his side

(a) They must own it
(b) They must rally to the standard
(c) They must be willing to be in a minority
(d) They must be forthright
(e) They must let God master all nature's ties
(f) They must do as they are commanded

## Encouragements which belong to the Lord's followers

(a) It is a cause of right and truth
(b) You are on God's side
(c) Jesus the crucified is with you
(d) All of God's saints are with you

## Enlisting in the Lord's army

(a) You must receive something
(b) Confess Christ openly by being baptised
(c) Submit to the discipline of the principles of the Christian faith
(d) Wear the clothes of holiness
(e) Expect to wage war for King Jesus

# The day of atonement

'This shall be an everlasting statute unto you, to make an atonement for the children of Israel for all their sins once a year' Leviticus 16:34

15

## Introduction

The Jews had many striking ceremonies which marvellously set forth the death of Jesus Christ as the salvation of our souls. One of the chief of these was the day of atonement, which I believe was pre-eminently intended to typify the great day of acceptance of our souls, when Jesus Christ 'died, the just for the unjust, to bring us to God'.

I now invite your attention to the ceremonies of this solemn day, taking the different parts in detail.

## The person who made the atonement

*Aaron, the high priest* At the outset, we note that Aaron, the high priest, did it. 'Thus shall Aaron come into the holy place; with a young bullock for a sin offering, and a ram for a burnt offering.' Inferior priests slaughtered the lambs; other priests at other times did almost all the work of the sanctuary; but on this day nothing was done by anyone, as part of the business of the great day of atonement, except by the high priest. So, beloved, Jesus Christ, the High Priest, and he only, works the atonement.

*A humbled priest* Then it is interesting to note that the high priest on this day was a humbled priest. You read in Leviticus 16:4, 'He shall put on the holy *linen* coat, and he shall have the linen breeches upon his flesh, and shall be girded with a linen girdle, and with the linen mitre shall he be attired: these are holy garments.' On other days he wore what the people were accustomed to call the golden garments. He had the mitre, with a plate of pure gold around his brow, tied with brilliant blue; the splendid breastplate, studded with gems, adorned with pure gold and set with precious stones; the glorious ephod, the tinkling bells, and all the other finery, in which he came before the people as the accepted high priest. But on this day he had none of them.

Jesus Christ, then, when he made atonement, was a humbled priest. He did not make atonement, arrayed in all the glories of his ancient throne in heaven. Upon his brow was no diadem

16

except the crown of thorns; around him was cast no purple robe except the one he wore when he was mocked; he held no sceptre except the reed they thrust in cruel contempt on him.

*A spotless high priest* In the next place, the high priest who offered the atonement must be a spotless high priest. Because there were no such people to be found, since Aaron was a sinner himself as well as the people, you will note that Aaron had to make atonement for his own sin before he could go in to make atonement for the sins of the people. Leviticus 16:3 says, 'Thus shall Aaron come into the holy place: with a young bullock for a sin offering, and a ram for a burnt offering.' These were for himself. Leviticus 16:6 says, 'And Aaron shall offer his bullock of the sin offering, which is for himself, and make an atonement for himself, and for his house.' He was also washed over and over again in the sacred bath, as Leviticus 16:24 shows. It was carefully arranged that Aaron should be a spotless high priest on that day.

> 'He was pure and spotless. Adore and love him, the spotless High Priest, who on the day of atonement took away your guilt.'

Beloved, we have a spotless high priest. He did not need to wash himself or make any atonement for himself, for he, for ever, might have sat down at the right hand of God, and never come on earth at all. He was pure and spotless. Adore and love him, the spotless High Priest, who on the day of atonement took away your guilt.

*A solitary high priest* Note again, the atonement was made by a solitary high priest – alone and unassisted. You read in Leviticus 16:17, 'And there shall be no man in the tabernacle of the congregation when he goeth in to make an atonement in the holy place, until he come out, and have made an atonement for himself, and for his household, and for all the congregation of Israel.' No other man was present, so that the people might be quite certain that everything was done by the high priest alone.

It is remarkable, as Matthew Henry, the eighteenth century Bible commentator, observes, that no disciple died with Christ. None but Jesus, none but Jesus, has wrought out the work of our salvation.

*A laborious high priest* Again, it was a laborious high priest who did the work on that day. It is astonishing how, after comparative rest, he should be so accustomed to his work as to be able to perform all that he had to do on that day. I have tried to count up how many creatures he had to kill, and I find that there were fifteen beasts which had to be slaughtered at different times. He toiled like a common Levite. Just so with our Lord Jesus Christ. Oh, what a labour the atonement was to him! The atonement was made by a labouring high priest that day; and Jesus toiled on that wondrous day of atonement.

## The sacrifice through which the atonement was made

And he shall take of the congregation of the children of Israel two kids of the goats for a sin offering, and one ram for a burnt offering . . . And he shall take the two goats, and present them before the LORD at the door of the tabernacle of the congregation. And Aaron shall cast lots upon the two goats; one lot for the LORD, and the other lot for the scapegoat. And Aaron shall bring the goat upon which the LORD's lot fell, and offer him for a sin offering. But the goat, on which the lot fell to be the scapegoat, shall be presented alive before the LORD, to make an atonement with him, and to let him go for a scapegoat into the wilderness. (Leviticus 16:7–10)

The first goat is the great type of Jesus Christ the atonement, which is not the case with the scapegoat. The first is the type by means of which the atonement was made, and we shall stay with this first one.

*A perfect, unblemished goat of the first year* Note that this goat must be a perfect, unblemished goat of the first year. In the same way our Lord was a perfect man, in the prime of his manhood.

*It was taken from the congregation of the children of Israel* This goat was an eminent type of Christ from the fact that it was taken from the congregation of the children of Israel. The public treasury paid for the goat. So, beloved, Jesus Christ was bought by the public treasury of the Jewish people before he died. Thirty pieces of silver they valued him at. His own led him forth to slaughter.

*God's decision* Note, again, that though this goat, like the scapegoat, was brought by the people, God's decision was in it still. Note, it is said, 'Aaron shall cast lots upon the two goats; one lot for the LORD, and the other lot for the scapegoat.' This mention of the lots teaches us that although the Jews bought Jesus Christ through their own will to die, yet Christ had been appointed to die. Christ's death was fore-ordained, and there was not only man's hand in it, but God's. 'The lot is cast into the lap, but the whole disposing thereof is of the LORD' (Proverbs 16:33).

*See it die* Next, observe the goat that destiny has marked out to make the atonement. Come and see it die. As the blood of the goat made the atonement typically, so, Christian, your Saviour dying for you made the great atonement for your sins, that you may go free.

## The results of the atonement

*The sanctification of the holy things which had been made unholy* One of the first effects of the death of this goat was the sanctification of the holy things which had been made unholy. 'Then shall he . . . sprinkle it upon the mercy seat . . . and he shall make an atonement for the holy place, because of the uncleanness of the children of Israel, and because of their transgressions in all their sins: and so shall he do for the tabernacle of the congregation, that remaineth among them in the midst of their uncleanness' (Leviticus 16:15–16).

The holy place was made unholy by the people. Where God dwelt should be holy. The goat's blood made the unholy place holy. Our holy service here today has been sprinkled by the blood of the great Jesus, and as such it will be accepted through him.

*Their sins were taken away* Observe the second great fact: their sins were taken away. This was set forth by the scapegoat.

And when he hath made an end of reconciling the holy place, and the tabernacle of the congregation, and the altar, he shall bring the live goat: And Aaron shall lay both his hands upon the head of the live goat, and confess over him all the iniquities of the children of Israel, and all their transgressions in all their sins, putting them upon the head of the goat, and shall send him away by the hand of a fit man into the wilderness: And the goat shall bear upon him all their iniquities unto a land not inhabited: and he shall let go the goat in the wilderness. (Leviticus 16:20–22)

'By the death of Christ there was full, free, perfect remission for all those whose sins are laid upon his head.'

When this was done the great and wonderful atonement was finished, and its effects were displayed to the people. But note, this goat did not sacrificially make the atonement; it was a type of the sins going away, and so it was a type of the atonement, for, you know, since our sins are thereby lost it is the fruit of the atonement; but the sacrifice is the means of making it. So we have this great and glorious thought before us, that by the death of Christ there was full, free, perfect remission for all those whose sins are laid upon his head. Note that on this day all sins were laid on the scapegoat's head – sins of presumption, sins of ignorance, sins of uncleanness, sins little and sins great, sins few and sins many, sins against the law, sins against morality, sins against ceremonies, sins of all kinds were taken away on that great day of atonement.

## Our response to the atonement

Now we note what our correct response should be to the day of atonement.

*Afflict your souls* 'And this shall be a statute for ever unto you: that in the seventh month, on the tenth day of the month, ye shall *afflict your souls*' (Leviticus 16:29). That is the one thing that we ought to do when we remember the atonement. Sure, sinner, there is nothing that should move you to repentance like the thought of that great sacrifice of Christ which is necessary to wash away your guilt. Drops of grief ought to flow. 'Afflict your souls', children of Israel, for the day of atonement has come. Weep o'er your Jesus; weep for him who died; weep for him who was murdered by your sins, and 'afflict your souls'.

# Lifting up the bronze snake

'And Moses made a serpent of brass, and put it upon a pole, and it came to pass, that if a serpent had bitten any man, when he beheld the serpent of brass, he lived' Numbers 21:9

## Introduction

In John's gospel we read the joyful words, 'As Moses lifted up the serpent in the wilderness, even so must the Son of man be lifted up: that whosoever believeth in him should not perish, but have eternal life' (John 3:14–15). We are going to speak about this act of Moses this morning, that we may all of us behold him of whom the bronze snake was a notable type; and may find the promise true, 'every one that is bitten, when he looketh upon the serpent of brass, shall live'.

### The person in mortal peril

Consider the person in mortal peril, for whom the bronze snake was made and lifted up. Our text says, 'It came to pass, that if a serpent had bitten any man, when he beheld the serpent of brass, he lived.'

*They had despised God's way and God's bread* Notice that these venomous snakes first of all came among the people because they spoke against the Lord and against Moses. They also complained about God's food.

*They had been actually bitten by the snakes* Observe carefully for whom the bronze snake was specially lifted up, they that had been actually bitten by the snakes. The Lord sent venomous snakes among them; but it was not the snakes being *among* them that involved the lifting up of the bronze snake; it was the snakes having actually poisoned them which led to the provision of the remedy. 'It shall come to pass, that *every one that is bitten*, when he looketh upon it, shall live.' The only people who did look and derive benefit from the wonderful cure lifted up in the middle of the camp were those who had been bitten by the snakes.

'God's medicine is for the sick, and his healing is for the diseased. The grace of God, through the atonement of our Lord Jesus Christ, is for men who are actually and really guilty.'

The common belief is that salvation is for good people, salvation is for those who fight against temptation, salvation is for the spiritually healthy; but how different is God's Word! God's medicine is for the sick, and his healing is for the diseased. The grace of God, through the atonement of our Lord Jesus Christ, is for men who are actually and really guilty.

*The bite of the snake was fatal* 'Much people of Israel died.'

*The promise had no qualifying clause* 'It came to pass, that if a serpent had bitten *any man*, when he beheld the serpent of brass, he lived.'

## The remedy provided for him

This was as singular as it was effective.

    (a) It was purely of divine origin
    (b) The remedy was exceedingly instructive
    (c) There was only one remedy
    (d) The healing snake was bright and shining
    (e) The remedy was an enduring one

## The application of the remedy

It was personal.

## The cure effected

    (a) He was healed at once
    (b) This remedy healed again and again
    (c) This cure was of universal efficacy to all who used it

## A lesson for those who love their Lord

We must preach him, teach him, and make him visible to all.

# Confession of sin – a sermon with seven texts

My sermon this morning will have seven texts, and yet I pledge myself that there will be but three different words in all of them, for it so happens that the seven texts are all alike,

occurring in seven different parts of God's holy Word. I shall
need to use them all as they illustrate different cases.

### The hardened sinner

Pharaoh: 'I have sinned' Exodus 9:27.

### The double-minded man

Balaam: 'I have sinned' Numbers 22:34.

### The insincere man

Saul: 'I have sinned' 1 Samuel 15:24.

### The doubtful penitent

Achan: 'I have sinned' Joshua 7:20.

### The repentance of despair

Judas: 'I have sinned' Matthew 27:4.

### The repentance of the saint

Job: 'I have sinned' Job 7:20.

### The blessed confession

The Prodigal: 'I have sinned' Luke 15:18.

# Canaan on earth

'For the land, whither thou goest in to possess it, is not as the
land of Egypt, from whence ye came out, where thou sowedst

thy seed, and wateredst it with thy foot, as a garden of herbs: but the land whither ye go to possess it, is a land of hills and valleys, and drinketh water of the rain of heaven: a land which the LORD thy God careth for: the eyes of the LORD thy God are always upon it, from the beginning of the year, even unto the end of the year' Deuteronomy 11:10–12

## Introduction

The journey through the desert is typical of that state of hoping, and fearing, and doubting, and wavering, and inconstancy, and distrust, which we usually experience between the period when we come out of Egypt and that time when we attain full assurance of faith. Many of you, my dear hearers, have come out of Egypt, but you are still wandering about in the wilderness. Though you have eaten of Jesus you have not so believed in him as to have entered into the Canaan of rest.

## The difference between the Christian's temporal condition and that of the worldly Egyptian

*The worldly person looks to secondary causes* The worldly person only looks to the water that flows from the river of this world. The Christian looks to heaven, from where he receives mercy.

*The worldly person toils* A worldly man, just like the Israelites in Egypt, has to water his land 'with his foot', which involved great effort. 'But,' says Moses, 'the land to which you are going is not a land which you will have to water with your foot. The water will come spontaneously; the land will be watered by the rain of heaven. You can sit in your own houses, or under your own vine, or your own fig tree, and God himself will be your irrigator.'

Here is the difference between the godly and the ungodly. The ungodly person toils and strives. The Christian rests content in the God who 'giveth his beloved sleep'.

*The worldly person does not understand the universality of God's*

25

*providence* In Egypt the land is nearly all flat. 'But,' says Moses, 'the land, whither ye go to possess it, is a land of hills and valleys.' Give the worldly Egyptian everything just as he likes it (flat land, easy to irrigate) and he can cope; but let him lose a friend (put a hill in his way), and he cannot water that. But the Christian lives in 'a land of hills and valleys', a land of sorrow as well as joys, but the hills drink the water, as well as the valleys.

## The special privilege given to those who have entered into Canaan

'The eyes of the Lord thy God are always upon it, from the beginning of the year even unto the end of the year.'

- (a) The eyes of the Lord are always upon you
- (b) The eyes of the Lord are upon us as a Church

# Honour for honour

'Them that honour me I will honour, and they that despise me shall be lightly esteemed' 1 Samuel 2:30

## Introduction

If we honour God, he will honour us; and if we despise him, we shall be lightly esteemed ourselves.

## Here is a plain duty – to honour God

- (a) By confessing his deity in all our prayers and praises, and, indeed, at all times
- (b) By confessing the dominion of God
- (c) By confessing sin, and so glorifying his justice
- (d) By submitting to his teaching

(e) When we have not any particular trouble, we ought to honour God by great joy

## Here is a very gracious reward

'Them that honour me I will honour.'

(a) This is true in the Church of God
(b) This is true in our own families
(c) This is true in society around us
(d) This is true throughout the world
(e) God honours those who honour him in their own consciences

## Conclusion

We never know, any of us, how much God is honouring us.

# The sound in the mulberry trees

'When thou hearest the sound of a going in the tops of the mulberry trees, that then thou shalt bestir thyself: for then shall the LORD go out before thee, to smite the host of the Philistines' 2 Samuel 5:24

## Introduction

David was not to go into battle until he heard the sound of a rustling in the tops of the mulberry trees. There was a calm, perhaps; and God's order to David was, 'Do not start fighting until you hear rustling through the tops of the mulberry trees.' There are certain signs which are indications to us about certain duties.

## Special duties

There are special duties, which are not everybody's duties, but are duties for just some people. I confine myself to one special duty, the office of the ministry. I do not believe that it is the business of every one of us to preach.

*'How do I know whether I am called to preach?'* Can you pray? Are you called by God's Spirit to preach? Do not preach if you are uncalled and unsent.

## Duties which belong to all Christians

There are certain duties which belong to all Christians which are to be practised at special times.

*The Christian Church at large* The whole of the Christian Church should always be seeking the divine unction of the Holy One to rest on their hearts. But there are times when God seems to favour Zion, when there are great movements made in the Church, when revivals start, when men are raised up whom God blesses; that ought to be to you like 'the sound of a going in the tops of the mulberry trees'. Then we ought to be doubly prayerful.

*Any particular congregation* Each congregation can ask itself, 'Have we not been too dilatory, too neglectful in not availing ourselves of favourable times and seasons, when the power of the Spirit has been in our midst?'

*Every individual* Keep this same idea in view with regard to every individual you meet with.

*With your own children* There are certain times in the lives of my own beloved children, when they seem more open than at other times. I beseech you never to lose the opportunity.

*With regard to yourself* There are times, you know, 'when thou hearest the sound of a going in the tops of the mulberry trees'.

You have a peculiar power in prayer; the Spirit of God gives you joy and gladness; the Scripture is open to you; walk in the light of God's countenance.

# The plea of faith

'Do as thou hast said' 2 Samuel 7:25

### How important it is to know what God has said

   (a) The errors of this present age stem from not reading the Bible
   (b) Bigotry and uncharitableness stem from not reading the Bible

### All that faith needs to build on is what God has said

The only solid foothold that faith has is 'It is written, God has said it.'

   (a) Do not build on what other people have said
   (b) Do not build on your own dreams

### Faith is a very bold thing

Faith is quite right in appealing to God to do as he has said.

### Conclusion

What has God said to you? There is always some special promise God has made to you.

# Prayer found in the heart

'Therefore hath thy servant found in his heart to pray this prayer unto thee' 2 Samuel 7:27

## How did David come by this prayer?

He tells us that he found it in his heart: 'Thy servant hath found in his heart to pray this prayer unto thee.'

(a) He looked for it in his heart
(b) The best place in which to find a prayer is to find it in your heart
(c) David's heart had been renewed by divine grace
(d) David's heart was a believing heart
(e) David's heart was a serious heart
(f) David's heart was a humble heart

## How did David's prayer come to be in his heart?

Because the Lord put it there.

## How does God put prayers into a man's heart?

(a) By inclining us to pray
(b) By encouragement
  You notice that my text begins with 'Therefore'. What does David mean by that 'therefore'? Why, God had promised to do great things for him. The Lord greatly encourages the needy soul to pray.
(c) By a sense of God's general goodness

## What must you and I do to find prayers in our hearts?

(a) Be renewed by grace
(b) Live near to God
(c) Read and study the Scriptures

# David's dying song

'Although my house be not so with God; yet he hath made with me an everlasting covenant, ordered in all things, and sure: for this is all my salvation, and all my desire, although he make it not to grow' 2 Samuel 23:5

## Introduction

'These be the last words of David' 2 Samuel 23:1.

## David had sorrow in his house

'Although my house be not so with God.'

I think that the principal meaning here is to David's family – especially his children. David had many trials with his children.

It is necessary that you have an 'although' in your lot.

Prayer can remove your troubles.

## David had confidence in the covenant

'Yet he hath made with me an everlasting covenant.'

(a) In its divine origin
(b) In its particular application
    'He hath made with me . . .'
(c) In its everlasting duration
(d) It is an orderly covenant
(e) It is a certain covenant

## The Psalmist's satisfaction in his heart

'This is all my salvation, and all my desire.'

(a) He is satisfied with his salvation
(b) He has all he can desire

# Elijah's appeal to the undecided

'How long halt ye between two opinions? If the LORD be God, follow him: if Baal, then follow him' 1 Kings 18:21

## Introduction

It was a day to be remembered, when the multitudes of Israel were assembled at the foot of Carmel, and when the solitary prophet of the Lord came to defy the four hundred and fifty priests of the false god. We have on that hill of Carmel and along the plain three types of people. First, the devoted servant of Jehovah, a solitary prophet; second, the definite servants of the evil one, the four hundred and fifty prophets of Baal; and third, those who had not made up their minds about worshipping Jehovah.

Now, we have these three categories of people here this morning. We have, I hope, a very large number who are on Jehovah's side, who fear God and serve him. We also have a number who are on the side of the evil one, who make no profession of religion because they are both inwardly and outwardly servants of the evil one. But the great majority of my hearers belong to the third category – the waverers.

## The distinction

The prophet insisted upon the distinction which existed between the worship of Baal and the worship of Jehovah. Most of the people who were brought before Elijah thought that Jehovah was God and that Baal was god too; and for this reason the worship of both was quite consistent.

'No,' said the prophet when he began, 'this will not do, these are two opinions; you can never make them one, they are two contradictory things which cannot be combined.' He would not allow any of his hearers to worship both. 'No,' said he, 'these are two opinions, and you are halting between the two.'

## Called to account

The prophet calls these waverers to an account for the amount of time which they had taken in making their choice. Some of them might have replied, 'We have not yet had the opportunity of judging between God and Baal, we have not yet had enough time to make up our minds.' But the prophet rejects this objection, saying, '*How long* halt ye between two opinions? How long? For three and a half years not a drop of rain has fallen, at Jehovah's command. Is that not proof enough? *How long*, then, halt ye between two opinions?'

I am speaking here not to the thoroughly worldly, but to those who are seeking to serve God and to serve Satan.

## An absurd position

The prophet charges these people with the absurdity of their position. 'What,' they reply, 'may we not continue to halt between two opinions? We are not desperately irreligious, so we are better than the profane; certainly we are not thoroughly pious, but isn't a little piety better than none?'

'How long halt ye between two opinions?
How long limp ye between two opinions?
How long wriggle ye between two opinions?
How long hop ye between two branches?'

'Now,' replies the prophet, 'how long halt ye?' Or, if you will allow the translation, 'How long *limp* ye between two opinions?' ('How long *wriggle* ye between two opinions?' would be a good word if I may use it.) The prophet says they are like a man whose legs are entirely out of joint; he first goes on one side, and then on the other, and cannot go far either way. The prophet laughs at them, as it were.

Another way to translate the Hebrew is: 'How long *hop* ye between two branches?' They are like birds which are perpetually flying from one branch to another. If a bird keeps on doing this it will never have a nest. And so with you; you keep leaping between two branches, from one opinion to another;

and so between the two you get no rest for the sole of your foot, no peace, no joy, no comfort, but are just a poor miserable thing all your life long.

## How do you know we do not believe that Jehovah is God?

The multitude who had worshipped Jehovah and Baal, and who were now undecided, might reply, 'How do you know that we have not made up our minds?' The prophet meets this objection by saying, 'I know because you are not decided in practice. If God be God, follow him; if Baal, follow him. You are not decided in practice.'

## How long halt ye?

And now I make my appeal to the halters and waverers, with some questions, which I pray the Lord to apply. Now I will put this question to them: 'How long halt ye?' You will never decide for God through the strength of your own will.

# The sin of unbelief

'And that lord answered the man of God, and said, Now, behold, if the LORD should make windows in heaven, might such a thing be? And he said, Behold, thou shalt see it with thine eyes, but shalt not eat thereof' 2 Kings 7:19

## Introduction

One wise man may deliver a whole city.

## Man's sin

His sin was unbelief. He doubted God's promise.

(a) Unbelief is the parent of every other iniquity
(b) Unbelief not only begets but fosters sin
(c) Unbelief disables a man for the performance of any good work
(d) Unbelief has been severely punished
(e) Unbelief is the damning sin

**Man's punishment**

'Thou shalt see it with thine eyes, but shalt not eat thereof.' People who have no faith come and listen to sermons, and see, and see, and see, but never eat.

# Manasseh

'Then Manasseh knew that the LORD he was God' 2 Chronicles 33:13

**Introduction**

Manasseh 'shed innocent blood very much' but also, at the eleventh hour, was forgiven and pardoned.

**Manasseh as a sinner**

(a) He sinned against great light, against a pious education and early training
(b) He was a very bold sinner
(c) He had power to lead others

**Manasseh as an unbeliever**

He believed in false gods, but he did not believe in the truth.

(a) Because of his unlimited power

(b) Because he was proud
(c) Because he loved sin too much

## Manasseh as a convert

What were the bases of Manasseh's faith?

(a) He had his prayer answered
(b) He had a sense of pardoned sin

# The death of a Christian

'Thou shalt come to thy grave in a full age, like as a shock of corn cometh in in his season' Job 5:26

## Introduction

We do not believe all that Job's friends said. They often spoke as uninspired men. But they also uttered many holy and pious sentences, which are well worth noting.

We shall consider the death of Christians in general; not of the aged Christian only, for we shall show that while this text does seem to bear upon the aged Christian, in reality it speaks with a loud voice to every believer.

## Death is inevitable

The text says, 'Thou *shalt* come.'

## Death is acceptable

The text does not read, 'I will make thee *go* to the grave', but, 'thou shalt *come* there'.

The old Bible commentator Caryl remarks on this verse: 'A willingness and cheerfulness to die. Thou shalt *come*, thou shalt not be dragged or hurried to thy grave, as it is said of the foolish rich man (Luke 12), "This night shall thy soul be taken from thee." But thou shalt come to thy grave, thou shalt die quietly and smilingly, as it were; thou shalt go to thy grave, as it were upon thine own feet.'

'The long-wished-for time has come at last, in which I shall see that glory in another manner than I have ever done, or was capable of doing in this world' (Dr Owen).

'I am ready to die – Lord, forsake me not now, my strength faileth; but grant me mercy for the merits of my Lord Jesus. And now Lord, receive my soul' (George Herbert).

'I am almost in eternity. I long to be there. My work is done. I have done with all my friends. All the world is now nothing to me. Oh, to be in heaven, to praise and glorify God with his holy angels' (Brainerd, missionary among American Indians).

> 'I am almost in eternity. I long to be there. My work is done. Oh, to be in heaven, to praise and glorify God with his holy angels.'

## Death is always timely

'Thou shalt come to thy grave in a full age.'

'Ah!' says someone, 'that is not true. Good people do not live longer than others. The most pious man may die in the prime of his youth.' But look at my text. It does not say, thou shalt come to thy grave in old age – but in 'a full age'. Well, who knows what 'a full age' is? 'A full age' is whenever God likes to take his children home.

(a) A Christian never dies too soon

(b) A Christian never dies too late

## The death of a Christian is always honourable

The promise declares to him, 'Thou shalt come to thy grave in a full age, like as a shock of corn cometh in his season.'

I think there are two funerals for every Christian. One, the funeral of the *body*; and the other, the *soul*. Funeral, did I say, of the soul? No, I meant not so; I meant not so; it is a marriage of the soul; for as soon as it leaves the body the angel reapers stand ready to carry it away.

# Job's sure knowledge

'For I know that my redeemer liveth' Job 19:25

## Introduction

I daresay you know that there are a great many difficulties about the translation of this passage. It is a very complicated piece of Hebrew, partly, I suppose, owing to its great antiquity, being found in what is probably one of the oldest books of the Bible. I am quite satisfied with the translation given in our Authorised Version; yet it has occurred to me that, possibly, Job himself may not have known the full meaning of all that he said.

Imagine the patriarch driven into a corner, badgered by his so-called friends, charged by them with all manner of evils until he is quite boiling over with indignation, and at the same time smarting under terrible bodily diseases and the dreadful losses which he has sustained; at last, he bursts out with this exclamation, 'I shall be vindicated one day; I am sure I shall. I know that my Vindicator liveth. I am sure that there is One who will vindicate me; and if he never clears my name and reputation as long as I live, it will be done afterwards. There must be a just God, in heaven, who will see me righted; and even though worms devour my body until the last relic of it has passed away, I do verily believe that, somehow, in the far-off ages, I shall be vindicated.'

## Job had a true Friend amid his mistaken friends

These men were miserable comforters, but Job had a real

Comforter; they were estranged from him, but he had a true Friend left; so he said, 'I know that my *goel* liveth.' This is the Hebrew word. It means the person's nearest relative, who was bound to take up his cause. If a person fell into debt, and was sold into slavery because of the debt, his *goel*, if he was able, had to redeem him; and hence we get the word 'redeemer'.

*Job had One whom he called his Kinsman* 'I know,' he said, 'that my Kinsman liveth.' We interpret that word 'Kinsman' as meaning our Lord Jesus Christ. I want you to think of Jesus Christ as your Kinsman.

- (a) Christ's kinship with his people brings great comfort because it is voluntary
- (b) This is a kinship of which Jesus is never ashamed
- (c) Your Kinsman will always be your Kinsman

*Job's Kinsman would become his Vindicator* There was a second meaning to the word *goel*, arising out of the first. Job's Kinsman would become his Vindicator. It was the kinsman's duty to defend the rights of his needy relative, so Job intended to say here, 'I know that my Vindicator liveth.' The Lord Jesus Christ is the Vindicator of his people from all false charges. He is also our Vindicator from all true charges, and our Vindicator from all the accusations of Satan.

*'I know that my redeemer liveth'* The third meaning of the word *goel* is certainly 'redeemer'. Let us think how the Lord Jesus Christ has redeemed us from bondage. There are two redemptions – redemption by price and redemption by power, and both of these Christ has wrought for us. By price is through his sacrifice on the cross of Calvary; and by power is through his divine Spirit coming into our heart, and renewing our soul.

## Job had real possession in the middle of absolute poverty

Job had lost everything – every stick and stone that he possessed. He had lost his children, and he had lost his

39

wife, too, for all practical purposes, for she had not acted like a wife to him in his time of trial. Poor Job, he had lost everything else, but he had not lost his Redeemer. He did not merely rejoice in Christ as *the* Redeemer, or *your* Redeemer, but as *'my* Redeemer'. Luther used to say that the marrow of the gospel is found in the pronouns, and I believe it is: *'my* Redeemer'. Job had something real and valuable left even when he had lost all his property.

### Job had a living Kinsman in the middle of a dying family

'I know that my redeemer *liveth.*'

### Job had absolute certainty in the middle of uncertain affairs

He said, 'I *know* that my redeemer liveth.' If Christ is your only hope, and you cling to him like a limpet clings to the rock, then all is right with you for ever, and you may know that he is your Redeemer as surely as Job knew that he was his. The Lord bless you, for Jesus' sake! Amen.

# Comfort for the discouraged

'Oh that I were as in months past' Job 29:2

### Introduction

For the most part the gracious Shepherd leads his people beside the still waters, and makes them to lie down in green pastures; but at times they wander through a wilderness, where there is no water, and they find no city to dwell in. Hungry and thirsty, their soul faints within them, and they cry unto the Lord in their trouble.

## A complaint

How many Christians look on the past with pleasure, on the future with dread, and on the present with sorrow! They cry out, 'Oh that I were as in months past!' Let us take distinct cases, one by one.

(a) The man who has lost the brightness of his evidence
(b) The man who does not enjoy perpetual peace of mind about other matters
(c) The man who has lost his enjoyment in the house of God and the means of grace
(d) The man whose conscience is not as tender as it used to be
(e) The man who does not have as much zeal for the glory of God and the salvation of men as he used to

## Its cause and cure

(a) Defect in prayer
(b) The fault of your minister
(c) Rarely eating spiritual food
(d) Idolatry
   Many have given their hearts to something other than God, and have set their affections on the things of earth, instead of the things in heaven.
(e) Self-confidence and self-righteousness

## An exhortation

(a) Of consolation
   Sing to the Lord, cry to the Lord, and he will deliver you from your iron cage.
(b) Be discontent with a moderation in religion

'To be moderately religious is to be irreligious.'

(c) To the indifferent
   Remember how far you have fallen.

# Indwelling sin

'Then Job answered the LORD, and said, Behold, I am vile'
Job 40:3-4

## Introduction

Surely, if any man had a right to say, 'I am *not* vile', it was Job;
for, according to the testimony of God himself, he was 'perfect
and upright, and one that feared God and eschewed evil'. Yet
we find even this eminent saint, when by his nearness to God
he had received light enough to discover his own condition,
exclaiming, 'Behold, I am vile.'

## Even the righteous have in them evil natures

It will be my business this morning to say something of that
evil nature which still abides in the righteous. *Job* said,
'Behold, I am vile.' He did not always know it. All through
the long controversy he had declared himself to be just and
upright. He said, 'My righteousness I will hold fast.' But when
God came to plead with him he put his finger on his lips and
would not answer God, but simply said, 'Behold, I am vile.'

> 'You will have found that in your best and happiest
> moments sin still dwells in you; that when you would
> serve God best, sin frequently works in you most
> furiously.'

I hardly need to demonstrate this to you, beloved. For all of
you, I am sure, who know anything about the experience of a
living child of God have found that in your best and happiest
moments sin still dwells in you; that when you would serve
God best, sin frequently works in you most furiously.

The best of men still have sin remaining in them.

## What does indwelling sin do?

*Indwelling sin exerts a checking power upon every good deed*

*Indwelling sin attacks us* Paul says, 'O, wretched man that I am, who shall deliver me from the body of this death?' (Romans 7:24). Now this proves that he was not attacking his sin, but his sin was attacking him.

*This sin reigns within us* The evil heart which still remains in the Christian, does always, when it is not obstructing or attacking, still reign and dwell within him. My heart is just as bad when no evil emanates from it as when it is completely vile. A volcano is ever a volcano; even when it sleeps, trust it not.

'A volcano is ever a volcano; even when it sleeps, trust it not.'

## The danger we are under from such evil hearts

Few people think what a solemn thing it is to be a Christian. Did you never think how great is the danger to which a Christian is exposed, from his indwelling sin?

(a) Sin is within us
    Sin is within us, and so has great power over us.
(b) Remember how many supporters your evil nature has
(c) Your evil nature is very powerful

## The discovery of our corruption

Job said, 'Behold, I am vile.' That word 'behold' implies that he was astonished. The discovery was unexpected.

'I believe we generally find out most of our failings when we have the greatest access to God.'

### How should we act?

(a)  It is wrong to suppose that all your work is done
(b)  You should be very watchful
(c)  You should still exhibit faith in God


# The Treasury of David


## Psalm 1

### Verse 1

'Blessed': See how the book of Psalms opens with a benediction. The word translated 'blessed' is plural, and it is a controverted matter whether it is an adjective or a substantive. Hence we may learn the multiplicity of the blessings which will rest on those whom God has justified, and the perfection and greatness of the blessedness they will enjoy. We might read it, 'Oh, the blessednesses!' and we may well regard it as a joyful acclamation of the gracious man's felicity. May the like benediction rest on us!

The gracious man is described both negatively (verse 1) and positively (verse 2). He is 'the man that walketh not in the counsel of the ungodly'. He takes wiser counsel, and walks in the commandments of the Lord his God. To him the ways of piety are paths of peace and pleasantness. His footsteps are ordered by the Word of God, and not by the cunning and wicked devices of carnal men. It is a rich sign of inward grace when the outward walk is changed, and when ungodliness is put far from our actions.

'Nor standeth in the way of sinners.' His company is of a choicer sort than it was. Although a sinner himself, he is now a blood-washed sinner, quickened by the Holy Spirit and renewed in heart. Standing by the rich grace of God in the congregation of the righteous, he dares not herd with the multitude who do evil.

'Nor sitteth in the seat of the scornful.' He finds no rest in the atheist's scoffings. Let others make a mock of sin, or eternity, of hell and heaven and of the Eternal God; this man has learned better philosophy than that of the infidel, and has too much sense of God's presence to endure to hear his name blasphemed. The seat of the scorner may be very lofty, but it is very near to the gate of hell; let us flee from it, for it will soon be empty, and destruction will swallow up the man who sits in it.

Note the gradation in the first verse:

| | | |
|---|---|---|
| He *walketh* not | in the *counsel* of the | *ungodly,* |
| Nor *standeth* | in the *way* of | *sinners,* |
| Nor *sitteth* | in the *seat* of the | *scornful.* |

When people are living in sin they go from bad to worse. At first they merely *walk* in the counsel of the careless and *ungodly*, who forget God – the evil is rather practical than habitual – but after that they become habituated to evil, and they *stand* in the way of open *sinners* who wilfully violate God's commandments; and if let alone they go one step further, and become themselves pestilent teachers and tempters of others, and thus they *sit in the seat of the scornful.* They have taken their degree in vice, and as true Doctors of Damnation they are installed, and are looked up to by others as Masters in Belial. But the blessed man, the man to whom all the blessings of God belong, can hold no communion with such characters as these. He keeps himself pure from these lepers; he puts away evil things from him as garments spotted by the flesh; he comes out from among the wicked, and goes outside the camp, bearing the reproach of Christ. Oh for grace to be thus separate from sinners.

## Verse 2

'But his delight is in the law of the LORD.' He is not *under* the law as a curse and condemnation, but he is *in* it, and he delights to be in it as his rule of life.

'And in his law doth he meditate day and night.' He delights to meditate in it, to read it by day and think upon it by night. He takes a text and carries it with him all day long; and in the night-watches, when sleep forsakes his eyelids, he muses upon the Word of God. In the day of his prosperity he sings psalms out of the Word of God, and in the night of his affliction he comforts himself with promises out of the same book. The law of the Lord is the daily bread of the true believer. And yet, in David's day, how small was the volume of inspiration, for they had scarcely anything save the first five books of Moses! How much more, then, should we prize the whole written Word which it is our privilege to have in all our houses! But, alas, what ill-treatment is given to this angel from heaven! We are not all Berean searchers of the Scriptures. How few among us can lay claim to the benediction of the text! Perhaps some of you can claim a sort of negative purity, because you do not walk in the way of the ungodly; but let me ask you, is your delight in the law of God? Do you study God's Word? Do you make it the man of your right hand – your best companion and hourly guide? If not, this blessing does not belong to you.

## Verse 3

'And he shall be like a tree planted.' Not a wild tree, but one planted, chosen, considered as property, cultivated and secured from the last terrible uprooting.

'By the rivers of water.' Even if one river should fail, he has another. The rivers of pardon and the rivers of grace, the rivers of the promise and the rivers of communion with Christ, are never-failing sources of supply.

'That bringeth forth his fruit in his season.' Not unseasonable graces, like untimely figs, which are never full-flavoured. But the man who delights in God's Word, being taught by it, brings forth patience in the time of suffering, faith in the day of trial and holy joy in the hour of prosperity. Fruitfulness is an essential quality of a gracious man, and that fruitfulness should be seasonable.

'His leaf also shall not wither.' His faintest word will be everlasting; his little deeds of love will be remembered. Not only will his fruit be preserved, but his leaf also. He will lose neither his beauty nor his fruitfulness, 'and whatsoever he doeth shall prosper'. Blessed is the man who has such a promise as this. But we must not always estimate the fulfilment of a promise by our own eyesight. How often, my brethren, if we judge by feeble sense, may we come to the mournful conclusion of Jacob, 'All these things are against me!' For though we know our interest in the promise, yet are we so tried and troubled that sight sees the very reverse of what the promise foretells. But to the eye of faith this word is sure, and by it we perceive that our works are prospered, even when everything seems to go against us. It is not outward prosperity which the Christian most desires and values; it is soul prosperity which he longs for. We often, like Jehoshaphat, make ships go to Tarshish for gold, but they are broken at Ezion-geber; yet even here there is a true prospering, for it is often for the soul's health that we should be poor, bereaved and persecuted. Our worst things are often our best things. As there is a curse wrapped up in the wicked man's mercies, so there is a blessing concealed in the righteous man's crosses, losses and sorrows. The trials of the saint are a divine husbandry, by which he grows and brings forth abundant fruit.

## Verse 4

'The ungodly are not so: but are like the chaff which the wind driveth away.' We have now come to the second head of the psalm. In this verse the contrast of the bad state of the wicked is employed to heighten the colouring of that fair and pleasant picture which precedes it. The more forcible translation of the Latin and Greek versions is, 'Not so the ungodly, not so.' And we are hereby to understand that whatever good thing is said of the righteous is not true in the case of the ungodly. Oh, how terrible it is to have a double negative put upon the promises! And yet this is just the condition of the ungodly. Mark the use of the term 'ungodly', for, as we have seen in the opening of the psalm, these are the beginners in evil, and are the least offensive of sinners. Oh, if such is the sad state of those who quietly continue in their morality and neglect their God, what must be the condition of open sinners and shameless unbelievers? The first sentence is a negative description of the ungodly, and the second is the positive picture. Here is their *character* – they are like chaff, intrinsically worthless, dead, unserviceable, without substance and easily carried away. Here, also, mark their *doom* – the wind drives them away; death will hurry them with its terrible blast into the fire in which they will be utterly consumed.

## Verse 5

'Therefore the ungodly shall not stand in the judgment.' They will stand there to be judged, but not be acquitted. Fear will lay hold upon them there; they will not stand their ground; they will flee away; they will not stand there in their own defence; for they will blush and be covered with eternal contempt.

Well may the saints long for heaven, for no evil men will dwell there, 'nor sinners in the congregation of the righteous'. All our congregatioṇs on earth are mixed. Every church has one devil in it. The tares grow in the same furrows as the wheat. There is no floor which is as yet thoroughly purged from chaff. Sinners mix with saints, as dross mingles with gold. God's precious diamonds still lie in the same field with pebbles. Righteous Lots are this side of heaven continually vexed by the men of Sodom. Let us rejoice, then, that in the general assembly and Church of the firstborn above, there shall by no means be admitted a single unrenewed soul. Sinners cannot live in heaven. They would be out of their element. Sooner could a fish live upon a tree than the wicked in Paradise. Heaven would be an intolerable hell to an impenitent man, even if he could be allowed to enter; but such a privilege will never be granted to the man who perseveres in his iniquities. May God grant that we may have a name and a place in his courts above!

## Verse 6

'For the LORD knoweth the way of the righteous.' The Hebrew puts this yet more fully: 'The LORD is knowing the way of the righteous.' He is constantly looking on their way, and though it may be often in mist and darkness, yet the Lord knows it. If it be in the clouds and tempest of affliction, he understands it. He numbers the hairs of our head; he will not let any evil come to us.

'But the way of the ungodly shall perish.' Not only will they perish themselves, but their way will perish too. The righteous carves his name upon the rock, but the wicked writes his remembrance in the sand. The righteous man ploughs the furrows of earth, and sows a harvest here which will never be fully reaped till he enters the enjoyments of eternity; but as for the wicked, he ploughs the sea, and though there may seem to be a shining trail behind his keel, yet the waves will pass over it, and the place that knew him will know him no more for ever. The very way of the ungodly will perish. If it exists in remembrance, it will be in the remembrance of the bad; for the Lord will cause the name of the wicked to rot, to become a stench in the nostrils of the good, and to be known to the wicked themselves only by its putridity.

May the Lord cleanse our hearts and our ways, that we may escape the doom of the ungodly, and enjoy the blessedness of the righteous!

# Psalm 22

## Verse 1

'My God, my God, why hast thou forsaken me?' This was the startling cry of Golgotha: 'Eloi, Eloi, lama sabachthani?' The Jews mocked, but the angels adored when Jesus cried this exceedingly bitter cry. Nailed to the tree we behold our great Redeemer in extremities, and what do we see? Let us gaze with holy wonder, and mark the flashes of light amid the awful darkness of that midday-midnight. First, our Lord's faith deserves our reverent imitation; he keeps his hold upon his God and cries twice, 'My God, my God'. The spirit of adoption was strong within the suffering Son of Man, and he felt no doubt about his interest in his God. Oh that we could imitate this cleaving to an afflicting God! Nor does the sufferer distrust the power of God to sustain him, for the title used – *El* – signifies strength, and is the name of the mighty God. He knows the Lord to be the all-sufficient support and succour of his spirit, and therefore appeals to him in the agony of grief, but not in the misery of doubt. He would like to know why he is left; he raises that question and repeats it, but neither the power nor the faithfulness of God does he mistrust. What an enquiry is this before us?

'Why hast thou forsaken me?' We must lay the emphasis on every word of this saddest of all utterances.

'Why?' There was no cause in him; why then was he deserted?

'Hast': it is done, and the Saviour is feeling its dread effect; it is surely true, but how mysterious! It was no threatening of forsaking which made the great Surety cry aloud: he endured that forsaking in very deed.

'Thou': I can understand why traitorous Judas and timid Peter should be gone, but *thou*, my God, my faithful friend, how canst thou leave me? This is worst of all, worse than all put together. Hell itself has for its fiercest flame the separation of the soul from God.

'Forsaken': if thou hadst chastened I might bear it, for thy face would shine; but to forsake me utterly, ah! why is this?

'Me': thine innocent, obedient, suffering Son, why leavest thou *me* to perish? A sight of self seen by penitence, and of Jesus on the cross seen by faith will best expound this question. Jesus is forsaken because our sins had come between us and God.

'Why art thou so far from helping me, and from the words of my roaring?' The Man of Sorrows had prayed until his speech failed him, and he could only utter moanings and groanings as people do in severe sicknesses, like the roarings of a wounded animal. To what extremity of grief was our Master driven! What a strong crying and tears were those which made him too hoarse for speech! What must have been his anguish to find his own beloved and trusted Father standing afar off, and neither granting help nor apparently hearing prayer! Yet there was a reason for all this which those who rest in Jesus as their Substitute will know.

## Verse 2

'O my God, I cry in the daytime, but thou hearest not; and in the night season, and am not silent.' For our prayer to appear to be unheard is no new trial. Jesus felt it before us. He still held fast on God, and cried still, 'My God', but his faith did not render him less importunate. Our Lord continued to pray even though no comfortable answer came, and in this he set us an example of obedience to the words, 'men ought always to pray, and not to faint'. No daylight is too glaring and no midnight too dark to pray in; no delay or apparent denial, however grievous, should tempt us to forbear from importunate pleading.

## Verse 3

'But thou art holy, O thou that inhabitest the praises of Israel.' However ill things may look there is no ill in thee, O God! We are very apt to think and speak hardly of God when we are under his affecting hand, but not so the obedient Son. He knows too well his Father's goodness to let outward circumstances libel his character. There is no unrighteousness with the God of Jacob. If prayer be unanswered it is not because God is unfaithful. If we cannot perceive any ground for the delay, we must leave the riddle unsolved, but we must not fly in God's face to invent an answer. While the holiness of God is acknowledged and adored, the afflicted speaker in this verse seems to marvel at how the holy God could forsake him, and be silent to his cries. The argument is: Thou art holy; oh, why is it that thou dost disregard thy holy One in his hour of sharpest anguish? We may not question the holiness of God, but we may argue from it, and use it as a plea in our petitions.

## Verse 4

'Our fathers trusted in thee: they trusted, and thou didst deliver them.' This is the rule of life with all the chosen family. Three times over is it mentioned that they trusted; they never left off trusting, for it was their very life, and they

51

fared well, too, for *thou didst deliver them*. Out of all their straits, difficulties and miseries faith brought them by calling their God to the rescue; but in the case of our Lord it appeared as if faith would bring no assistance from heaven; he alone of all the trusting ones was to remain without deliverance. The experience of other saints may be a great consolation to us when in deep waters, if faith can be sure that their deliverance will be ours; but when we feel ourselves sinking, it is poor comfort to know that others are swimming. Our Lord here pleads the past dealings of God with his people as a reason why he should not be left alone; here again he is an example to us in the skilful use of the weapon of all prayer. The use of the plural pronoun 'our' shows how one with his people Jesus was even on the cross. We say, 'Our Father which art in heaven,' and he calls those 'our fathers' through whom we came into the world, although he was without father as to the flesh.

## Verse 5

'They cried unto thee, and were delivered; they trusted in thee, and were not confounded.' As if he had said, 'How is it that I am now left without succour in my overwhelming griefs, while all others have been helped?' We may remind the Lord of his former lovingkindnesses to his people, and beseech him to be still the same. This is true wrestling; let us learn the art. Observe that ancient saints *cried* and *trusted*, and that in times of trouble we must do the same; and the inevitable result was that they were not ashamed of their hope, for deliverance came in due time; this same happy portion will be ours. The prayer of faith can do the deed when nothing else can. Let us wonder when we see Jesus using the same pleas as ourselves, and immersed in grief far deeper than our own.

## Verse 6

'But I am a worm, and no man.' How could the Lord of glory be brought to such abasement as to be not only lower than the angels, but even lower than men? What a contrast between 'I AM' and 'I am a worm'! Yet such a double nature was found in the person of our Lord Jesus when bleeding on the tree. He felt himself to be comparable to a helpless, powerless, downtrodden worm, passive while crushed, and unnoticed and despised by those who trod on him. He selects the weakest of creatures, which is all flesh; and becomes, when trodden upon, writhing, quivering flesh, utterly devoid of any might except strength to suffer. This was a true likeness of himself when his body and soul had become a mass of misery – the very essence of agony – in the dying pangs of crucifixion. Man by nature is but a worm; but our Lord puts himself beneath even man, on account of the scorn which was heaped upon him and the weakness which he felt, and therefore he adds 'and no man'. The privileges and blessings which belonged to the fathers he could not obtain while deserted by God, and common acts of humanity were not allowed him, for he was rejected of men; he was outlawed from the society of earth, and shut out from the smile of heaven. How utterly did the Saviour empty himself of all glory, and become of no reputation for our sakes!

'A reproach of men.' Their common butt and jest; a byword and a proverb unto them; the sport of the rabble, and the scorn of the rulers. Oh the caustic power of reproach, to those who endure it with patience, yet smart under it most painfully!

'And despised of the people.' The very people who would once have crowned him then condemned him, and they who were benefited by his cures sneered at him in his woes. Sin was worthy of all reproach and contempt, and for this reason Jesus, the Sinbearer, was given up to be thus unworthily and shamefully treated.

## Verse 7

'All they that see me laugh me to scorn: they shoot out the lip, they shake the head.' Read the evangelistic narrative of the ridicule endured by the Crucified One, and then consider how it grieved him. The iron entered into his soul. The scornful ridicule of our Lord was unanimous. Which shall we wonder at more, the cruelty of man or the love of the bleeding Saviour? How can we ever complain of ridicule after this? Pouting, grinning, shaking of the head, thrusting out of the tongue and other modes of derision were endured by our patient Lord; men made faces at him before whom angels veil their faces and adore. They punned upon his prayer; they made matter for laughter of his sufferings and set him utterly at nought.

## Verse 8

'He trusted on the LORD that he would deliver him: let him deliver him, seeing he delighted in him.' Here the taunt is cruelly aimed at the sufferer's faith in God, which is the tenderest point in a good man's soul, the very apple of his eye. They must have learned the art from Satan himself, for they made rare proficiency in it. There were five forms of taunt hurled at the Lord Jesus (Matt. 27:39–44); this mockery is probably mentioned in this psalm because it is the most bitter of the whole. When we are tormented in the same manner, let us remember him who endured such contradiction of sinners against himself. We must not lose sight of the truth which was unwittingly uttered by the Jewish scoffers. They themselves are witnesses that Jesus of Nazareth trusted in God: why then was he permitted to perish? Jehovah had previously delivered those who rolled their burdens upon him; why was this man deserted? Oh that they had understood the answer! Their principal jest, 'seeing he delighted in him', was true. The Lord did delight in his dear Son, and when he became obedient unto death, he still was well pleased in him. Jehovah delights in him, and yet slays him.

## Verse 9

'Thou art he that took me out of the womb.' Kindly providence attends with the surgery of tenderness at every human birth; but the Son of Man, who was marvellously begotten of the Holy Spirit, was in an especial manner watched over by the Lord when brought forth by Mary. The destitute state of Joseph and Mary, far away from friends and home, led them to see the cherishing hand of God in the safe delivery of the mother. Her child, now fighting the great battle of his life, uses the mercy of his nativity as an argument with God. Faith finds weapons everywhere. The person who desires to believe will never lack reasons for believing.

'Thou didst make me hope when I was upon my mother's breasts.' Was our Lord one of those babes and sucklings out of whose mouths strength is ordained? Early piety gives particular comfort in our later trials, for surely he who loved us when we were children is too faithful to cast us off in our riper years. Some give the text the sense of 'gave me cause to trust, by keeping me safely', and assuredly there was a special providence which preserved our Lord's infant days from the fury of Herod, the dangers of travelling and the ills of poverty.

## Verse 10

'I was cast upon thee from the womb.' Into the almighty arms he was first received, as into those of a loving parent. God begins his care over us from the earliest hour.

'Thou art my God from my mother's belly.' The psalm begins with 'My God, my God,' and here not only is the claim repeated but its early date is urged. Our birth was our weakest and most perilous period of existence; if we were then secured by omnipotent tenderness, surely we have no cause to suspect that divine goodness will fail us now.

## Verse 11

'Be not far from me.' This is the petition for which he has been using such varied and powerful pleas. His great woe was that God had forsaken him; his great prayer is that he would be near him. A lively sense of the divine presence is a mighty stay to the heart in times of distress.

'For trouble is near; for there is none to help.' 'For' is repeated, as though faith gave a double knock at mercy's gate; that is a powerful prayer which is full of holy reasons and thoughtful arguments. The nearness of trouble is a weighty motive for divine help; this moved our heavenly Father's heart, and brings down his helping hand. It is his glory to be our very present help in trouble. Our Substitute had trouble in his inmost heart, for he said, 'The waters have come in, even unto my soul'; well might he cry, 'Be not far from me.' The absence of all other helpers is another telling plea. In our Lord's case none either could or would help him; yet it was a sore aggravation to find that all his disciples had forsaken him, and lover and friend were put far from him. There is an awfulness about absolute friendlessness which is crushing to the human mind, for man was not made to be alone, and is like a dismembered limb when he has to endure heart-loneliness.

## Verse 12

'Many bulls have compassed me: strong bulls of Bashan have beset me round.' The mighty ones in the crowd are here marked by the tearful eye of their victim. The priests, elders, scribes, Pharisees, rulers and captains bellowed round the cross like wild cattle, full of strength and fury. The Rejected One was all alone, and bound naked to the tree.

## Verse 13

'They gaped upon me with their mouths, as a ravening and a roaring lion.' Like hungry cannibals they opened their blasphemous mouths as if they were about to swallow the man whom they abhorred. They could not commit forth their anger fast enough, and therefore set the doors of their lips wide open like those who gape. Our Lord's faith must have passed through a most severe conflict while he found himself abandoned to the tender mercies of the wicked, but he came off victorious by prayer, the very danger to which he was exposed being used to add prevalence to his entreaties.

## Verse 14

Turning from his enemies, our Lord describes his own personal condition in language which should bring the tears into every loving eye.

'I am poured out like water.' He was utterly spent, like water poured upon the earth; his heart failed him, and had no more firmness in it than running water, and his whole being was made a sacrifice, like a libation poured out before the Lord. He had long been a fountain of tears; in Gethsemane his heart welled over in sweat, so that he was reduced to the most feeble and exhausted state.

'All my bones are out of joint', as if distended upon a rack. Is it not most probable that the fastening of the hands and feet, and the jar occasioned by fixing the cross in the earth, may have dislocated the bones of the Crucified One? If this is not intended, we must refer the expression to that extreme weakness which would occasion relaxation of the muscles and a general sense of parting asunder throughout the whole system.

'My heart is like wax; it is melted in the midst of my bowels.' Excessive debility and intense pain made his inmost life to feel like wax melted in the heat. The Greek liturgy uses the expression 'thine unknown sufferings', and well it may. The fire of almighty wrath would have consumed our souls for ever in hell; it was no light work to bear as a substitute the heat of an anger so justly terrible.

## Verse 15

'My strength is dried up like a potsherd; and my tongue cleaveth to my jaws; and thou hast brought me into the dust of death.' Most complete disability is here portrayed; Jesus likens himself to a broken piece of earthenware, or an earthen pot, baked in the fire till the last particle of moisture is driven out of the clay. No doubt a high degree of feverish burning afflicted the body of our Lord. All his strength was dried up in the tremendous flames of avenging justice, just as the paschal lamb was roasted in the fire. Thirst and fever fastened his tongue to his jaws, so that he could scarcely speak. So, tormented in every single part as to feel dissolved into separate atoms, and each atom full of misery, the full price of our redemption was paid, and no part of the Surety's body or soul escaped its share of agony. The Lord of Glory stoops to the dust of death.

## Verse 16

We are to understand every item of this sad description as being urged by the Lord Jesus as a plea for divine help; and this will give us a high idea of his perseverance in prayer.

'For dogs have compassed me.' Here he marks the more ignoble crowd, who were howling like hungry dogs. Hunters frequently surround their game with a circle, and gradually encompass them with an ever-narrowing ring of dogs and men. Such a picture is before us. In the centre stands, not a panting stag, but a bleeding, fainting man, and around him are the enraged and unpitying wretches who have hounded him to his doom. Here we have the 'hind of the morning' of whom the psalm so plaintively sings, hunted by bloodhounds, all thirsting to devour him.

The assembly of the wicked have enclosed me.' Thus the Jewish people, which called itself an assembly of the righteous, is justly for its sin marked upon the forehead as an assembly of the wicked. This is not the only occasion when professed churches of God have become synagogues of Satan, and have persecuted the Holy One and the Just.

'They pierced my hands and my feet.' This can by no means refer to David, or to anyone but Jesus of Nazareth. Pause, and view the wounds of the Redeemer.

## Verse 17

So emaciated was Jesus by his fastings and suffering that he says, 'I may tell all my bones.' He could count and re-count them. The zeal of his Father's house had eaten him up. Oh that we cared less for the body's enjoyment and ease and more for our Father's business! It is better to count the bones of an emaciated body than to bring leanness into our souls.

'They look and stare upon me.' Unholy eyes gazed insultingly upon the Saviour's nakedness. The sight of the agonising body ought to have ensured sympathy from the throng, but it only increased their savage mirth as they gloated over our Redeemer's shame. The first Adam made us all naked, and therefore the Second Adam became naked that he might clothe our naked souls.

## Verse 18

'They part my garments among them, and cast lots upon my vesture.' The garments of the executed were the perquisites of the executioners in most cases, but it was not often that they cast lots at the division of the spoil; this incident shows how clearly David in vision saw the day of Christ, and how surely the Man of Nazareth is he of whom the prophets spoke. It may be noted that the habit of gambling is of all others the most hardening, for men could practise it even at the cross-foot while besprinkled with the blood of the Crucified. No Christian will endure the rattle of the dice when he thinks of this.

## Verse 19

'But be not thou far from me, O God.' Invincible faith returns to the charge, and uses the same means, namely, importunate prayer. He repeats the petition offered before. He wants nothing but his God, even in his lowest state. He does not ask for the most comfortable or nearest presence of God; he will be content if he is not far from him; humble requests speed at the throne.

'O my strength, haste thee to help me.' Hard cases need timely aid; when necessity justifies it we may be urgent with God as to time, but we must not do this out of wilfulness. In the last degree of weakness he calls the Lord 'my strength'; after this fashion the believer can sing, 'When I am weak, then am I strong.'

## Verse 20

'Deliver my soul from the sword.' By 'the sword' is probably meant entire destruction, which as man he dreaded; or perhaps he sought deliverance from the enemies round him, who were like a sharp and deadly sword to him. The Lord has said, 'Awake, O sword', and now from the terror of that sword the

Shepherd wanted to be delivered as soon as justice should see fit.

'My darling from the power of the dog', meaning his soul, his life, which is most dear to every person. The origin is 'my only one', and therefore is our soul dear, because it is our only soul. Would that everyone made their souls their darlings, but many treat them as if they were not worth so much as the mire of the streets. The dog may mean Satan, or else the whole company of Christ's foes, who though many in number were but one. If Jesus cried for help against the dog of hell, much more may we. Beware of the dog, for his power is great, and only God can deliver us from him. When he fawns upon us, we must not put ourselves in his power; and when he howls at us, we may remember that God holds him with a chain.

## Verse 21

'Save me from the lion's mouth; for thou hast heard me from the horns of the unicorns.' Having experienced deliverance in the past from our enemies, who were strong as the unicorns, the Redeemer utters his last cry for rescue from death, which is fierce and mighty as the lion. This prayer was heard, and the gloom of the cross departed. Thus faith, though sorely beaten, and even cast beneath the feet of her enemy, ultimately wins the victory. It was so in our Head; it shall be so in all the members. We have overcome the unicorn, we shall conquer the lion, and from both lion and unicorn we shall take the crown.

## Verses 22–31

The transition is very marked; from a horrible tempest all is changed into calm. The darkness of Calvary at length passed away from the face of nature, and from the soul of the Redeemer, beholding the light of his triumph and its future, results the Saviour's smile. It will be well still to regard the words as a part of our Lord's soliloquy upon the cross, uttered in his mind during the last few moments before his death.

## Verse 22

'I will declare thy name unto my brethren.' The delights of Jesus are always with his Church, and hence his thoughts, after much distraction, return at the first moment of relief to their usual channel; he forms fresh designs for the benefit of his loved one. He is not ashamed to call them brethren. He anticipates happiness in having communion with his people; he intends to be their teacher and minister, and fixes his mind upon the subject of his discourse. The name, i.e. the character and conduct of God, are by Jesus Christ's gospel proclaimed to all the holy brotherhood; they behold the fullness of the Godhead dwelling bodily in him, and rejoice greatly to see all the infinite perfections manifested in one who is bone of their bone and flesh of their flesh. What a precious subject is the name of our God! It is the only one worthy of the only Begotten, whose meat and drink it was to do the Father's will. We may learn from this resolution of our Lord that one of the most excellent methods of showing our thankfulness for deliverance is to tell to our brethren what the Lord has done for us. We mention our sorrows readily enough; why are we so slow in declaring our deliverances?

'In the midst of the congregation will I praise thee.' Not in a little household gathering merely does our Lord resolve to proclaim his Father's love, but in the great assemblies of his saints, and in the general assembly and Church of the first-born. This he is always doing by his representatives, who are the heralds of salvation and labour to praise God. In the great universal Church Jesus is the one authoritative teacher, and all others are nothing but echoes of his voice. Jesus declares the divine name so that God may be praised. The Church continually magnifies Jehovah for revealing himself in the person of Jesus, and Jesus himself leads the song, and is both leader and preacher in his Church. Delightful are the seasons when Jesus communes with our hearts concerning divine truth; joyful praises are the sure result.

## Verse 23

'Ye that fear the LORD, praise him; all ye the seed of Jacob, glorify him; and fear him, all ye the seed of Israel.' Imagine the Saviour as addressing the congregation of the saints. He exhorts the faithful to unite with him in thanksgiving. The description of 'fearing the Lord' is very frequent and very instructive; it is the beginning of wisdom, and is an essential sign of grace. Humble awe of Gid is so necessary a preparation for praising him that none are fit to sing his honour but such as reverence his Word; but this fear is consistent with the highest joy, and is not to be confounded with legal bondage, which is a fear which perfect love casteth out. Jew and Gentile saved by sovereign grace should be eager in magnifying the God of our salvation: *all* saints should unite in the song. The spiritual Israel all *fear* him, and we hope the day will come when the bodily Israel will be brought to the same mind. The more we praise God the more reverently shall we fear him, and the sweeter will be our songs.

## Verse 24

'For he hath not despised nor abhorred the affliction of the afflicted.' Here is good matter and motive for praise. The experience of our covenant Head and Representative should encourage all of us to bless the God of grace. Never was man so afflicted as our Saviour in body and soul from friends and foes, by heaven and hell, in life and death; he was the foremost in the ranks of the afflicted, but all those afflictions were sent in love, and not because his Father despised and abhorred him. It is true that justice demanded that Christ should bear the burden which as a substitute he undertook to carry, but Jehovah always loved him, and in love laid that load upon him with a view to his ultimate glory and to the accomplishment of the dearest wish of his heart. Under all his woes our Lord was honourable in the Father's sight.

'Neither hath he hid his face from him.' The hiding was but temporary, and was soon removed; it was not final and eternal.

'But when he cried unto him, he heard.' Jesus was heard in that he feared. He cried from the depths, and was speedily answered; he therefore bids his people to join him in singing a gloria.

Every child of God should seek refreshment for his faith in this testimony of the Man of Sorrows. What Jesus here witnesses is as true today as when it was first written. It shall never be said that anyone's affliction or poverty prevented his being an accepted suppliant at Jehovah's throne of grace.

## Verse 25

'My praise shall be of thee in the great congregation.' The one subject of our Master's song is the Lord alone. The word in the original is 'from thee' – true praise is of celestial origin. The rarest harmonies of music are nothing unless they are sincerely consecrated to God by hearts sanctified by the Spirit. The cleric says, 'Let us sing to the praise and glory of God,' but the choir often sing to the praise and glory of themselves. Oh when shall our service of song be a pure offering? Observe how Jesus loves the public praises of the saints. It would be wicked on our part to despise the twos and threes; but, on the other hand, let not the little companies snarl at the greater assemblies as though they were necessarily less pure and less approved, for Jesus loves the praise of the great congregation.

'I will pay my vows before them that fear him.' Jesus dedicates himself anew to the carrying out of the divine purpose in fulfilment of his vows made in anguish. Did our Lord when he ascended to the skies proclaim amid the redeemed in glory the goodness of Jehovah? And was that the vow meant here? Undoubtedly the publication of the gospel is the constant fulfilment of covenant engagements. The Messiah vowed to build up a spiritual temple for the Lord, and he will surely keep his word.

## Verse 26

'The meek shall eat and be satisfied.' Mark how the dying Lover of our souls solaces himself with the result of his death. The spiritually poor find a feast in Jesus, to the satisfaction of their hearts. The thought of the joy of his people gave comfort

63

to our expiring Lord. Note the characters who partake of the benefit of his passion: the *meek*, the humble and lowly. Lord, make us so. Note also the certainty that gospel provisions will not be wasted – *they shall eat* – and the sure result of such eating – and *be satisfied.*

'They shall praise the LORD that seek him.' For a while they may keep a fast, but their thanksgiving days must and will come.

'Your heart shall live for ever.' Your spirits will not fail through trial. Thus Jesus speaks even from the cross to the troubled seeker. If his dying words are so assuring, what consolation may we not find in the truth that he ever liveth to make intercession for us! Those who eat at Jesus' table receive the fulfilment of the promise, 'Whosoever eateth of this bread shall live for ever.'

## Verse 27

'All the ends of the world shall remember and turn unto the LORD: and all the kindreds of the nations shall worship before thee.' One is struck with the Messiah's missionary spirit. It is evidently his grand consolation that Jehovah will be known throughout all places of his dominion. Out from the inner circle of the present Church the blessing is spread in growing power until the remotest parts of the earth will be ashamed of their idols, mindful of the true God, penitent for their offences, and unanimously earnest for reconciliation with Jehovah. Then shall false worship cease. This is a stimulus to those who fight his battles.

It is well to mark the order of conversion: they shall *remember* – this is reflection, like the Prodigal who came to himself; *and turn unto Jehovah* – this is repentance, like Manasseh who left his idols; and *worship* – this is holy service, as Paul adored the Christ whom once he abhorred.

## Verse 28

'For the kingdom is the LORD's: and he is the governor among the nations.' As an obedient Son the dying Redeemer rejoiced to know that his Father's interests would prosper through his pains. He who by his own power reigns supreme in creation and providence has set up a new kingdom of grace, and by the conquering power of the cross that kingdom will grow until all people proclaim that 'he is the governor among the nations'. Amid the tumults and disasters of the present the Lord reigns; but in the halcyon days of peace the rich fruit of his dominion will be apparent to every eye.

## Verse 29

'All they that be fat upon the earth.' The rich and great are not shut out. Grace now finds most of its jewels among the poor, but in the latter days the mighty of the earth shall eat, with all their hearts, the God who deals so bountifully with us in Christ Jesus. Those who are spiritually fat with inward prosperity will be filled with the marrow of communion, and worship the Lord with especial fervour. In the covenant of grace Jesus has provided good cheer for our high estate, and taken equal care to console us in our humiliation: 'all they that go down to the dust shall bow before him.' There is relief and comfort in bowing before God when our case is at its worst; even amid the dust of death prayer kindles the lamp of hope.

'None can keep alive his own soul.' While all who come to God by Jesus Christ are thus blessed, whether rich or poor, none who despise him may hope for a blessing. This is the stern counterpart of the gospel message of 'look and live'. We must have life as Christ's gift, or we shall die eternally. This should be proclaimed in every corner of the earth, that it may break in pieces all self-confidence.

## Verse 30

'A seed shall serve him; it shall be accounted to the Lord for a generation.' Posterity will perpetuate the worship of the Most High. The kingdom of truth on earth will never fail. The Lord will reckon the ages by the succession of the saints. Generations of sinners come not into the genealogy of the skies. God's family register is not for strangers, but for the children only.

## Verse 31

'They shall come.' Sovereign grace will bring out from among men the blood-bought ones. Nothing will thwart the divine purpose. In this the dying Saviour finds a sacred satisfaction.

'And shall declare his righteousness unto a people that shall be born.' None of the people brought to God by the irresistible attractions of the cross will be dumb; they will be able to tell out the righteouness of the Lord, so that future generations know the truth. Fathers will teach their sons, who will hand it down to their children; the burden of the story always being 'that he hath done this', or that 'It is finished'. Salvation's glorious work is done, there is peace on earth, and glory in the highest.

# Psalm 23

## Verse 1

'The LORD is my shepherd.' It should be the subject of grateful admiration that the great God allows himself to be compared to anything which will set forth his great love and care for his own people. David had himself been a keeper of sheep, and understood both the needs of the sheep and the many cares of a shepherd. He compares himself to a creature weak, defence-less and foolish, and he takes God to be his Provider, Preserver, Director and indeed his everything. No one has a right to consider himself the Lord's sheep unless his nature has been renewed, for the scriptural description of the un-converted does not picture them as sheep but as wolves or goats. A sheep is an object of property, not a wild animal; its owner sets great store by it, and frequently it is bought with a great price. It is well to know, as certainly David did, that we belong to the Lord. There is no 'if' or 'but' or even 'I hope so' in this sentence. We must cultivate the spirit of assured dependence on our heavenly Father.

The sweetest word of the whole is 'my'. He does not say, 'The Lord is the shepherd of the world at large, and leadeth forth the multitude as his flock.' If he is a Shepherd to no one else, he is a Shepherd to *me*. The words are in the present tense. Whatever the believer's position, he is under the pastoral care of Jehovah now.

'I shall not want.' These positive words are a sort of inference from the first statement. When the Lord is my Shepherd he is able to supply my needs, and he is certainly willing to do so, for his heart is full of love. I shall not lack temporal things: does he not feed the ravens, and cause the lilies to grow? How then can he leave his children to starve? I shall not lack spiritual things; I know that his grace will be sufficient for me. I may not possess all that I wish for; but I shall not lack. Others may, far wealthier and wiser than I, but I shall not. 'The young lions do lack, and suffer hunger: but they that seek the LORD shall not want any good thing' (Psalm 34:10). It is not only 'I do not want' but 'I shall not want'. Come what may, if famine should devastate the land, or calamity destroy the city, 'I shall not want'. Old age with its feebleness will not bring me any lack, and even death with its gloom will not find me destitute. I have all things and abound; not because I have a good store of money in the bank, not because I have skill and wit with which to win my bread, but because 'The LORD is my shepherd'. The wicked always want, but the righteous never; a sinner's heart is far from satisfaction, but a gracious spirit dwells in the place of content.

## Verse 2

'He maketh me to lie down in green pastures: he leadeth me beside the still waters.' The Christian life has two elements in it, the contemplative and the active, and both are richly provided for. What are the green pastures but the Scriptures of truth – always fresh, and never exhausted? When by faith we are enabled to find rest in the promises, we are like the sheep that lie down in the pasture; we find at the same moment both rest and refreshment. It is the Lord who graciously enables us to perceive the preciousness of his truth, and to feed upon it. How grateful ought we to be for the power to appropriate the promises! There are some distracted souls who would give worlds if they could only do this. They know the blessedness of it, but they cannot say that this blessedness is theirs. Those believers who have for years enjoyed a 'full assurance of faith' should greatly bless their gracious God.

The second part of a vigorous Christian's life consists in gracious activity. We are not always lying down to feed, but are journeying onward towards perfection. What are the still waters but the influences and graces of his blessed Spirit? His Spirit attends us in various operations, like waters – in the plural – to cleanse, to refresh, to fertilise, to cherish. They are still because the Holy Spirit loves peace, and sounds no trumpet of ostentation in his operations. He may flow into our soul, but not into our neighbour's, and therefore our neighbour may not perceive the divine presence. Our Lord leads us beside these still waters; we could not go there of ourselves, we need his guidance. He does not drive us. Moses drives us by the law, but Jesus leads us by his example, and the gentle drawing of his love.

## Verse 3

'He restoreth my soul.' When the soul grows sorrowful he revives it; when it is sinful he sanctifies it; when it is weak he strengthens it. *He* does it. His ministers could not do it if he did not. His Word would not avail by itself. He *restoreth*: do we feel that our spirituality is at its lowest ebb? He who turns the ebb into the flood can soon restore our soul. Pray to him, then, for the blessing.

'He leadeth me in the paths of righteousness for his name's sake.' The Christian delights to be obedient, but it is the obedience of love, to which he is constrained by the example of his Master. He is not obedient to some commandments and neglectful of others; he does not pick and choose, but yields to all. Observe that the plural is used – the *paths* of righteousness. Whatever God may give us to do we would do it, led by his love. Some Christians overlook the blessing of sanctification, and yet to a thoroughly renewed heart this is one of the sweetest gifts of the covenant. If we could be saved from wrath, and yet remain unregenerate, impenitent sinners, we should not be saved as we desire, for we mainly and chiefly pant to be saved from sin and led in the way of holiness. All this is done out of pure free grace, *for his name's sake*. It is to the honour of our great Shepherd that we should be a holy people, walking in the narrow way of righteousness. If we are so led and guided, we must not fail to adore our heavenly Shepherd's care.

## Verse 4

'Yea, though I walk through the valley of the shadow of death, I will fear no evil: for thou art with me; thy rod and thy staff they comfort me.' This has been sung on many a dying bed, and has helped to make the dark valley bright times out of mind. Every word in it has a wealth of meaning. 'Yea, though I walk', as if the believer did not quicken his pace when he came to die, but still calmly walked with God. To walk indicates the steady advance of a soul which knows its road, knows its end, resolves to follow the path, feels quite safe and is therefore perfectly calm and composed.

It is not walking in the valley but *through* the valley. We go through the dark tunnel of death and emerge into the light of immortality. We do not die; we only sleep, to wake in glory. Death is not the goal but the passage to it. The storm breaks on the mountain, but the valley is a place of quietude, and thus often the last days of the Christian are the most peaceful in his whole career; the mountain is bleak and bare, but the valley is rich with golden sheaves, and many a saint has reaped more joy and knowledge when he came to die than he ever knew while he lived. And, then, it is not 'the valley of death' but 'the valley of the *shadow* of death', for death in its substance has been removed, and only the shadow of it remains. Someone has said that when there is a shadow there must be light somewhere. Death stands by the side of the highway in which we have to travel, and the light of heaven shining upon him throws a shadow across our path; let us then rejoice that there is a light beyond. A shadow cannot stop a man's pathway even for a moment. Let us not, therefore, be afraid.

'I will fear no evil.' He does not say there will not be any evil; he had got beyond even that high assurance, and knew that

Jesus had put all evil away; but his fears, those shadows of evil, were gone for ever. The worst evils of life are those which do not exist except in our imagination. We feel a thousand deaths in fearing one, but the psalmist was cured of the disease of fearing. 'I will fear no evil', not even the evil one himself; I will look upon him as a conquered foe, an enemy to be destroyed, 'for thou art with me'. This is joy of the Christian! The little child out at sea in the storm is not frightened like all the other passengers; it is asleep in its mother's bosom; it is enough for it that its mother is with it; and it should be enough for the believer to know that Christ is with him; 'thy rod and thy staff', by which thou governest and rulest thy flock, the ensigns of thy sovereignty and of thy gracious care, 'they comfort me'.

Many people profess to receive much comfort from the hope that they will not die. Certainly there will be some who will be 'alive and remain' at the coming of the Lord, but is there so very much of advantage in such an escape from death as to make it the object of a Christian desire? Those who 'shall be caught up together with the Lord in the air' will lose that actual fellowship with Christ in the tomb which dying saints will have, and we are expressly told they will have no preference beyond those who are asleep. Let us be of Paul's mind when he said that 'to die is gain', and think of 'departing to be with Christ, which is far better'. This psalm is as sweet in a believer's ear now as it was in David's time.

## Verse 5

'Thou preparest a table before me in the presence of mine enemies.' The good man has his enemies. He would not be like his Lord if he had not. If we were without enemies we might fear that we were not the friends of God, for the friendship of the world is enmity to God. Yet see the quietude of the godly man in spite of, and in the sight of, his enemies. How refreshing is his calm bravery! When a soldier is in the presence of his enemies, if he eats at all he snatches a hasty meal, and away he hastens to the fight. But observe: 'Thou preparest a table', just as a servant does when unfolding the damask cloth and displaying the ornaments of the feast on an ordinary peaceful occasion. Nothing is hurried, the enemy is at the door, and yet God prepares a table, and the Christian sits down and eats as if everything were in perfect peace.

'Thou anointest my head with oil.' May we receive a fresh anointing for every day's duties. Every Christian is a priest, but must go day by day to God the Holy Spirit. A priest without oil misses the chief qualification for his office, and the Christian priest lacks his chief fitness for service when he is devoid of new grace from on high.

'My cup runneth over.' He had not only enough, but more than enough. A poor man may say this as well as those in higher circumstances. A man may be ever so wealthy, but if he is discontented his cup cannot run over; it is cracked and leaks.

## Verse 6

'Surely goodness and mercy shall follow me all the days of my life.' This is indisputable, and therefore a heavenly 'surely' is set as a seal upon it. This sentence may be read, 'Only goodness and mercy', for there will be unmingled mercy in our story. These twin guardian angels will always be with me. Just as when great princes go abroad and must not go unattended, so it is with the believer. Goodness and mercy follow him always – the black days as well as the bright days. Goodness supplies our needs, and mercy blots out our sins.

'And I will dwell in the house of the LORD for ever.' A servant does not stay in the house for ever, but the son abides for ever. While I am here I will be a child at home with my God; the whole world will be his house to me; and when I ascend into the upper room I will not change my company, nor even change the house.

# Psalms 42 and 43

## Psalm 42

### Verse 1

'As the hart panteth after the water brooks, so panteth my soul after thee, O God.' As the hunted hart instinctively seeks the river to bathe its smoking flanks and to escape the dogs, so my weary, persecuted soul pants after the Lord my God. Debarred from public worship, David was heartsick. Ease he did not seek, honour he did not covet, but the enjoyment of communion with God was an urgent and absolute necessity, like water to a stag. Have you personally felt the same? The next best thing to living in the light of the Lord's love is to be unhappy till we have it, and to pant hourly after it. Thirst is a perpetual appetite. When it is as natural for us to long after God as for an animal to thirst, it is well with our souls, however painful our feelings. The eagerness of our desires may be pleaded with God, and the more so because there are special promises for the importunate and fervent.

### Verse 2

'My soul': all my nature, my inmost self.

'Thirsteth': hunger you can palliate, but thirst is awful, insatiable, deadly.

'For God': not merely for the temple and the ordinances, but for fellowship with God himself. None but the spiritual can sympathise with this thirst.

'For the living God': because he lives, and gives the living water, therefore we with greater eagerness desire him.

'When shall I come and appear before God?' He who loves the Lord loves also the assemblies wherein his name is adored. Vain are all claims to religion where the outward means of grace have no attraction. David was never so much at home as in the house of the Lord; he was not content with private worship; he did not forsake the place where saints assemble, as the manner of some is. After God, his *Elohim* (his God to be worshipped, who had entered into covenant with him), he pined as the drooping flowers for the dew. If all our resortings to public worship were viewed as appearances before God, it would be a sure mark of grace to delight in them. Alas, how many appear before the minister, or their fellow-men, and think that enough! 'To see the face of God' is a nearer translation of the Hebrew; but the two ideas may be combined – he would see his God and be seen by him; this is worth thirsting after!

## Verse 3

'My tears have been my meat day and night.' Salty meats, but healthful to the soul. Those who come to tears, plenteous tears, are in earnest indeed. There is a dry grief far more terrible than showery sorrows. David's tears, since they were shed because God was blasphemed, were 'honourable dew', drops of holy water, such as Jehovah puts in his bottle.

'While they continually say unto me, Where is thy God?' Cruel taunts come naturally from cowardly minds. Surely they might have left the mourner alone; he could weep no more than he did – it was a supererogation of malice to pump more tears from a heart which already overflowed. Note how incessant was the jeer, and how artfully they framed it! It cut the good man to the bone to have the faithfulness of his God impugned. The wicked know that our worst misfortune would be to lose God's favour; hence their diabolical malice leads them to declare that such is the case. Glory be to God, they lie in their throats, for our God is in the heavens, and in the furnace too, succouring his people.

## Verse 4

'When I remember these things, I pour out my soul in me.' When he harped upon his woes his heart melted into water and was poured out upon itself. God hidden, and foes raging, a pair of evils enough to bring down the stoutest heart! Yet why let reflections so gloomy engross us, since the result is of no value: merely to turn the soul on itself, to empty it from itself into itself, is useless; how much better to pour out the heart before the Lord! The prisoner's treadwheel might sooner land him in the skies than mere inward questioning raise us nearer to consolation.

'For I had gone with the multitude, I went with them to the house of God.' Painful reflections were awakened by the memory of past joys; he had mingled in the pious throng, their numbers had helped to give him exhilaration and to awaken holy delight, their company had been a charm to him as with them he ascended the hill of Zion. With frequent strains of song, he and the people of Jehovah had marched in reverent ranks up to the shrine of sacrifice, the dear abode of peace and holiness. Far away from such goodly company the holy man pictures the sacred scene and dwells upon the details of the pious march.

'With the voice of joy and praise, with a multitude that kept holyday.' Perhaps he alludes to the removal of the ark and to the glorious gatherings of the tribes on that grand national holy day and holiday. How changed his present place! For Zion, a wilderness; for the priests in white linen, soldiers in garments of war; for the song, the sneer of blasphemy; for the festivity, lamentation; for joy in the Lord, a mournful dirge over his absence. David appears to have had a peculiarly tender remembrance of the *singing* of the pilgrims, and assuredly it is the most delightful part of worship and that which comes nearest to the adoration of heaven. What a degradation to supplant the intelligent song of the whole congregation by the theatrical prettinesses of a quartet, the refined niceties of a choir, or inanimate bellows and pipes! We might as well pray by machinery as praise by it.

## Verse 5

'Why art thou cast down, O my soul?' As though he were two men, the psalmist talks to himself. These present troubles, are they to last for ever? The rejoicings of my foes, are they more than empty talk? My absence from the solemn feasts, is that a perpetual exile? Why this deep depression? To search out the causes of our sorrow is often the best surgery for grief. Self-ignorance is not bliss; in this case it is misery. The mist of ignorance magnifies the causes of our alarm; a clearer view will make monsters dwindle into trifles.

'Why art thou disquieted within me?' Why is my quiet gone? If I cannot keep a public Sabbath, yet wherefore do I deny my soul her indoor Sabbath? Why am I agitated like a troubled sea, and why do my thoughts make a noise like a tumultuous multitude? The causes are not enough to justify such utter yielding to despondency. Up, my heart! Your castings down will turn to liftings up, and your disquietudes to calm.

'Hope thou in God.' If every evil is let loose from Pandora's box, yet is there hope at the bottom. God is unchangeable, and therefore his grace is the ground for unshaken hope. If everything be dark, yet the day will come, and meanwhile hope carries stars in her eyes; her lamps are not dependent upon oil from without, her light is fed by secret visitations of God, which sustain the spirit.

'For I shall yet praise him for the help of his countenance.' Salvation comes from the propitious face of God, and he will yet lift up his countenance upon us. Note well that the main hope and chief desire of David rest in the smile of God. This verse, like the singing of Paul and Silas, looses chains and shakes prison walls. He who can use such heroic language in his gloomy hours will surely conquer.

## Verse 6

'O my God, my soul is cast down within me.' Perhaps the spasm of despondency returned. The singer was also a little more tranquil. Outward expression of desire was gone; there was no visible panting; the sorrow was now all restrained within doors. Within or upon himself he was cast down; it may well be so while our thoughts look more within than upward. If self were to furnish comfort, we should have but poor provender. There is no solid foundation for comfort in such fickle frames as our heart is subject to. It is well to tell the Lord how we feel, and the more plain the confession the better.

'Therefore will I remember thee': blessed downcasting which drives us to so sure a rock of refuge as thee, O Lord!

'From the hill Mizar': he recalls his seasons of choice communion by the river and among the hills, and especially that dearest hour upon the little hill where love spoke her sweetest language and revealed her nearest fellowship. It is great wisdom to store up in memory our choice occasions of converse with heaven; we may want them another day, when the Lord is slow in bringing back his banished ones, and our soul is aching with fear. Or does David mean that even where he was he would think of his God; does he declare that, forgetful of time and place, he would count Hermon as holy as Zion, and even Mizar, that insignificant rising ground, as glorious as the mountains which are round about Jerusalem?

### Verse 7

'Deep calleth unto deep at the noise of thy waterspouts.' Thy severe dealings with me seem to excite all creation to attack me; heaven and earth and hell call to each other, stirring each other up in dreadful conspiracy against my peace. As in a waterspout, the deeps above and below clasp hands, so it seemed to David that heaven and earth united to create a tempest around him. His woes were incessant and overwhelming. His soul seemed drowned as in a universal deluge of trouble, over whose waves the providence of the Lord moved as a watery pillar, in dreadful majesty inspiring the utmost terror. As for the afflicted one, he was like a mariner floating on a mast, almost every moment submerged.

'All thy waves and thy billows are gone over me.' David thought that every trouble in the world had met in him, but he exaggerated, for 'all' the breaking waves of Jehovah have passed over none but the Lord Jesus. Yet what a plight to be in! Most of the heirs of heaven have experienced the like. This is a deep experience unknown to babes in grace, but common enough to such as do business on great waters of affliction: to such it is some comfort to remember that the waves and billows are the Lord's – '*thy* waves and *thy* billows' – they are all sent and directed by him, and achieve his purposes.

## Verse 8

'Yet the LORD will command his lovingkindness in the day-time': lovingkindness is a noble life-belt in a rough sea. The day may darken into a strange and untimely midnight, but the love of God ordained of old to be the portion of the elect shall be by sovereign grace meted out to them. No day shall ever dawn on an heir of grace and find him altogether forsaken of his Lord; the Lord reigns, and as a sovereign he will with authority command mercy to be reserved for his chosen.

'And in the night': both divisions of the day will be illuminated with special love, and no stress of trial will prevent it. Our God is God of the nights as well as the days.

'His song shall be with me': songs of praise for blessings received will cheer the gloom of the night. The belief that we shall yet glorify the Lord for mercy given in extremity is a delightful stay to the soul.

'And my prayer unto the God of my life': prayer is yoked with praise. The living God is the God of our life; from him we derive it, with him in prayer and praise we spend it, to him we devote it, in him we shall perfect it. To be assured that our sighs and songs will both have free access to our glorious Lord is to have reasons for hope in the most deplorable condition.

## Verse 9

'I will say unto God my rock, Why hast thou forgotten me?' Faith is allowed to inquire of her God the causes of his displeasure, and she is even permitted to expostulate with him and remind him of his promises, and ask why apparently they are not fulfilled. If the Lord be indeed our refuge, when we find no refuge it is time to be raising the question, 'Why is this?' Yet we must not let go our hold; the Lord must be 'my' rock still.

'Why go I mourning because of the oppression of the enemy?' Surely God can have no pleasure in seeing the faces of his servants stained and squalid with their tears; he can find no contentment in the harshness with which their foes assail them. How can the strong God, who is as firm and abiding as a rock, be also as hard and unmoved as a rock towards those who trust in him? Such inquiries humbly pressed often afford relief to the soul. To know the reason for sorrow is in part to know how to escape it, or at least to endure it. Lack of attentive consideration often makes adversity appear to be more mysterious and hopeless than it really is. It is a pitiable thing for anyone to have a limb amputated, but when we know that the operation was needed in order to save life, we are glad to hear that it has been successfully performed.

## Verse 10

'As with a sword in my bones, mine enemies reproach me': cruel mockeries cut deeper than the flesh; they reach the soul. The tongue cuts to the bone, and its wounds are hard to cure.

'While they say daily unto me, Where is thy God?' This is the unkindest cut of all, reflecting as it does both upon the Lord's faithfulness and his servant's character. Such was the malice of David's foes that they repeated the cruel question 'daily'. Surely this was enough to madden him, and perhaps would have done so had he not resorted to prayer.

## Verse 11

'Why art thou cast down, O my soul? and why art thou disquieted within me?' He finds after all no sufficient ground for being disquieted. Looked in the face, his fears were not so overwhelming as they seemed when shrouded in obscurity.

'Hope thou in God': let the anchor still keep its hold. God is faithful, God is love, there is room and reason for hope.

'Who is the health of my countenance, and my God': this is the same hopeful expression as that contained in verse 5, but the addition of 'and my God' shows that the writer was growing in confidence, and was able defiantly to reply to the question, 'Where is thy God?' Here he is, ready to deliver me. I am not ashamed to own him amid your sneers and taunts, for he will rescue me out of your hands. Thus faith closes the struggle, a victor in fact by anticipation and in heart by firm reliance. The saddest countenance will yet be made to shine, if there be a taking of God at his word and an expectation of his salvation.

## Psalm 43

### Verse 1

'Judge me, O God': others are unable to understand my motives, and unwilling to give me a just verdict. My heart is clear as to its intent, and therefore I bring my case before thee, content that thou wilt impartially weigh my character and right my wrongs. If thou wilt judge, thy acceptance of my conduct will be enough for me; I can laugh at human misrepresentation if my conscience knows that thou art on my side; thou art the only one I care for; and besides, thou wilt see practical justice done to thy slandered servant.

'And plead my cause against an ungodly nation': one such advocate as the Lord will more than suffice to answer a nation of brawling accusers. When people are ungodly, no wonder they are unjust; those who are not true to God himself cannot be expected to deal rightly with his people.

'O deliver me from the deceitful and unjust man': from such devils none can deliver us but God. His wisdom can outwit the craft of the vilest serpent, and his power can overmatch the most raging lion. If we try to fight them with our own weapons we shall suffer more serious injury from ourselves than from them. Vengeance belongeth not to us, but to our Lord. Turn to him in prayer, and ere long you will publish abroad the remembrance of his salvation.

### Verse 2

'For': here is argument, which is the very sinew of prayer. If we reasoned more with the Lord we should have more victories in supplication.

'Thou art the God of my strength': all my strength belongs to thee. I will not, therefore, use it on my own behalf against my personal foes; I seek help from thee; I leave the task of combating my foes entirely in thy hands. Note the assurance of David: 'thou art', not 'I hope and trust so', but 'I know it is so'.

'Why dost thou cast me off?' There are many reasons why the Lord might cast us off, but no reason will prevail to make him do so. He has not cast off his people, though he for a while treats them as castoffs. It is well to inquire into dark providences, but we must inquire of God, not of our own fears. He who is the author of a mysterious trial can best expound it to us.

'Why go I mourning because of the oppression of the enemy?' Why do I wander hither and thither like a restless spirit? Why do I wear the weeds of sorrow on my body, and the lines of grief on my face? Oppression makes a wise man mad; why, Lord, am I called to endure so much of it for so long a time? Here again is a useful question, addressed to the right quarter. The answer will often be because we are saints, and must be made like our Head, and because such sorrow is chastening to the spirit, and yields fruit. We are not to cross-question the Lord in peevishness, but we may ask of him in humility; God help us to observe the distinction so as not to sin through stress of sorrow.

## Verse 3

'O send out thy light and thy truth.' The joy of thy presence and the faithfulness of thy heart – let both of these be manifest to me. Reveal my true character by thy light, and reward me according to thy truthful promise. As the sun darts out his beams, so does the Lord send out his favour and his faithfulness towards all his people, lighting up even our darkest surroundings with delightful splendour.

'Let them lead me': be these my star to guide me to my rest.

'Let them bring me unto thy holy hill, and to thy tabernacles': first in thy mercy bring me to thy earthly courts, and end my weary exile, and then in due time admit me to thy celestial palace above. We seek not light to sin by, nor truth to be exalted by it, but that they may become our practical guides to the nearest communion with God: only such light and truth as are sent us from God will do this; common light is not strong enough, nor will mere moral or physical truths assist to the holy hill; but the light of the Holy Spirit, and the truth as it is in Jesus, these are elevating, sanctifying, perfecting; and hence their virtue in leading us to the glorious presence of God. It is beautiful to observe how David's longing to be away from the oppression of man always leads him to sigh more intensely for communion with God.

## Verse 4

'Then will I go unto the altar of God.' If David might be permitted to return, it would not be his own house which would be his first resort, but the altar of God. With what exultation should believers draw near to Christ, who is the antitype of the altar!

'Unto God my exceeding joy': It was not the altar as such that the psalmist cared for, but fellowship with God himself. What are all the rites of worship unless the Lord be in them? God is not David's 'joy' alone, but his 'exceeding' joy; not the fountain of joy, the giver of joy or the maintainer of joy, but that joy itself. The margin has 'the gladness of joy', that is, the soul, the essence of my joy. To draw near to God, who is such a joy to us, may well be the object of our hungering and thirsting.

'Yea, upon the harp will I praise thee': when God fills us with joy we ought ever to pour it out at his feet in praise, and all the skill and talent we have should be laid under contribution to increase the divine revenue of glory.

'O God, my God': how he dwells upon the name which he loves so well! To have God in possession, and to know it by faith, is the heart's heaven.

## Verse 5

'Why art thou cast down, O my soul?' If God be thine, why this dejection?

'And why art thou disquieted within me?' Wherefore indulge unreasonable sorrows, which benefit no one, fret yourself and dishonour your God? Why overburden yourself with forebodings?

'Hope in God', or 'wait for God': there is need of patience, but there is ground for hope. The Heavenly Father will not stand by and see his children trampled upon for ever; light must arise for the people of God, though for a while they may walk in darkness. Why, then, should we not be encouraged, and lift up our head with comfortable hope?

'For I shall yet praise him': times of complaint will soon end and seasons of praise begin.

'Who is the health of my countenance, and my God': my God will clear the furrows from my brow and the tear-marks from my cheek; therefore will I smile in the face of the storm. The psalm has a blessed ending, such as we would like to imitate when death puts an end to our mortal existence.

# Psalm 80

## Verse 1

'Give ear, O Shepherd of Israel': the name is full of tenderness: broken hearts delight in names of grace. We may be quite sure that he who deigns to be a shepherd to his people will not turn a deaf ear to their complaints.

'Thou that leadest Joseph like a flock': the people are called here by the name of that renowned son who became a second father to the tribes, and kept them alive in Egypt; possibly they were known to the Egyptians under the name of 'the family of Joseph'.

'Thou that dwellest between the cherubims, shine forth': the Lord's especial presence was revealed upon the mercy-seat between the cherubim, and in all our pleadings we should come to the Lord by this way: only upon the mercy-seat will God reveal his grace, and only there can we hope to commune with him. Let us ever plead the name of Jesus, who is our true mercy-seat, to whom we may come boldly, and through whom we may look for a display of the glory of the Lord on our behalf. Our greatest dread is the withdrawal of the Lord's presence, and our brightest hope is the prospect of his return.

## Verse 2

'Before Ephraim and Benjamin and Manasseh stir up thy strength, and come and save us.' It is wise to mention the name of the Lord's people in prayer, for they are precious to him. Jesus bears the names of his people on his breast-plate. Just as the mention of the names of his children has power with a father, so is it with the Lord. The prayer is that the God of Israel would be mighty on behalf of his people, chasing away their foes and saving his people.

## Verse 3

'Turn us again, O God': it is not so much said, 'turn our captivity', but 'turn *us*'. All will come right if we are right. When the Lord turns his people he will soon turn their condition. It needs the Lord himself to do this, for conversion is as divine a work as creation; and those who have been once turned unto God, if they at any time backslide, as much need the Lord to turn them again as to turn them at the first. The word may be read, 'restore us'.

'And cause thy face to shine': be favourable to us; smile upon us. This was the high priest's blessing upon Israel: what the Lord has already given us by our High Priest and Mediator we may right confidently ask of him.

'And we shall be saved': all that is wanted for salvation is the Lord's favour. No matter how fierce the foe or dire the captivity, the shining face of God ensures both victory and liberty. This verse is a very useful prayer, since we too often turn aside.

## Verse 4

'O LORD God of hosts, how long wilt thou be angry against the prayer of thy people?' How long will the smoke of thy wrath drown the smoking incense of our prayers? Prayer would enter thy holy place, but thy wrath battles with it and prevents its entrance. That God should be angry with us when sinning seems natural enough; that he should be angry even with our prayers is a bitter grief.

## Verse 5

'Thou feedest them with the bread of tears': their meals, which were once such pleasant times of social merriment, are now like funeral feasts to which each person contributes a bitter morsel.

'And givest them tears to drink in great measure': not because their enemies have them in their power by force of arms, but because their God refuses to interpose; but it will by divine love be turned into a greater blessing by ministering to our spiritual health.

## Verse 6

'Thou makest us a strife unto our neighbours': a neighbour's jeer is ever most cutting, especially if we have been superior to them and claimed to possess more grace.

'And our enemies laugh among themselves': they find mirth in our misery, comedy in our tragedy, salt for their wit in the brine of our tears; it is the constant habit of the world to make merry with the saints' tribulations.

## Verse 7

'Turn us again, O God of hosts.' The prayer rises in the form of its address to God. He is here the God of Hosts. The more we approach the Lord in prayer and contemplation, the higher will our ideas of him become.

## Verse 8

'Thou hast brought a vine out of Egypt': there it was in unfriendly soil: the waters of the Nile were as death to its shoots, while the inhabitants of the land despised it and trampled it down. Glorious was the right hand of the Lord when with power and great wonders he removed his pleasant place from the teeth of those who sought its destruction.

'Thou hast cast out the heathen, and planted it': seven nations were dug out to make space for the vine of the Lord;

the old trees, which long had engrossed the soil, were torn up root and branch. The chosen vine was securely placed in its position with divine prudence and wisdom. Small in appearance, very dependent, exceeding weak and apt to trail on the ground, yet the vine of Israel was chosen by the Lord, because he knew that by incessant care and abounding skill, he could make of it a goodly fruitbearing plant.

## Verse 9

'Thou preparedst room before it': the weeds, brambles and huge stones were cleared; the Amorites and their brothers in iniquity were made to quit the scene, their forces were routed, their kings slain, their cities captured, and Canaan became like a plot of land made ready for a vineyard.

'And didst cause it to take deep root, and it filled the land': Israel became settled and established as a vine well rooted, and then it began to flourish and to spread on every side. This analogy might be applied to the experience of every believer in Jesus. The Lord has planted us, we are growing downward, 'rooting roots', and by his grace we are also growing visibly bigger. The same is true of the Church, for at this moment through the goodwill of the dresser of the vineyard her branches spread far and wide.

## Verse 10

'The hills were covered with the shadow of it': Israel dwelt up to the mountains' summits, cultivating every foot of soil. The nation multiplied and became so great that other lands felt its influence, or were shadowed by it.

'And the boughs thereof were like the goodly cedars': the nation itself was so great that even its tribes were powerful and worthy to take rank among the mighty. A more accurate rendering describes the cedars as covered with the vine, and we know that in many lands vines climb the trees and cover them. In Solomon's time the little land of Israel occupied a high place among the nations. There have been times when the

Church of God also has been eminently conspicuous, and her power has been felt far and near.

## Verse 11

'She sent out her boughs unto the sea': along the Mediterranean and, perhaps, across its waters, Israel's power was felt.

'And her branches unto the river': on her eastern side she pushed her commerce right to the Euphrates. Those were brave days for Israel, and would have continued had not sin cut them short. When the Church pleases the Lord, her influence becomes immense, far beyond the proportion which her numbers or her power would lead us to expect; but alas, when the Lord leaves her she becomes worthless.

## Verse 12

'Why hast thou then broken down her hedges?' Thou hast withdrawn protection from her after caring for her with all this care; why is this, O Lord? A vine unprotected is exposed to every form of injury: such was Israel when given over to her enemies; such has the Church often been.

'So that all they which pass by the way do pluck at her.' Her cruel neighbours have a pluck at her, and marauding bands, like roaming beasts, must pick at her. With God no enemy can harm us; without him none are so weak as to be unable to do us damage.

## Verse 13

'The boar out of the wood doth waste it': such creatures are famous for rending and devouring vines. Fierce peoples, comparable to wild swine of the forest, warred with the Jewish nation, until it was gored and torn like a vine destroyed by greedy hogs.

'And the wild beast of the field doth devour it': first one foe and then another wreaked vengeance on the nation, and God did not interpose to chase them away. Ruin followed ruin. See what evils follow in the train of sin, and how terrible a thing it is for a people to be forsaken by God.

## Verse 14

'Return, we beseech thee, O God of hosts.' Turn thyself to us as well as us to thee. Thou hast gone from us because of our sins; come back to us, for we sigh and cry after thee. Or, if it be too much to ask thee to come, then do at least give us some consideration and cast an eye upon our griefs.

'Look down from heaven, and behold, and visit this vine.' Do not close thine eyes; it is thy vine; at least note the mischief which the beasts have done, for then it may be thy heart will pity, and thy hand will be outstretched to deliver.

## Verse 15

'And the vineyard which thy right hand hath planted': thou hast done so much; wilt thou lose thy labour? With thy power and wisdom thou didst great things for thy people, wilt thou now utterly give them up?

'And the branch that thou madest strong for thyself': a prayer for the leader whom the Lord had raised up, or for the Messiah whom they expected. Though the vine had been left, yet one branch had been regarded by the Lord, as if to furnish a scion for another vine. Let us pray the Lord, if he will not in the first place look upon his Church, to look on the Lord Jesus, and then behold her in mercy for his sake.

## Verse 16

'It is burned with fire': The vineyard was like a forest which has been set on fire; the choice vines were charred and dead.

'It is cut down': the cruel axe had hacked after its murderous fashion, the branches were lopped, the trunk was wounded, desolation reigned supreme.

'They perish at the rebuke of thy countenance': God's rebuke was to Israel what fire and axe would be to a vine. His favour is life, and his wrath is as messengers of death.

## Verse 17

'Let thy hand be upon the man of thy right hand': give a commission to some chosen man by whom thou wilt deliver. Honour him, save us, and glorify thyself. There is no doubt here an outlook to the Messiah, for whom believing Jews had learned to look as the Saviour in time of trouble.

'Upon the son of man whom thou madest strong for thyself': send forth thy power with him whom thou shalt strengthen to accomplish thy purposes of grace. It is by the man Christ Jesus that fallen Israel is yet to rise, and indeed through him, who deigns to call himself the Son of Man, the world is to be delivered from the dominion of Satan and the curse of sin. O Lord, fulfil thy promise to the man of thy right hand, who participates in thy glory, and give him to see the pleasure of the Lord prospering in his hand.

## Verse 18

'So will not we go back from thee.' Under the leadership of one whom God had chosen the nation would be kept faithful, grace would work gratitude, and so cement them to their allegiance. It is in Christ that we abide faithful: because he lives we live also. There is no hope of our perseverance apart from him.

'Quicken us, and we will call upon thy name.' If the Lord gives life out of death, his praise is sure to follow. The Lord Jesus is such a leader that in him is life, and the life is the light of men. When he visits our souls anew we shall be revivified, and our praise will ascend to the name of the Triune God.

## Verse 19

'Turn us again, O LORD God of hosts': here we have another advance in the title, and the incommunicable name of Jehovah, the I AM, is introduced. Faith's prayers grow more full and mighty.

'Cause thy face to shine; and we shall be saved': even we who were so destroyed. No extremity is too great for the power of God. He is able to save at the last point, and that too by simply turning his face upon his afflicted. People can do little, but God can do all things with a glance. Oh, to live for ever in the light of his countenance!

# Psalm 100

## Verse 1

'Make a joyful noise unto the LORD, all ye lands.' This is a repetition of Psalm 98:4. The original word signifies a glad shout, such as loyal subjects give when their king appears among them. Our happy God should be worshipped by a happy people; a cheerful spirit is in keeping with his nature, his acts and the gratitude which we should cherish for his mercies. In every land Jehovah's goodness is seen; therefore in every land should he be praised. Never will the world be in its proper condition until with one unanimous shout it adores the only God.

## Verse 2

'Serve the LORD with gladness.' He is our Lord, and therefore he is to be served; he is our gracious Lord, and therefore to be served with joy.

'Come before his presence with singing.' We ought in worship to realise the presence of God, and by an effort of the mind to approach him. This is an act which must to every rightly instructed heart be one of great solemnity, but at the same time it must not be performed in the servility of fear, and therefore we come before him with psalms and hymns. Singing, as it is a joyful, and at the same time a devout, exercise, should be a constant form of approach to God.

## Verse 3

'Know ye that the LORD he is God.' Our worship must be intelligent. We ought to know whom we worship and why. Only those who practically recognise his Godhead are at all likely to offer acceptable praise.

'It is he that hath made us, and not we ourselves.' Some men call themselves 'self-made men', and they adore their supposed creators; but Christians recognise the origin of their being and their well-being, and take no honour to themselves either for being, or for being what they are. Neither in our first or second creation dare we put so much as a finger upon the glory, for it is the sole right and property of the Almighty. To disclaim honour for ourselves is as necessary a part of true reverence as to ascribe the glory to the Lord. For our part, we find it far more easy to believe that the Lord made us than that we were developed by a long chain of natural selections from floating atoms which fashioned themselves.

'We are his people, and the sheep of his pasture.' It is our honour to have been chosen from all the world besides to be his own people, and our privilege to be therefore guided by his wisdom, tended by his care and fed by his bounty. Sheep gather around their shepherd and look up to him; in the same manner let us gather around the great Shepherd of mankind. The avowal of our relation to God is in itself praise; when we recount his goodness we are rendering to him the best adoration. The simple narration of the mercies of the Lord is more astonishing than the productions of imagination. That we are the sheep of his pasture is a plain truth, and at the same time the very essence of poetry.

## Verse 4

'Enter into his gates with thanksgiving.' In all our public service the rendering of thanks must abound; it is like the incense of the temple, which filled the whole house with smoke. Expiatory sacrifices are ended, but those of gratitude will never be out of date. So long as we are receivers of mercy we must be givers of thanks. Mercy permits us to enter his gates; let us praise that mercy.

'And into his courts with praise.' The innermost court is now open to believers, and we enter into that which is within the veil; it is incumbent upon us that we acknowledge the high privilege by our songs.

'Be thankful unto him.' Let the praises be in your heart as

well as on your tongue, and let it all be for him to whom it all belongs.

'And bless his name.' He blessed you; bless him in return. Bless his name, his character, his person. Whatever he does, be sure that you bless him for it: bless him when he takes away as well as when he gives; bless him as long as you live, under all circumstances; bless him in all his attributes, from whatever point of view you consider him.

## Verse 5

'For the LORD is good.' This sums up his character and contains a mass of reasons for praise. He is good, gracious, kind, bountiful, loving. Whoever does not praise the good is not good himself.

'His mercy is everlasting.' God is not mere justice, stern and cold: he has compassion, and wills not the sinner's death. Towards his own people mercy is still more conspicuously displayed. Everlasting mercy is a glorious theme for sacred song.

'And his truth endureth to all generations.' He has entered into covenant with his people, and he will never revoke it. Our heart leaps for joy as we bow before One who has never broken his word or changed his purpose. Resting on his sure word, we feel that joy which is here commanded, and in the strength of it we come into his presence even now, and speak good of his name.

# Psalm 121

## Verse 1

'I will lift up mine eyes unto the hills, from whence cometh my help.' It is wise to look to the strong for strength. Dwellers in valleys are subject to many disorders for which there is no cure but a sojourn in the uplands, and it is well then they shake off their lethargy and resolve upon a climb. Down below they are the prey of marauders, and to escape from them the surest method is to fly to the strongholds upon the mountains. Often before the actual ascent the sick and plundered people looked towards the hills and longed to be upon their summits. The holy man who here sings looked away from the slanderers by whom he was tormented to the Lord, who saw all from the high places and was ready to pour down succour for his injured servant. Help comes to saints only from above; they look elsewhere in vain. Let us lift up our eyes with hope, expectancy, desire and confidence. Satan will endeavour to keep our eyes upon our sorrows that we may be disquieted and discouraged; be it ours firmly to resolve that we will look out and up, for there is good cheer for the eyes, and those who lift up their eyes to the eternal hills will soon have their hearts lifted up also. The purposes of God; the divine attributes; the immutable promises; the covenant, ordered in all things and sure; the providence, to which we must lift up our eyes, for from these our help must come. It is our resolve that we will not be bandaged and blindfolded, but will lift up our eyes.

Or is the text in the interrogative? Does he ask, 'Shall I lift up mine eyes to the hills?' Does he feel that the highest places of the earth can afford him no shelter? Or does he renounce the idea of recruits hastening to his standard from the hardy mountaineers? Does he again enquire, 'Whence cometh my help?'? If so, the next verse answers the question, and shows whence all help must come.

## Verse 2

'My help cometh even from the LORD, which made heaven and earth.' What we need is help – help powerful, efficient, constant: we need a very present help in trouble. What a mercy that we have it in our God. Our hope is in Jehovah, for our help comes from him. Help is on the road, and will not fail to reach us in due time, for he who sends it to us is equal to every emergency; heaven and earth are at the disposal of him who made them, therefore let us be very joyful in our infinite helper. He will sooner destroy heaven and earth than permit his people to be destroyed, and the perpetual hills themselves will bow rather than he fail whose ways are everlasting. We are bound to look beyond heaven and earth to him who made them both; it is vain to trust the creatures: it is wise to trust the Creator.

## Verse 3

'He will not suffer thy foot to be moved.' Though the paths of life are dangerous and difficult, yet we shall stand fast, for Jehovah will not permit our feet to slide; and if he will not suffer it we shall not suffer it. If our feet will be thus kept we may be sure that our head and heart will be preserved also. In the original the words express a wish or prayer – 'May he not suffer thy foot to be moved'. Promised preservation should be the subject of perpetual prayer; and we may pray believingly, for those who have God for their keeper will be safe from all the perils of the way. Among the hills and ravines of Palestine the literal keeping of the feet is a great mercy; but in the slippery ways of a tried and afflicted life the boon of upholding is of priceless value, for a single false step might cause us a fall fraught with awful danger. To stand erect and pursue the even tenor of our way is a blessing which only God can give, which is worthy of the divine hand and worthy also of perennial gratitude. Our feet will move in progress, but they will not be moved to their overthrow.

'He that keepeth thee will not slumber', or, 'thy keeper will not slumber'. We should not stand a moment if our keeper were to sleep; we need him by day and by night; not a single step can be safely taken except under his guardian eye. This is a choice stanza in a pilgrim song. God is the convoy and bodyguard of his saints. When dangers are awake around us we are safe, for our Preserver is awake also, and will not permit us to be taken unawares. No fatigue or exhaustion can cast our God into sleep; his watchful eyes are never closed.

## Verse 4

'Behold, he that keepeth Israel shall neither slumber nor sleep.' The consoling truth must be repeated: it is too rich to be dismissed in a single line. It were well if we always imitated the sweet singer, and would dwell a little upon a choice doctrine, sucking the honey from it. What a glorious title is in the Hebrew – 'the Keeper of Israel' – and how delightful to think that no form of unconsciousness ever steals over him, neither the deep slumber nor the lighter sleep. He will never let the house be broken up by the silent thief; he is ever on the watch, and speedily perceives every intruder. This is a subject of wonder, a theme for attentive consideration; therefore the word *behold* is set up as a waymark. Israel fell asleep, but his God was awake. Jacob had neither walls nor curtains nor bodyguard around him; but the Lord was in that place though Jacob knew it not, and therefore the defenceless man was safe as in a castle. In after days he mentioned God under this enchanting name – 'the God that led me all my life long': perhaps David alludes to that passage in this expression. The word *keepeth* is also full of meaning: he keeps us as a rich man keeps his treasures, as a captain keeps a city with a garrison, as a royal guard keeps his monarch's head. If the previous verse is in strict accuracy a prayer, this is the answer to it. In verse 3 the Lord is spoken of as the personal keeper of one individual, and here of all those who are in his chosen nation, described as Israel: mercy to one saint is the pledge of blessing to them all. Happy are the pilgrims to whom this psalm is a safe-conduct; they may journey all the way to the celestial city without fear.

## Verse 5

'The LORD is thy keeper.' Here the preserving One, who had been spoken of by pronouns in the two previous verses, is distinctly named – Jehovah. Here is a glorious person – 'Jehovah' – assuming a gracious office – 'keeper' – and fulfilling it in person on behalf of a favoured individual – 'thy' – and a firm assurance of revelation that it is so at this hour – 'is'. We may journey through the valley of the shadow of death and fear no evil.

'The LORD is thy shade upon thy right hand.' A shade gives protection from burning heat and glaring light. We cannot bear too much blessing; even divine goodness, which is a right-hand disposition, must be toned down and shaded to suit our infirmity, and this the Lord will do for us. God is as near us as our shadow, and we are as safe as angels.

## Verse 6

'The sun shall not smite thee by day, nor the moon by night.' Doubtless there are dangers of the light and of the dark, but in both and from both we shall be preserved – literally from excessive heat and from baneful chills; mystically from any injurious effects which might follow from doctrine; spiritually from the evils of prosperity and adversity; eternally from the strain of overpowering glory and from the pressure of terrible events, such as judgment. Day and night make up all time: thus the ever-present protection never ceases. All evil may be ranked as under the sun or the moon, and if neither of these can smite us we are indeed secure. God has not made a new sun or a fresh moon for his chosen; they exist under the same outward circumstances as others, but the power to smite is in their case removed from temporal agencies; saints are en-riched, and not injured, by the powers which govern the earth's condition; to them has the Lord given 'the precious things brought forth by the sun, and the precious things brought forth by the moon', while at the same moment he has removed from them all bale and curse of heat or damp, or glare or chill.

## Verse 7

'The LORD shall preserve thee from all evil.' It is a great pity that our admirable translation did not use the word 'keep' all through the psalm, for all along it is one. God not only keeps his own in all evil times but from evil influences and opera-tions, indeed from evils themselves. The wings of Jehovah amply guard his own from evils great and small, temporary and eternal. There is a most delightful double personality in this verse: Jehovah keeps the believer, not only by agents, but by himself; and the person protected is definitely pointed out by the word *thee* – it is not our estate or name which is shielded, but the proper person. To make this even more intensely real and personal another sentence is added: The LORD shall preserve thee from all evil: he shall preserve thy soul, or 'Jehovah will keep thy soul'. Soulkeeping is the soul of keeping. If the soul be kept all is kept. Our soul is kept from the dominion of sin, the infection of error, the crush of despondency, the puffing up of pride; kept from the world, the flesh and the devil; kept for holier and greater things; kept in the love of God; kept unto the eternal kingdom and glory. What can harm a soul that is kept by the Lord?

## Verse 8

'The LORD shall preserve thy going out and thy coming in from this time forth, and even for evermore.' When we go out in the morning to labour and come home at eventide to rest, Jehovah will keep us. When we go out in youth to begin life and come in at the end to die, we shall experience the same keeping. Our exits and our entrances are under one protection. Three times we have the phrase, 'Jehovah shall keep', as if the sacred Trinity thus sealed the word to make it sure: ought not all our fears to be slain by such a three-fold flight of arrows? This keeping is eternal, continuing from this time forth for evermore. The whole Church is thus assured of everlasting security: the final perseverance of the saints is thus ensured, and the glorious immortality of believers is guaranteed. Under the aegis of such a promise we may go on pilgrimage without trembling, and venture into battle without dread. None are so safe as those whom God keeps, none so much in danger as the self-secure. To goings out and comings in belong particular dangers, since every change of position turns a fresh quarter to the foe, and it is for these weak points that an especial security is provided: Jehovah will keep the door when it opens and closes, and this he will perseveringly continue to do so long as there is left a single person who trusts in him, as long as a danger survives, and in fact as long as time endures. Glory be unto the Keeper of Israel, who is endeared to us under that title, since our growing sense of weakness makes us feel more deeply than ever our need of being kept.

# Psalm 127

## Verse 1

'Except the LORD build the house, they labour in vain that build it.' The word 'vain' is the keynote here, and we hear it ring out clearly three times. People desiring to build know that they must labour, and accordingly they exert all their skill and strength; but let them remember that if Jehovah is not with them their designs will prove failures. So was it with the Babel builders; they said, 'Go to, let us build us a city and a tower'; and the Lord returned their words, saying, 'Go to, let us go down and there confound their language.' In vain they toiled, for the Lord's face was against them. When Solomon resolved to build a house for the Lord, matters were very different, for all things united under God to aid him in his great under-taking: even the heathen were at his beck and call that he might erect a temple for the Lord his God. In the same manner God blessed him in the erection of his own palace; for this verse evidently refers to all sorts of house-building. Without God we are nothing. Great houses have been erected by ambitious men; but like the baseless fabric of a vision they have passed away, and scarce a stone remains to tell where once they stood.

'Except the LORD keep the city, the watchman waketh but in vain.' Note that the psalmist does not bid the builder cease from labouring, nor suggest that watchmen should neglect their duty, nor that people should show their trust in God by doing nothing; he supposes that they will do all that they can and assures them that all creature effort will be in vain unless the Creator exerts his power.

In scriptural language a dispensation or system is called a house. Moses was faithful as a servant over all his house; and as long as the Lord was with that house it stood and prospered; but when he left it, the builders of it became foolish and their labour was lost. They sought to maintain the walls of Jerusalem, but sought in vain: they watched around every ceremony and tradition, but their care was idle. Of every church, and every system of religious thought, this is equally true: unless the Lord is in it, and is honoured by it, the whole structure must sooner or later fall in hopeless ruins.

## Verse 2

'It is vain for you to rise up early, to sit up late, to eat the bread of sorrows.' We are bound to be diligent, for this the Lord blesses; we ought not to be anxious, for that dishonours the Lord, and can never secure his favour. Some deny themselves needful rest. They threaten to bring themselves into the sleep of death by neglect of the sleep which refreshes life. They stint themselves in their meals, they eat the commonest kind of food and the smallest possible quantity of it, and what they do swallow is washed down with the salty tears of grief, for they fear that daily bread will fail them. Hard earned is their food, scantily rationed, and scarcely ever sweetened, but perpetually smeared with sorrow; and all because they have no faith in God, and find no joy except in hoarding up the gold which is their only trust. Not thus, not thus would the Lord have his children live. He would have them, as princes of the race, lead a happy and restful life.

'For so he giveth his beloved sleep.' Through faith the Lord makes his chosen ones to rest in him in happy freedom from care. The text may mean that God gives blessings to his beloved in sleep, just as he gave Solomon the desire of his heart while he slept. The meaning is much the same: those whom the Lord loves are delivered from the fret and fume of life. God is sure to give the best thing to his beloved, and we here see that he gives them sleep – a laying aside of care, a forgetfulness of need, a quiet leaving of matters with God: this kind of sleep is better than riches and honour. Note how Jesus slept amid the hurly-burly of a storm at sea. He knew that he was in his Father's hands.

## Verse 3

'Lo, children are an heritage of the LORD.' This points to another mode of building up a house, namely by leaving descendants to keep our name and family alive upon the earth. Without this what is a man's purpose in accumulating wealth? Yet in this matter a man is powerless without the Lord.

'And the fruit of the womb is his reward', or a reward from God. He gives children, not as a penalty nor as a burden, but as a favour. They are a token for good if people know how to receive them and educate them. Where society is rightly ordered, children are regarded not as an encumbrance but as an inheritance; and they are received not with regret but as a reward. With all the straits of limited incomes, our best possessions are our own dear offspring, for whom we bless God every day.

## Verse 4

'As arrows are in the hand of a mighty man; so are children of the youth.' Children born to men in their early days by God's blessing become the comfort of their riper years. A man of war is glad of weapons which may fly where he cannot; good sons are their father's arrows speeding to hit the mark which their parents aim at. What wonders a good man can accomplish if he has affectionate children to second his desires, and lend themselves to his desires! To this end we must have our children in hand while they are yet children, or they are never likely to be so when they are grown up; and we must try to point them and straighten them so as to make arrows of them in their youth, lest they should prove crooked and useless in later life. Let the Lord favour us with loyal, obedient, affectionate offspring, and we shall find in them our best helpers. We shall see them shot into life to our comfort and delight if we take care from the very beginning that they are directed to the right point.

## Verse 5

'Happy is the man that hath his quiver full of them.' Those who have no children bewail the fact. The writer of this comment gives it as his own observation that he has seen

the most frequent unhappiness in marriages which are un-
fruitful; that he has himself been most grateful for two of the
best of sons; but as they have both grown up, and he has no
child at home, he has without a tinge of grumbling, or even
wishing that he were otherwise circumstanced, felt that it
might have been a blessing to have had a more numerous
family. He therefore heartily agrees with the psalmist's verdict
here. A quiver may be small and yet full; and then the blessing
is obtained. In any case we may be sure that a man's life
consists not in the abundance of children that he possesses.

'They shall not be ashamed, but they shall speak with the
enemies in the gate.' They can meet foes both in law and in
fight. Nobody cares to meddle with a man who can gather a
clan of brave sons about him. Does not the Lord Jesus thus
triumph in his offspring? Looked at literally, this favour
comes of the Lord: without his will there would be no
children to build up the house, and without his grace there
would be no good children to be their parents' strength. If
this must be left with the Lord, let us leave every other thing
in the same hands. He will undertake for us and prosper our
trustful endeavours, and we shall enjoy a tranquil life, and
prove ourselves to be our Lord's beloved by the calm and
quiet of our spirit. We need not doubt that if God gives us
children as a reward he will also send us the food and raiment
which he knows they need.

He who is the father of a host of spiritual children is
unquestionably happy. He can answer all opponents by
pointing to souls who have been saved by his means. Converts
are emphatically the heritage of the Lord, and the reward of
the preacher's soul-travail. By these, under the power of the
Holy Spirit, the city of the Church is built up and watched, and
the Lord has the glory of it.

# Pride and humility

'Before destruction the heart of man is haughty, and before honour is humility' Proverbs 18:12

## Pride

(a) What is it?
It is a groundless thing
It is a brainless thing
It is the maddest thing that can exist
It is a protean thing (readily assuming different shapes or roles)
(b) The seat of pride
The heart
(c) The consequence of pride
Destruction

## Humility

(a) What is it?
To think rightly of ourselves
(b) What is the centre or throne of humility?
The heart
(c) What comes from humility?
Honour

# A faithful friend

'There is a friend that sticketh closer than a brother' Proverbs 18:24

### Introduction

Cicero has well said, 'Friendship is the only thing in the world concerning the usefulness of which all mankind are agreed.'

We believe that the 'friend' in this text is the blessed Redeemer, Jesus Christ.

### Christ is 'a friend that sticketh closer than a brother'

In order to prove this from facts, we appeal to such of you as have had him for a friend.

### Why we may depend on Christ being a faithful friend

(a) True friendship can only be between true people
(b) Faithfulness to us in our faults
   This is a certain sign of fidelity in a friend.
(c) There are some aspects of his friendship which make us certain that we are not deceived, when we put our confidence in him
(d) A lasting friendship does not come from the lap of luxury

'Give me a friend who was born in the winter time, whose cradle was rocked in the storm; he will last.'

(e) A friend who is acquired by folly is never a lasting friend
   The friendship of ignorance is not a very desirable one.
(f) Friendship and love, to be real, must not lie in words, but in deeds
(g) A bought friendship never lasts long

(h)  There cannot, by any possibility, arise any cause which could make Christ love us less

## An inference to be derived from this

The Bible commentator Lavater says, 'The qualities of your friends will be those of your enemies: cold friends, cold enemies; half friends, half enemies; fervid enemies, warm friends.' Then we draw this inference, that if Christ sticks close, and he is our friend, then our enemies will stick close, and never leave us till we die.

**'The dog of hell will never cease his howlings, till you reach the other side of Jordan.'**

# Tomorrow

'Boast not thyself of to morrow; for thou knowest not what a day may bring forth' Proverbs 27:1

## Introduction

God's most holy Word was principally written to inform us of the way to heaven, and to guide us in our path through this world, to the realms of eternal life and light. But as if to teach us that God is not disinterested about our present life, he has given us some excellent and wise maxims, which we may put into practice, not only in spiritual matters, but in temporal affairs also.

## The abuse of tomorrow

The abuse of tomorrow is forbidden by this text, 'Boast not thyself of to morrow.'

(a) Because it is extremely foolish to boast at all
(b) Tomorrow is one of the frailest things in all creation
(c) To boast about tomorrow is exceedingly harmful
   I never knew a man who was always hoping to do great things in the future, who ever did much in the present. Boasting about tomorrow harms you now. Some people were led into extraordinary extravagance from their hopes of the future.
   Boasting about tomorrow will hurt you tomorrow.

## A spiritual approach

Never boast about tomorrow with regard to your soul's salvation.

(a) People who do this think that it will be easier to repent in the future than today
(b) He who boasts about tomorrow supposes that he has plenty of time to return to God

## The value of the future

(a) Patience and confidence
   We can look forward to tomorrow with patience and confidence.
(b) Joy
(c) Ecstasy
(d) Take out an insurance policy
(e) Provide for the poor and distressed
(f) One thing a Christian has not to do
   You must not boast about today's grace, as though it were enough for tomorrow. 'Sufficient unto the day is the evil thereof' (Matthew 6:34).

# Five fears

'Yet surely I know that it shall be well with them that fear God, which fear before him' Ecclesiastes 8:12

## Introduction

An old Puritan says, 'Jesus Christ would shake hands with a man that had the palsy.' I must try and do the same this morning. Some of you have the palsy of fear. I want to come after you and to say to you, 'Fear not'; to bid you to be of good cheer, because God would comfort you. There are five different kinds of fear that people are labouring under which I would now endeavour to address.

## The fear caused by an awakened conscience

This is the lowest grade of godly fear. Here all true piety begins. By nature, the sinner does not dread the wrath of God. No sooner, however, is he awakened by God's Spirit than fear takes possession of his heart. He feels his life to be uncertain. He dreads death, because he knows that death to him would be the prelude to destruction; he dreads life, for life itself is intolerable when the wrath of God is poured out into his soul. Be comforted, this is not a desert island; others have been there too; and like them, you will pass through this and win the crown.

I will tell you something else to comfort you. I put it to you in the form of a question: Do you wish to return to what you were? Ask the poor stricken conscience, in the first agonies and throes of his grief, whether he would like to be a hardened sinner? 'No,' he says. He says, 'Lord, I thank you for my miseries, if they deliver me from my hardness of heart.'

## The fear of anxiety

There are many who have believed, and are truly converted,

who have a fear which I may call the fear of anxiety. They are afraid that they are not converted. They are converted, there is no doubt about it. Sometimes they know they are so themselves, but, for the most part, they are afraid.

First, they will tell you they are afraid they never repented enough. Then they are quite sure they never came to Christ aright, they think they came the wrong way. How that can be no one knows, for they could not come at all except the Father drew them; and the Father did not draw them the wrong way. Still they hold that they did not come aright. Then if that idea is knocked on the head, they say they do not believe aright; but when that is got rid of, they say, if they were converted they would not be the subject of so much sin.

> 'There are some of these poor creatures who are the holiest and most heavenly minded people in the world.'

Now what shall I say to these souls? Why, I will say this, 'Surely I know that it shall be well with them that fear God, which fear before him.' Not only those who believe, but those who fear, have got a promise. I would to God that they had more assurance, and even attain to a perfect confidence; but if they cannot, shall I utter a word that would hurt them? God forbid. 'Surely it shall be well even with them that fear God, with them that fear before him.' There are some of these poor creatures who are the holiest and most heavenly minded people in the world. I have seen men who, with poor, desponding spirits, have exhibited the most lovely graces.

You who are fearing, I would not say a word to hurt you, but I would say a word to comfort you if I could. I would remind you that you are not fit to judge yourself. You have just examined yourself and concluded that you are not a child of God. Now, you will not be offended with me, but I would not give one single farthing for your opinion of yourself. We are not qualified to judge ourselves; our poor scales are out of order, that they will not tell the truth. Now, then, just give up your own judgement, except thus far. Can you say that you 'are a poor sinner and nothing at all, and that Jesus Christ is your all in all?' Then be comforted.

Did you know that the greatest of God's people are often in the same condition as you are now? Those who enjoy the greatest assurance have times when they would give all the world to know that they possessed grace. Now, little one, if the giants go there, what wonder if the dwarfs must.

## Fear which works caution

When we advance a little further in the Christian life our present state is not so much an anxiety as our future state. We believe that we will never totally fall from grace. But we often think that we will bring dishonour on the cause of Christ. I am afraid that in some moment of temptation, I shall be left to go astray. One bad result of this fear is that such people say, 'I dare not join the Church, because I am afraid that I shall fall.' I will ask you this question: Where do you think a man is safest – in the paths of obedience, or in the paths of disobedience? Friends, I believe that union with the Christian Church is often a means, under God, of preserving men from sin.

> '**I believe that union with the Christian Church is often a means, under God, of preserving men from sin.**'

I daresay that the poor creature who has been uttering this thinks that I am about to condemn him. God forbid! My text belongs to him. You are afraid you will fall into sin – 'Surely I know that it shall be well with them that fear God, which fear before him.' If you should tell me that you were not afraid of falling, I would not have you in the Church for the world; you would be no Christian. All Christians, when they are in a right frame of mind, are afraid of falling into sin. Holy fear is the proper condition of a child of God. Seek then, my friends, to grow in this fear of caution; obtain more and more of it; and whilst you do not distrust the Saviour, learn to distrust yourself more and more every day.

## The fear of jealousy

Strong love will usually promote jealousy. We cannot love

strongly without feeling some jealousy – I mean, not jealousy against the object of our love, but jealousy against ourselves. The true believer, when he gets his Saviour in full possession, is so jealous lest any rival should intrude in his heart. He is afraid lest his dearest friend should get more of his heart than the Saviour has. He is afraid of his wealth; he trembles at his health, at his fame, at everything that is dear to him, lest it should engross his heart. I tell you the more he loves the more he fears lest he provoke his Saviour. Seek, my brethren, to know the meaning of fellowship, and you must know, then, the meaning of fear; for fear and fellowship must, to a great degree, go together.

## The fear that is felt when we have had divine manifestations

Have you never viewed the stars and felt that you could say with Jacob, 'How dreadful is this place! This is none other than the house of God, and the very gate of heaven'? How fearful it must be to come into the presence of the King of kings, and to feel oneself near him. Why, I believe that even in heaven we shall have this kind of fear. Certainly the angels have it. They dare not look on God. They hide their faces with their wings, while they cry aloud, 'Holy, holy, holy, Lord God of Hosts', yet they dare not view him. The very sight of him might destroy them, and they tremble at his presence. Now this kind of fear, if you have ever felt it, if it has been produced in your heart by contemplation of God, is a high and hallowed thing, and to you this promise is addressed – 'Surely I know that it shall be well with them that fear God, which fear before him.'

# The desire of the soul in spiritual darkness

'With my soul have I desired thee in the night' Isaiah 26:9

## For established Christians

*Christians do not always have a bright shining sun* I am about to address this text to established Christians. The first fact I deduce from it, a truth I am sure they will readily agree with, is that the Christian does not always have a bright shining light, but rather *he has seasons of darkness and of night*. Experience tells us that if the course of the just is 'as the shining light, that shineth more and more unto the perfect day', yet sometimes that light is eclipsed. We need clouds and darkness to exercise our faith; to cut off self-dependence, and make us put more faith in Christ, and less in evidence, less in experience, less in frames and feelings. The best of God's children – I repeat it again for the comfort of those who are suffering depression of spirits – have their nights. Sometimes it is a night over the whole Church at once. I think, when a man says, 'I never doubt', it is quite time for us to doubt him.

'The best of God's children have their nights.'

*A Christian's religion will keep its colour in the night* 'With my soul have I desired thee in the night.' Demas and Mr Hold-the-world, and a great many others, are very pious people in easy times. But they will not go with Christ in the night. The stars are not visible by daylight, but they become apparent when the sun sets. Put a trouble on the Christian, and his endurance proves him to be of the true seed of Israel.

*All the Christian wants in the night is his God* 'With *desire* have I desired *thee* in the night.' By day there are many things that a Christian will desire besides his Lord; but in the night he wants nothing but his God.

*There are times when all the saints can do is to desire* There are
seasons when Christians find few witnesses to testify to their
piety. But there is one witness that is seldom gagged, even in
the night: and that is, 'I have *desired* thee – I have desired thee
in the night.' 'Yes, Lord, if I have not believed in thee, I have
*desired* thee; and if I have not spent and been spent in thy
service, yet one thing I know, and the devil cannot beat me out
of it, I have *desired* thee – that I do know – and I have desired
thee in the night, too, when no one saw me, when troubles
were round about me.'

## For newly awakened souls

I will now endeavour to answer three questions to those who
are newly awakened.

*How am I to know that my desires are proofs of a work of grace
in my soul?* Some of you may say, 'I think I can go so far as the
text – I have desired God; I know I have desired to be saved.
But how am I to know that it is a desire sent from God, and
how can I tell whether it will end in conversion?' I suggest
three tests.

You can tell whether your desires are from God by their
*constancy.* Many people hear a stirring sermon, have a very
strong desire to be saved; but go home and forget it. I admit
there will be variations even to our more sincere desires, but a
certain measure of constancy is essential to their real value as
evidence of divine work.

You can discern whether your desires are right or wrong by
their *efficacy.* Some people desire heaven very earnestly, but
they do not desire to leave off drunkenness. But if your desires
are practical desires you are on the right road and may take
comfort.

You can tell if these desires are from God by their *urgency.*
The Bible commentator Tillotson well remarks: 'To be always
intending to live a new life, but never to find time to set about
it; this is as if a man should put off eating and drinking, and
sleeping, from one day and night to another, till he is starved
and destroyed.'

*If I have desired God, why have I not obtained my desire before now?* You have hardly a right to ask the question. For God has a right to grant your petition or not, as he pleases. There is no penitent who loves mercy so well as he who has been waiting for it for a season.

Perhaps it has already come. I think some of you are pardoned and do not know it. People have the strangest ideas in the world about conversion. Some people fancy that they are not pardoned because they have never heard a voice in their ears.

*Will God grant my desire at last?* Yes, poor soul, verily he will. It is quite impossible that you should have desired God and should be lost, if you have desired him with the desire I have described.

# The withering work of the Spirit

'The voice said, Cry. And he said, What shall I cry? All flesh is grass, and all the goodliness thereof is as the flower of the field: the grass withereth, the flower fadeth: because the Spirit of the Lord bloweth upon it: surely the people is grass. The grass withereth, the flower fadeth: but the word of our God shall stand for ever' Isaiah 40:6–8

## Introduction

This passage in Isaiah may be used as a very eloquent description of our mortality, and if a sermon was preached from it about the frailty of human nature, the brevity of life and the certainty of death, no one could dispute the appropriateness of the text. Yet I venture to question whether such a discourse would strike the central teaching of the prophet. Something more than the decay of our material flesh is intended here; the carnal mind, the flesh in another sense,

111

was intended by the Holy Spirit when he bade his messenger proclaim those words.

The Spirit blows on the flesh, and what seemed vigorous becomes weak, what was fair to look at is smitten with decay; the true nature of the flesh is thus discovered, its deceit is laid bare, its power is destroyed, and there is space for the dispensation of the ever-abiding Word, and for the rule of the Great Shepherd, whose words are spirit and life. There is a withering wrought by the Spirit which is the preparation for the sowing and implanting by which salvation is wrought.

The subject this morning is the withering work of the Spirit upon the souls of men, and when we have spoken about this, we will conclude with a few words about the implanting work, which always follows where this withering work has been performed.

## The work of the Spirit in causing the ungodliness of the flesh to fade

*It is very unexpected* Let us first observe that the work of the Holy Spirit on the soul of man in withering up what is of the flesh, is *very unexpected*. You will observe in our text that even the speaker himself, though doubtless taught by God, when he was told to speak out, said, 'What shall I say?' Even he did not know that in order to comfort God's people, a preliminary visitation must first be experienced. Many preachers of God's gospel have forgotten that the law is the schoolmaster to bring people to Christ. They have sown on the unbroken fallow ground, and forgotten that the plough must break the clods. Only the sick welcome the doctor. It is the work of God's Spirit to convince men of sin, and until they are convinced about sin, they will never be led to seek the righteousness which is of God through Jesus Christ. I am persuaded that wherever there is a real work of grace in any soul, it begins with a pulling down: the Holy Spirit does not build on the old foundation.

'I am persuaded that wherever there is a real work of grace in any soul, it begins with a pulling down.'

The convicting work of the Spirit, wherever it comes, is unexpected, and even to the child of God in whom this process has still to go on, it is often startling. We begin again to build what God's Spirit had destroyed. Having begun in the spirit, we act as if we would be made perfect in the flesh; and then when our mistaken edifice has to be levelled with the earth, we are almost as astonished as we were when the scales first fell from our eyes. In a similar condition to this John Newton wrote:

> I asked the Lord that I might grow
> In faith and love and every grace,
> Might more of his salvation know,
> And seek more earnestly his face.

> 'Twas he who taught me thus to pray,
> And he, I trust, has answered prayer;
> But it has been in such a way
> As almost drove me to despair.

> I hop'd that in some favour'd hour,
> At once he'd answer my request,
> And by his love's constraining power,
> Subdue my sins, and give me rest.

> Instead of this, he made me feel
> The hidden evils of my heart;
> And let the angry powers of hell
> Assault my soul in ev'ry part.

Ah, marvel not, for thus the Lord is wont to answer his people. The voice which says, 'Comfort ye, comfort ye my people,' achieves its purpose by first making them hear the cry, 'All flesh is grass, and all the goodliness thereof is as the flower of the field.'

113

*This withering is after the usual order of the divine operation* If we consider God's ways we will not be surprised that he begins by reminding his people of his acts of righteousness.

Remember the redemption of the children of Israel out of Egypt: it occurred when they were in the saddest plight, and their cry went up to heaven because of their slavery. When no arm brought salvation, then with a high hand and an out-stretched arm the Lord brought out his people. Everywhere before the salvation there comes the humbling of the creature, the overthrow of human hope. So when these witherings and fadings occur in our souls, we should only say, 'It is the Lord, let him do as seems good to him.'

*The universality of this process* I want you to notice, third, that we are taught in our text how universal this process is in its scope, over the hearts of those on whom the Spirit works. The withering is a withering of what? Of part of the flesh and some portion of its tendencies? No, observe, '*All* flesh is grass; and *all* the goodliness thereof' – the very pick of the bunch – 'is as the flower of the field', and what happens to the grass? Does any of it live? 'The grass withereth', all of it. The flower, will not that abide? So fair a thing, has not that an immortality? No, it fades: it utterly falls away. So wherever God's Spirit breathes on the soul of man, there is a withering of everything that is of the flesh, and it is seen that to be carnally minded is death.

When the withering of the Spirit moves over the carnal mind, it reveals the death of the flesh in all respects, especially in the matter of power towards what is good. We then learn that word of our Lord: 'Without me ye can do nothing.' This is a humbling revelation of God's Holy Spirit, but a necessary one; for the faith of the flesh is not the faith of God's elect. The faith which justifies the soul is God's gift and does not come from us. The flower of the flesh must wither; only the seed of the Spirit will produce fruit to perfection.

*The completeness of the withering of the Holy Spirit* You see, then, the universality of this withering work within us, but I beg you also to notice the completeness of it. The grass, what does it do? Droop? No. It withers. The flower of the field: what about it? Does it hang its head a little? No. According to Isaiah it fades, and Peter says it falls away. It is not revived with showers, it has come to an end. In this way are the awakened led to see that in their flesh there dwells no good thing. What dying and withering work some of God's servants have had in their souls! Look at John Bunyan, as he describes himself in his *Grace Abounding*. For how many months, even years, was the Spirit engaged in writing death on all that was the old Bunyan, in order that he might become by grace a new man fitted to track the pilgrims along their heavenly way. We have not all endured the ordeal so long, but in every child of God there must be a death to sin, to the law and to self, which must be fully accomplished before he is perfected in Christ and taken to heaven. Corruption cannot inherit incorruption; it is through the Spirit that we mortify the deeds of the body, and therefore live.

*The withering work of the Holy Spirit is painful* As you read these verses do they not strike you as having a very funereal tone? 'All flesh is grass, and all the goodliness thereof is as the flower of the field: the grass withereth, the flower fadeth.' This is mournful work, but it must be done.

I think those who experience much of it when they first come to Christ have good reason to be thankful. Their course in life will, in all probability, be much brighter and happier, for I have noticed that people who are converted very easily, and come to Christ with comparatively little knowledge of their own depravity, have to learn it afterwards, and they remain for a long time babes in Christ, and are perplexed with matters that would not have troubled them if they had experienced a deeper work at first.

## The implantation

According to Peter (1 Peter 1:23–5) although the flesh withers and the flower falls away, yet in God's children there is an unfading something of another kind. 'Being born again, not of corruptible seed, but of incorruptible, by the word of God, which liveth and abideth for ever . . . The word of the Lord endureth for ever. And this is the word which by the gospel is preached unto you.' Now, the gospel is beneficial to us because it has no human origin. If it was of the flesh, all it could do for us would not land us beyond the flesh; but the gospel of Jesus Christ is superhuman, divine and spiritual. If you, my hearer, believe a gospel which you have thought out for yourself, or if you believe a gospel thought up by another human brain, it is of the flesh, and will wither, and you will die, and be lost through trusting in it. The only word that can bless you and be a seed in your soul must be the living and incorruptible Word of the eternal Spirit.

**'Pluck the sun out of the heavens, and you will not even then be able to pluck grace out of a regenerate heart.'**

Now observe, wherever this new life comes through the Word, it is incorruptible, it lives and abides for ever. To get the good seed out of a true believer's heart and to destroy the new nature in him is a thing attempted by earth and hell, but never achieved. Pluck the sun out of the heavens, and you will not even then be able to pluck grace out of a regenerate heart. It 'liveth and abideth for ever', says the text. You have a spiritual life, about which is written, 'Whosoever liveth and believeth in me shall never die.' You are now within the noblest and truest immortality: you must live as God lives, in peace and joy, and happiness.

# Fear not

'Fear not, thou worm Jacob, and ye men of Israel; I will help thee, saith the Lord, and thy redeemer, the Holy One of Israel'
Isaiah 41:14

116

## Introduction

I shall speak this morning to those that are discouraged, depressed in spirit and sore troubled in the Christian life.

## Know our own weakness

Before we can do any great things for Christ there must be a sense of weakness. 'Worm Jacob.' The first qualification for serving God with any amount of success, and for doing God's work well and triumphantly, is a sense of our own weakness.

*He knows his weakness by contemplation* He who thinks will always think himself little. Men who have not brains are always great men; but those who think must think their pride down – if God is with them in their thinking. Labour, O soul, to know thy nothingness, and learn it by contemplating God's greatness.

*To know your own weakness consider what you are in suffering* Great sorrow will always make a man think little of himself, if God blesseth it to him.

*To know your own weakness try some hard work for Christ* Go and do something, some of you, and I will be bound to say it will be the means of pricking that fair bubble of your pride.

## Believe God's strength

Before devoting ourselves to Christ, or doing any great labour for the Saviour, it is necessary there should be trust in the promised strength. 'I will help thee, saith the Lord, and thy redeemer, the Holy One of Israel.' It is a certain fact that though men be worms, they do what worms never could do. Brother, what an all-sufficient promise that is – '*I* will help thee.'

117

Though men be worms, they do what worms never could do.

## Labour to be free from fear

We must then work to get rid, as much as possible, of fear, when we are not certain we are serving our Master.

*Fear is painful* Get rid of fear, because fear is painful. How it torments the spirit! When the Christian trusts, he is happy; when he doubts, he is miserable. Fear never helped you yet, and it never will.

*Fear is weakening* Make a man afraid – he will run at his own shadow; make a man brave, and he will stand before an army and overcome them. We must not fear, for fear is weakening.

*Fear dishonours God* God is too wise to err, too good to be unkind; leave off doubting him.

*You lower yourself if you doubt* If you crouch, and cringe, and dread, and doubt, you have lost your Christian dignity and are no longer what you should be. You do not honour God. 'Fear not, thou worm Jacob; I will help thee, saith the Lord.'

# Trials expected and overcome

'When thou passest through the waters, I will be with thee; and through the rivers, they shall not overflow thee; when thou walkest through the fire, thou shalt not be burned; neither shall the flame kindle upon thee. For I am the Lord thy God, the Holy One of Israel, thy Saviour: I gave Egypt for thy ransom, Ethiopia and Seba for thee' Isaiah 43:2–3

## Introduction

Every promise in the Scriptures, of a spiritual nature, which is made to the literal people of Israel and to the descendants after the flesh, is, according to the inspired teaching of the apostle Paul, yet more fully made to the descendants of Abraham after the spirit, for all believers are his spiritual descendants. Christian martyrologists have told us how often Christian martyrs have gone through fire and water; but the flames have not consumed them and the waters have not drowned them.

The promise in this text applies to the whole Church of God as well as to every individual in that Church.

## Trials are to be expected by believers

I suppose that some young Christians imagine that the favourites of heaven will never be tried, but it is not so.

(a) These trials will be of various kinds
(b) These trials will be very terrible ones
(c) These trials will be repeated many times
(d) These trials are inevitable

## Trials will not destroy believers

(a) Trials will not separate believers from their God
(b) Neither the waters nor the fires shall stop the believer's march
    The text does not say, 'When you get to the waters, you shall stop there.' They cannot stop us; we are to go through them.
(c) Some trials which threaten to overwhelm us will not be able to do so

## The arguments and assurances which go to prove that this will be the case with believers

(a) 'For I am Jehovah'
(b) 'Thy God'

(c) 'Thy Saviour'
(d) 'I gave Egypt for thy ranson, Ethiopia and Seba for thee'
  This last assurance is, in some respects, the strongest of
  all. By it the Lord means, 'I will surely preserve you,
  because I have bought you at such a great price that I
  cannot afford to lose you.'

# Forgiveness

'I, even I, am he that blotteth out thy transgressions for mine
own sake, and will not remember thy sins' Isaiah 43:25

## Introduction

There are some passages of sacred writ which have been more
abundantly blessed to the conversion of souls than others.
These passages of God's Word especially attract attention,
and direct the sinner to the cross of Christ. It so happens that
this text is one of the chief of them.

## The recipients of mercy

*They were a prayerless people* If you turn to your Bibles you
will find who is spoken about here. Look for example at Isaiah
43:22, and you will see that they were a prayerless people,
'Thou has not called upon me, O Jacob.' Prayerless souls are
Christless souls; for you can have no real fellowship with
Christ, no communion with the Father, unless you approach
his mercy-seat, and be often there.

*They were despisers of religion* Observe the language of the
same verse, 'Thou hast been weary of me, O Israel.' Not only is
religion unlovely to you, but it is a weariness.

*They were thankless people* 'Thou hast not brought me the
small cattle of thy burnt offerings.' They had their cattle and

their flocks all increased manyfold, but they did not bring even one of the small cattle to him in return. Some of you have never sung a hymn to God's praise.

*They were a useless people* 'Neither hast thou filled me with the fat of thy sacrifices; but thou hast made me to serve with thy sins.' It is well said, the chief end of man is to glorify God. Ask yourselves, what have you done?

*They were sanctuary sinners* There are some who may be termed sanctuary sinners – sinners in Zion – and these are the worst of sinners. O yes, the worst of sinners are sinners in Zion, because they sin against the light and knowledge; they force their way to hell, as John Bunyan says, over the cross of Christ; and the worst way to hell is to go by the cross to it.

Many of you now before me were consecrated to God by a beloved mother, or your father taught you to read and love the Scriptures of truth. Your sentence will be eternal banishment from the presence of him who has said to every repenting sinner, 'I, even I, am he that blotteth out thy transgressions, and will not remember thy sins.'

## The deed of mercy

We have found out the people to whom God will give mercy; now what is mercy's deed?

*Divine forgiveness* It is a deed of forgiveness, and, first, I shall speak of its being a divine forgiveness – 'I, even I, am he.' Divine pardon is the only forgiveness possible.

*A present forgiveness* The text does not say, 'I am he that *will* blot out your transgressions,' but 'I blot them out *now*'. If you have been the chief of sinners, you may have the chief of sinner's forgiveness, and God can bestow it now.

*The completeness of this forgiveness* Suppose you call on your creditor, and say to him, 'I have nothing to pay with.' 'Well,' says he, 'I can issue a distress against you, and place you in prison and keep you there.' You still reply that you have nothing and he must do what he can. Suppose he should then say, 'I will forgive all.' You now stand amazed and say, 'Can it be possible that you will give me that great debt of a thousand pounds?' He replies, 'Yes, I will.' 'But how am I to know it?' There is a bond. He takes it and crosses it all out and hands it back to you, and says, 'There is a full discharge, I have blotted it all out.'

So does the Lord deal with penitents. He has a book in which all your debts are written; but with the blood of Christ he crosses out the handwriting of ordinances which is written there against you. The bond is destroyed, and he will not demand payment for it again.

The devil will sometimes insinuate to the contrary, as he did to Martin Luther. 'Bring me a catalogue of my sins,' said Luther; and the devil brought a scroll black and long. 'Is that all?' said Luther. 'No,' said the devil; and he brought yet another. 'And now,' said the heroic saint of God, 'write at the foot of the scroll: "The blood of Jesus Christ his Son cleanseth from all sin." That is a full discharge.'

## The reason for mercy

One poor sinner says, 'Why should God forgive me? I am sure there is no reason why he should, for I have never done anything to deserve his mercy.' Hear what God says, 'I am not about to forgive you for your own sake, but for my own sake.' 'I am not about to forgive you for your own sake, but for my own sake.' 'But, Lord, I shall not be thankful enough.' 'I am not about to pardon you because of your gratitude, but for my name's sake.' So God says, I desire to have a name for mercy; so that the worse you are, the more God is honoured in your salvation. Go then to Christ, poor sinner – naked, filthy, poor, wretched, vile, lost, dead – come as you are, for there is nothing required from you, except the need of him. 'For mine own sake,' says God, 'I will forgive.'

### The promise of mercy

'And will not remember thy sins.' How are we to understand God's forgetfulness of our sins?

(a) He will not exact punishment for them when we come before his judgment bar at last
(b) The Lord says, 'I will not remember your sins and hold them against you as you serve me'
(c) He will not remember our sins in his distribution of the recompense of the reward

# Sovereignty and salvation

'Look unto me, and be ye saved, all the ends of the earth; for I am God, and there is none else' Isaiah 45:22

### Introduction

Six years ago today, as near as possible at this very hour of the day, I was 'in the gall of bitterness and in the bonds of iniquity', but had yet, by divine grace, been led to feel the bitterness of that bondage, and to cry out by reason of the soreness of its slavery. Seeking rest and finding none, I stepped within the house of God, and sat there, afraid to look upward, lest I should be utterly cut off, and lest his fierce wrath should consume me.

The minister rose in his pulpit, and, as I have done this morning, read this text – 'Look unto me, and be ye saved, all the ends of the earth: for I am God, and there is none else.' I looked that moment; the grace of faith was vouchsafed to me in the self-same instant. I shall never forget that day, while memory holds its place; nor can I help repeating this text, whenever I remember that hour when first I knew the Lord.

It has always been one of the objects of the great Jehovah to

123

teach mankind that he is God, and beside him there is none else.

## How God has been teaching this lesson to mankind

    (a) To false gods, and to the idolaters who are bowed down before them

    (b) God has taught this truth to empires
Babylon.

    (c) God has taught this truth to monarchs
Nebuchadnezzar.

    (d) God has taught this truth to the wise men of this world

    (e) God has taught this truth to the Church of God

## The special way God teaches about salvation

Salvation is God's greatest work; and therefore, in his greatest work, he specially teaches us this lesson – that he is God, and that beside him there is none else. Our text tells us *how* he teaches it. He tells us the person to whom he directs us, the means he tells us to use to obtain mercy, and the people whom he calls to 'look'.

    (a) To whom does God tell us to look for salvation?
'Look to *me*.'

    (b) The means of salvation
'*Look* unto me.'

    (c) The people he has called to look
'All the ends of the earth.'

# God's people in the furnace

'I have chosen thee in the furnace of affliction' Isaiah 48:10

## Introduction

*All people in the furnace of affliction are not chosen* The text says, 'I have chosen thee in the furnace of affliction', and it implies that there may be, and there doubtless are, some in the furnace who are not chosen. How many people suppose that because they are tried, afflicted and tempted, therefore they are God's children, whereas they are no such thing. It is a great truth that every child of God is afflicted; but it is a lie that every afflicted man is a child of God. Afflictions are no proof of sonship, though sonship always ensures affliction.

> 'It is a great truth that every child of God is afflicted; but it is a lie that every afflicted man is a child of God.'

*God's love to his people cannot change* 'I have chosen thee in the furnace of affliction.' God says, 'I chose you before you were here. I chose you at your birth. I loved you when you were dead in your trespasses and sins.' Rejoice then, O Christian, that God's love does not fail in the furnace, but is as hot as the furnace, and hotter still.

## If you want God's people you must generally look for them in the furnace

In the days of Noah you will find a man who is laughed at, hissed at, hooted as a fool, building a ship on dry land, standing in the furnace of slander and laughter: that is Noah, the elect of God. In the days of Christ, I point you to the despised fishermen and the persecuted apostles.

It is a fact, I say, that you will find religion in the furnace. If I were asked to find religion in London I should generally go among the poor, among the despised, where the furnace blazed the hottest; there I should expect to find saints – but not among the respectable and fashionable churches of our land. This is a fact, that God's people are often in the furnace.

## The reason for this

Why is it that God's children get there? Why does God see fit to put them in the furnace?

    (a)  This is the stamp of the covenant
         See Genesis 15:17.
    (b)  All precious things have to be tried
         See Proverbs 17:3; Numbers 31:23.
    (c)  The Christian is said to be a sacrifice to God
    (d)  If we were not like this we would not be at all like Jesus Christ

## The benefits of the furnace

    (a)  It purifies us
    (b)  It makes us more ready to be moulded
    (c)  God's people get more light in the furnace than anywhere else
    (d)  It is useful for bringing plagues on our enemies

## The comforts of the furnace

    (a)  Election
    (b)  You have the Son of Man with you in the furnace

# Healing by the stripes of Jesus

'With his stripes we are healed' Isaiah 53:5

## Introduction

Being one evening in Exeter Hall, I heard our late beloved
brother, Mr Mackay, of Hull, make a speech in which he told
us of a person who was under very deep concern of soul and
felt that he could never rest till he found salvation. So, taking
the Bible in his hand, he said to himself, 'Eternal life is to be
found somewhere in this Word of God; and if it be here, I will
find it, for I will read the book right through, praying to God
over every page of it, if perhaps it may contain some saving
message for me.'

He told us that the earnest seeker read on through Genesis,
Exodus, Leviticus and so on; and though Christ is there very
evidently, he could not find him in the types and symbols.
Neither did the holy histories yield him comfort, nor the book
of Job. He passed through the Psalms, but did not find the
Saviour there; and the same was the case with the other books
till he reached Isaiah. In this prophet he read on till near the
end, and then, in the fifty-third chapter, these words arrested
his delighted attention: 'With his stripes we are healed.' 'Now I
have found it,' he said. 'Here is the healing that I need for my
sin-sick soul, and I see how it comes to me through the
sufferings of the Lord Jesus Christ. Blessed be his name, I
am healed!'

## God, in infinite mercy, here treats sin as a disease

'With his stripes' – that is, the stripes of the Lord Jesus – 'we
are healed.' Through the sufferings of our Lord, sin is
pardoned, and we are delivered from the power of evil: this
is regarded as the healing of a deadly malady. The Lord in this
present life treats sin as a disease.

(a) It is not essential to mankind
   The disease of sin was not part of human nature as God created it.
(b) It puts the whole system of mankind out of order
(c) Sin, like disease, operates to weaken mankind
(d) Sin is a disease which in some cases causes extreme pain and anguish, but in other instances deadens sensibility
(e) Sin is a disease which pollutes a man
(f) This disease is fatal

## God declares the remedy which he has provided

I ask you very solemnly to accompany me in your meditations for a few minutes, while I bring before you *the stripes of the Lord Jesus.*

(a) Our Saviour's physical sufferings
(b) Our Saviour's soul-sufferings

## This remedy is immediately effective wherever it is applied

(a) The character is healed
(b) The conscience is healed
(c) The heart is healed

'Sin is no longer loved, but God is loved, and holiness is desired.'

Sin is no longer loved, but God is loved, and holiness is desired. *The whole person is healed,* and the whole life is changed. Many of you know how lighthearted faith in Jesus makes you, how the troubles of life lose their weight and the fear of death ceases to cause slavery. You rejoice in the Lord, for the blessed remedy of the stripes of Jesus is applied to your soul by faith in him.

# God in the covenant

'I will be their God' Jeremiah 31:33

## Introduction

What a glorious covenant the second covenant is! Well might it be called 'a better covenant, which was established upon better promises' (Heb. 8:6).

It is better because it is founded on *a better principle*.

It surpasses the other in *stability*.

It surpasses the other in *the mighty blessings* it conveys.

> 'In the covenant of grace God himself conveys himself to you and becomes yours.'

Stop just one moment and think over this text, 'I will be their God', before we start. In the covenant of grace God himself conveys himself to you and becomes yours. Understand it: *God* – all that is meant by that word: eternity, infinity, omnipotence, omniscience, perfect justice, infallible rectitude, immutable love – all that is meant by God: Creator, Guardian, Preserver, Governor, Judge – all that that great word can mean, all of goodness and of love, all of bounty and of grace – all that this covenant gives you to be your absolute property as much as anything you can call your own: 'I will be their God.'

## How is God especially the God of his own children?

For God is the God of all men, of all creatures; he is the God of the worm, of the flying eagle, of the star and of the cloud; he is God everywhere. How then is he more my God and your God than he is God of all created things? We answer that in some things God is the God of all his creatures; but even there, there is a special relationship between himself and his chosen creatures, whom he has loved with an everlasting love. And in the next place, there are certain relationships in which God does not exist towards the rest of his creatures, but only towards his own children.

*God is the God of all his creatures* God is the God of all his creatures seeing that *he has the right to decree* and to do with them as he pleases.

Also, God is the God of all his creatures in the sense that *he has a right to command obedience of all.*

God also has a universal power over all his creatures *in the character of a Judge.*

*How God is our God, as he is to no one else* God is my God because he is the God of my *election.*

The Christian can call God his God from the fact of his *justification.*

God is the believer's God by *adoption.*

## The exceeding preciousness of this great mercy

(a) Compare this with the lot of your fellow men
(b) Compare this with what you require, Christian

## The certainty of this promise

The text does not say, 'I *may* be their God' but 'I *will* be their God.'

## Make use of your God

It is strange that spiritual blessings are our only possessions that we do not use. Delight yourself in God. Remember that it is a command: 'Rejoice in the Lord, always, and again I say rejoice.'

# Cry out in the night

'Arise, cry out in the night; in the beginning of the watches pour out thine heart like water before the face of the Lord' Lamentations 2:19

## Introduction

This was originally spoken to Zion, when in her sad and desolate condition Jeremiah, the weeping prophet, had wept his eyes dry for the slain of the daughter of his people. When he had done all he could himself to pour out tears for poor Jerusalem, he then begged Jerusalem to weep for herself.

We leave Zion, however, to speak to those who need exhortation more than Zion does. From our text we gather the following points:

(a) It is never too soon to pray
(b) It is never too late to cry to the Lord
(c) We cannot pray too vehemently
(d) We cannot pray too simply

# The minister's true ordination

'Son of man, I have made thee a watchman unto the house of Israel: therefore hear the word at my mouth, and give them warning from me' Ezekiel 3:17

## Introduction

The office of gospel minister in some respects resembles that of the ancient prophets. Though we cannot, like Elisha, raise the dead; nor, like Isaiah, pour forth eloquent predictions; nor, as

Ezekiel, foretell certain coming and immediate judgments; yet, like them, we are commanded to teach, to warn and to encourage. So much are we like Ezekiel that his commission will suit any gospel minister even of our day. Let us consider:

## The minister's commission

Here is a scrap of ancient writing worthy of a place in a museum. It ought to be in every minister's study. It is the ultimatum of the King of Heaven to us in our doubts as to our calling. It is our Emperor's protocol to all his legions. It is *the minister's true ordination*; a real installation, worth more than all the charters of universities, or the appointments of arch-bishops. Notice:

*The wording of this ancient commission* It is worded in the court language of heaven, and each letter is divine. 'Son of man.' Here is the title by which Ezekiel is addressed: not Right Reverend, nor the Very Venerable; but he has given to him a graciously-humbling title. Ezekiel is called 'son of man' no less than ninety times. This is the name Jesus often took to himself when he was on earth, and therefore it is a truly glorious one. The gracious and all-wise Father saw that too lofty an eminence might tempt Ezekiel to pride. He therefore styles him 'son of man', as much as to say, 'Your visions, rank, talents and office, must not exalt you, for you are, after all, only man. You must not lean on self, for you are utter weakness, being only the "son of man". You must sympathise with each of your fellow-creatures, and deal with him, not as if you were a prince, or a master, but as being, like him, a "son of man".'

'I have made thee a watchman.' Here we read, on this ancient manuscript, a true account of the making of a minister. God alone can do it. Two things are absolutely requisite to make a man a preacher.

1  Special gifts – such as perception of truth, simplicity, aptness to impart instruction, some degree of eloquence and intense earnestness.

2  Special call – every man who is rightly in the ministry must

have been moved thereto by the Holy Spirit. He must feel an irresistible desire to spend his whole life in his Master's cause. No college, no bishop, no human ordination, can make a man a minister; but he who can feel, as did Bunyan, Whitefield, Berridge or Rowland Hill, the struggles of an impassioned longing to win the souls of men, may hear in the air God's voice saying, 'Son of man, I have made *thee* a watchman.'

'Unto the house of Israel.' Ezekiel's was a limited commission; but ours is not, it is as wide as the earth, and as long as time. The world is our parish. We are not ordered to cast the net alone in the pools of Heshbon, or the streams of Jordan, or the Lake of Gennesaret; but we may cover all seas and rivers with the gospel fishing-boats – the navy of Jesus. Yet, still, it is for the sake of the true Israel that we go.

> 'We may cover all seas and rivers with the gospel fishing-boats – the navy of Jesus.'

'Therefore hear the word at my mouth.' The ancient seers did not speak randomly, but they declared what God had taught them. Sometimes, in dreams, they heard heaven's message; sometimes, by a voice from on high; but most commonly by vision did the Word of the Lord come to them. The soul, inspired by God, seems at times to leave the body, and that narrow tube of vision which we call eyesight, with its own eagle eye, seems to pierce the thick cloud and to mount into that remote region which the ordinary eye cannot see.

The prophets heard the spoken Word, but we have the written Word; and this we must devoutly read. It becomes a minister diligently to study the Scriptures, with all the assistance he can gain from holy men who have gone before, but chiefly from the most excellent of all instructors, the true Interpreter, the Holy Spirit.

'And give them warning from me.' There are other duties; but as this is the most arduous, it is specially mentioned. We are to warn the Christian if he is found backsliding, or sinning; and to warn the sinner of the consequences of his sin, of the strict justice of God, and of the fearful hell in which the ungodly shall suffer.

*The high office conferred by this commission* It is that of
'watchman'. Every soldier of the cross is bound to watch;
but the minister is in a double sense a watchman. He is so
called because:
1   The ministry requires great vigilance. We must not sleep:
we must watch against false doctrine and false brethren. The
true minister is to sit like the shepherd in the wilderness by
night, or like the whisper-hearing sentinel.
2   The ministry involves toil and trouble. Few think of the
watchman who tramps by their door. Hark! there is a scuffle, a
fight! Who is sure to be in it? The watchman. How the wind
blows! The snow must be a foot deep; pray stir the fire. Surely
no one is out of doors tonight – except the watchman! His
exposed face is cut by the driving sleet, his fingers are numbed
with the cold, his eyelids are almost frozen. Some of you come
here and sit and smile and criticise. The minister must bear it
all, for he is the watchman.
3   The ministry should be arousing. If there is a fire, or a
thief, or a door or shutter unfastened, the watchman must cry
aloud. We must cry out with all our might and not be afraid
to disturb, or alarm, or hurt the feelings of the sleepers. We
may as well be asleep if all we do is mumble. Everyone who
labours in the Word and God's teaching should ponder over
this commission, and wear it next to his heart and on his
brow. It is to be feared that many who profess to preach the
gospel are not alive in a sense of their position; but, having
the next presentation to a living, or having bought a benefice,
they rush in where angels, if, like them, uncalled, would fear
to venture.

## The minister's responsibility

The watchman holds a responsible office. If the sentinel, by
sleeping, causes the death of a single person, he is a murderer.
If the prisoner escapes from his charge, he shall be required to
answer for his neglect. So, if the ungodly man is not warned,
he will suffer for his own guilt, but my unfaithfulness will lie as
a crime on me. If the professing Christian falls, his fall is his
own; but if I have not warned him, I also am guilty. If I do not

utter the whole truth, the warnings, the promises and the invitations of God, I shall be a sleeping sentinel, a careless captain, a negligent railway guard, and I shall be the murderer of my fellow-creatures. Or if, to the professor [one who professes to be a Christian], I give wine instead of medicine, or a stone for bread, I shall be a guilty wretch, and God help me then, for no one more requires help than an unfaithful minister!

## The minister's comfort

(a) The Lord's call to the office
'Son of man, I have made thee a watchman.'
(b) The promises peculiar to that call
For every call from God has the strength to perform it enclosed within itself.
(c) The blessed brow-hardening Spirit
He makes us despise alike the frown or the smile of man, and thus keeps us from unfaithfulness.
(d) The fact that success is not required of us
What is required from us is faithfulness.

O my Father, keep me clear of the blood of all men! Amen.

# The fruitless vine

'And the word of the Lord came unto me, saying, Son of man, What is the vine tree more than any tree, or than a branch which is among the trees of the forest?' Ezekiel 15:1–2

## Introduction

The Jewish nation had arrogant ideas of themselves; when they sinned against God, they supposed that on account of the superior sanctity of their forefathers they would be

135

delivered. So they sinned as they pleased. They thought God would never cast them away. God, therefore, in order to humble their pride, tells them that they in themselves are nothing more than any other nation; and he asks them what there is about them to recommend them. 'I have often called you a vine; I have planted you, and nurtured you in a very fruitful hill, but now you bring forth no fruit.' 'What is the vine tree more than any tree, or than a branch which is among the trees of the forest?'

## A lesson of humility

First, there is a lesson of humility for all you who have 'tasted that the Lord is gracious'. 'What is the vine tree more than any tree, or than a branch which is among the trees of the forest?' Let this humble you, Christian, that the vine is nothing more than any other tree, except for the fruitfulness which God has given it.

## A lesson of search

As the vine without its fruit is useless, so, too, the professor, without fruit, is worthless.

- (a) Where do we find fruitless professors?
  Everywhere.
- (b) Why are these men fruitless, and must be cast away?
  Because they have no roots.
- (c) What is God's estimation of the fruitless professor?
  He is the most useless thing in the world.
- (d) What is to become of this fruitless tree?
  It will be devoured in the fire.

I confess, I should dread above all things the unutterable hell of hells of hypocritical apostles, of men that stand in the ranks, profess to love God, prate of godliness, that sit in the pews and uphold Christianity, that take the sacrament and speak about communion, that stand up to pray and talk about being heard for their faith, who are all the while committing abominations, and under cover of their profession are cheating the poor, robbing the fatherless and doing all kinds of iniquity.

# The Bible

'I have written to him the great things of my law, but they were counted as a strange thing' Hosea 8:12

## Introduction

This is God's complaint against Ephraim. It is no mean proof of his goodness, that he stoops to rebuke his erring creatures.

Concerning the Bible, I have three things to say tonight, and they are all in my text. First, its author – '*I* have written'; second, its subjects – the great things of God's law; and third, its common treatment – it has been accounted by most men a strange thing.

## Who is the author?

Concerning this book, who is the author? The text says that it is God. '*I* have written to him the great things of my law.' Sometimes I see David as the penman, at other times Solomon, yet each letter was penned by an almighty finger. The Bible is God's Bible.

(a)  Admire its authority
(b)  Mark its truthfulness

## Its teaching

(a)  All things in the Bible are great
(b)  While all things in the Bible are important, all are not equally important

## How the Bible is received

The Bible is accounted a strange thing.

(a) They never read it
(b) They say it is so horribly dry
(c) Some people hate the Bible

# The plumbline

'Thus he shewed me: and, behold, the Lord stood upon a wall made by a plumbline, with a plumbline in his hand. And the Lord said unto me, Amos, what seest thou? And I said, A plumbline. Then said the Lord, Behold, I will set a plumbline in the midst of my people Israel: I will not again pass by them any more' Amos 7:7–8

## Introduction

God usually speaks by men according to their natural capacity. Amos was a herdsman. He was not a man of noble and priestly rank, like Ezekiel, nor a man of gigantic intellect and mightly eloquence, like Isaiah. He was a simple herdsman. God's rule is, 'Every man in his own order.' So when Amos had a vision, he simply saw a piece of string with a plumb of lead at the bottom of it – a plumbline – a thing which he could easily understand. There was a mystery about the vision, but the vision itself was not mysterious. We have nothing before us but this plumbline, but there is a great deal to be learnt from it.

## The plumbline is used in construction

We are told in the text that 'the Lord stood upon a wall made by a plumbline', that is to say, a wall which had been constructed with the help of a plumbline.

(a) God always uses it in his building
(b) We also should use the plumbline in our building

## The plumbline is to be used for testing the building when it is built

(a) We must continually use on ourselves the plumbline of God's Word
(b) God will use the plumbline, on the last great day, to test everything

## The plumbline is used in the work of destruction

(a) God goes about the work of destruction slowly
(b) Not a soul, on that great day, will be sent to hell who does not deserve to go there

# Salvation of the LORD

'Salvation is of the LORD' Jonah 2:9

## Introduction

Jonah learned this sentence of good theology in a strange college. He learned it in the whale's belly, at the bottom of the mountains, with the weeds wrapped about his head, when he supposed that the earth with her bars was about him for ever. Most of the grand truths of God have to be learned by trouble.

By salvation here we do not merely understand this special salvation which Jonah received from death; for according to the Bible commentator Dr Gill, there is something so special in the original that we can only understand it here as relating to the great work of the salvation of the soul which endures for ever.

## The teaching expounded

Salvation is from the Lord. By this we understand that the whole of the work whereby men are saved from their natural state of sin, and are translated into the kingdom of God and made heirs of eternal happiness, is of God, and of him only. 'Salvation is of the LORD.'

*The plan of salvation is entirely of God* No human intellect and no created intelligence assisted God in the planning of salvation. He contrived the way, even as he himself carried it out. God devised it, because without God it could not have been devised.

*Salvation was executed by the Lord* No one has helped to provide salvation; God has done it all himself. 'Salvation is of the LORD' as to its provisions; Jehovah – Father, Son and Spirit – has provided everything.

*The application of salvation is of the Lord* We are all agreed on the first two points. But now we separate a little. 'Salvation is of the LORD' *in its application.* 'No,' says the Arminian, 'it is not; salvation is of the Lord, inasmuch as he does all for man that he can do; but there is something that man must do, which if he does not do, he must perish.' That is the Arminian way of salvation.

If God does require of the sinner – dead in sin – that he should take the first step, then he requires just that which renders salvation as impossible under the gospel as ever it was under the law, seeing that man is as unable to believe as he is to obey, and is just as much without power to come to Christ as he is without power to go to heaven without Christ. The power must be given to him by the Spirit.

Well then, says one, that will make people sit still and fold their arms. Sir, it will not. But if men did so I could not help it; my business is not to prove to you the reasonableness of any truth, nor to defend any truth from its consequences; all I do here is just to assert the truth, because it is in the Bible.

*The sustaining work in any man's heart* When a man is made a child of God he does not have a stock of grace given to him with which to go on for ever, but he has grace for that day; and he must have grace for the next day, and grace for the next, and grace for the next, until days shall end, or else the beginning shall be of no avail.

> For day by day the manna fell,
> Oh to learn that lesson well.

*The ultimate perfection of salvation is of the Lord* So, soon, the saints of earth shall be saints in light.

## How God has hedged this doctrine about

I shall now try to show how God has guarded us from making any mistakes, and has hedged us around to make us believe the gospel.

*Natural temperament* Some have said salvation in some cases is the result of natural temperament. God has unanswerably met this objection since most people who are saved are just the most unlikely people in the world to have been saved.

*The minister* Some say it is the minister they hear who converts men. If I could convert you all, anyone else might unconvert you; what any man can do another man can undo; it is only what God does that is abiding.

## The influence of this truth on men

    (a) A great battering-ram against their pride
    (b) Grace to nerve you to work for God

## What is the obverse of this truth?

Damnation is of man: if salvation is of God, damnation is of man.

# The incarnation and birth of Christ

'But thou, Bethlehem Ephratah, though thou be little among
the thousands of Judah, yet out of thee shall he come forth
unto me that is to be ruler in Israel; whose goings forth have
been from of old, from everlasting' Micah 5:2

## Who sent Jesus Christ?

The answer is given in the words of the text. 'Out of thee,' says
Jehovah, speaking through the mouth of Micah, 'out of thee
shall he come forth unto me.' It is a sweet thought that Jesus
Christ did not come forth without his Father's permission,
authority, consent and assistance. He was sent of the Father,
that he might be the Saviour of men.

> **He was sent of the Father, that he might be the Saviour
> of men.**

The Father sent him! Contemplate that subject. Let your soul
get hold of it, and in every period of his life think that he
suffered what *the Father* willed; that every step of his life was
marked with the approval of the great I AM.

## Where did he come to?

A word or two concerning Bethlehem. It seemed right that our
Saviour should be born in Bethlehem because of its history,
name and position – 'little in Judah'.

*Bethlehem's history* It seemed necessary that Christ should be
born in Bethlehem, because of Bethlehem's history. Dear to
every Israelite was the little village of Bethlehem.
   Rachel died there (Genesis 35). It was in Bethlehem that
Ruth went to glean in the fields of Boaz (Ruth 2). Boaz
became the father of Obed, and Obed the father of Jesse,
and Jesse the father of David. This last fact gilds Bethlehem

with glory – the fact that David was born there. Little as Bethlehem was, it was much to be esteemed.

*Bethlehem's name* There is something in the name of the place, 'Bethlehem Ephratah'. The word Bethlehem had a double meaning. It signifies 'the house of bread' and 'the house of war'.

Jesus is Bread to his people, on which they feed. But while he is food to the righteous he wages war on the wicked, according to his own Word – 'Think not that that I am come to send peace on earth; I came not to send peace, but a sword' (Matthew 10:34).

Ephratah means 'fruitfulness' or 'abundance'. It is Jesus who makes us fruitful. 'If a man abide in me,' he says, 'and my words abide in him, he shall bring forth much fruit.'

*Bethlehem's position* Bethlehem is said to be 'little among the thousands of Judah'. Why is this? Because Jesus Christ always goes among the little ones. He is the Christ of the little ones.

We cannot pass from this without another thought here, which is, how wonderfully mysterious was that providence which brought Jesus Christ's mother to Bethlehem at the very time when she was to be delivered. Caesar Augustus issues a decree that they are to be taxed. It is for us to believe, that man does as he pleases, yet notwithstanding he always does as God decrees.

## What did Jesus come for?

He came to be 'ruler in Israel'. A very singular thing is this, that Jesus Christ was said to have been 'born the King of the Jews'. Very few have ever been 'born king'. The moment that he came on earth he was a king.

# Building for God

'Yet now be strong, O Zerubbabel, saith the LORD; and be strong, O Joshua, son of Josedech, the high priest; and be strong, all ye people of the land, saith the LORD, and work: for I am with you, saith the LORD of hosts: according to the word that I covenanted with you when ye came out of Egypt, so my spirit remaineth among you: fear ye not' Haggai 2:4–5

## Introduction

Satan is always doing his utmost to hamper God's work. He hindered these Jews from building the temple; and today he endeavours to hinder God's people from spreading the gospel.

In the case of the Jewish people on their return from captivity he sought to prevent the building of the temple by making them selfish and worldly, so that everyone was eager to build his own house, and cared nothing for the house of the Lord. Like some in our day, they saw to themselves first, and God's turn was very long in coming; hence the prophet cried, 'Is it time for you, O ye, to dwell in your cieled houses, and this house lie waste?'

By the mouth of his servant Haggai stern rebukes were uttered, and the whole people were aroused. We read, 'Then Zerubbabel the son of Shealtiel, and Joshua the son of Josedech, the high priest, with all the remnant of the people, obeyed the voice of the LORD their God, and the words of Haggai the prophet, as the LORD their God has sent him, and the people did fear before the LORD' (Haggai 1:12).

I will enter fully into the subject, by the assistance of the Holy Spirit, by calling your attention to *discouragement forbidden*. Then I shall speak of *encouragement imparted*; and, having done so, I shall linger with this blessed text which overflows with comfort, and will speak, third, of *encouragement further applied*.

## Discouragement forbidden

Discouragement comes readily enough to us poor mortals who are occupied in God's work, seeing it is a work of faith, a work of difficulty, a work above our capacity, and a work much opposed.

*Discouragement is very natural* Discouragement is a native of the soil of manhood. To believe is supernatural, faith is the work of the Spirit of God; to doubt is natural to fallen men, for we have within us an evil heart of unbelief. It is abominably wicked, I grant you; but still it is natural, because of the downward tendency of our depraved hearts.

> 'To believe is supernatural, faith is the work of the Spirit of God; to doubt is natural to fallen men.'

Discouragement may come and does come to us, as it did to these people, from a consideration of the great things which God deserves at our hands and the small things which we are able to render. When in Haggai's days the people thought of Jehovah and of a temple for him, and then looked on the narrow space which had been enclosed and the common stones which had been laid for foundations, they were ashamed. Where were those hewn stones and costly stones which, in times gone by, Solomon brought from afar? They said to themselves, 'This house is unworthy of Jehovah: what do we by labouring thus?' Have you not felt the depressing weight of what is so surely true? Brethren, all that we do is little for our God; far too little for him that loved us and gave himself for us.

When we have prayed for his kingdom we have been disgusted with our own prayers; and all the efforts we have put forth in connection with any part of his service have seemed too few, too feeble for us to hope for acceptance. Thus have we been discouraged. The enemy has worked upon us by this means, yet he has made us argue very wrongly. Because we could not do much, we have half resolved to do nothing! Because what we did was so poor, we were inclined to quit the work altogether! This is evidently absurd and wicked. The enemy can use humility for his purposes as well as pride. Whether he makes us think too much or too little of our work, it is all the same so long as he can get us off from it.

Moreover, the enemy contrasts our work with that of others and with that of those who have gone before us. We are doing so little in comparison with other people, therefore let us give up. We cannot build like Solomon, therefore let us not build at all. Yet, brethren, there is a falsehood in all this; for, in truth, nothing is worthy of God. The great works of others, and even the amazing productions of Solomon, all fall short of his glory. What house could man build for God? What are cedar and marble and gold as compared with the glory of the Most High? Though the house was 'exceeding magnifical', yet the Lord God has of old dwelt within curtains, and never was his worship more glorious than within the tent of badgers' skins; indeed, as soon as the great house was built, true religion declined. What of all human work can be worthy of the Lord? Our little labours do but share the insignificance of greater things, and therefore we ought not to withhold them: yet here is the temptation from which we must pray to be delivered.

*Wherever discouragement comes in it is dreadfully weakening* I am sure it is weakening, because the prophet was told to say three times to the governor, high priest and people, 'Be strong.' This proves that they had become weak. Being discouraged, their hands hung down and their knees were feeble. Faith girds us with omnipotence, but unbelief makes everything hang loose and limp about us. Distrust, and you will fail in everything; believe and according to your faith so will it be unto you.

We want Christian people who have faith in their principles, faith in the doctrines of grace, faith in God the Father, God the Son and God the Holy Spirit; and who therefore contend earnestly for the faith in these days when piety is mocked at from the pulpit, and the gospel is sneered at by professional preachers. We need people who love the truth, to whom it is dear as their lives; people into whose hearts the old doctrine is burned by the hand of God's Spirit through a deep experience of its necessity and of its power. We need no more people who will parrot what they are taught, but we want people who will speak what they know. Oh, for a troop of men like John Knox, heroes and martyrs and covenanter stock! Then would Jehovah of hosts have a people to serve him who would be strong in the Lord and in the power of his might.

*Discouragement deflects people from God's service* It is significant that the prophet said to them, 'Be strong, all ye people of the land, saith the Lord, *and work.*' They had ceased to build: they had begun to talk and argue, but they had laid down the trowel. They were extremely wise in their observations and criticisms and prophecies; but the walls did not rise.

It is always so when we are discouraged. We stop doing the Lord's work and and waste time in chatter and nonsensical refinements. May the Lord take away discouragement from any of you who now suffer from it! Blessed is the person who is able to stand fast by his God in these evil days. Let us not in any way be discouraged. 'Be strong; be strong; be strong,' sounds as a threefold voice from the triune God. 'Fear not,' comes as sweet refreshment to the faint. Therefore let nobody's heart fail him. So much for discouragement.

### Encouragement imparted

Second, here is encouragement imparted, which is the major part of our text. 'According to the word that I covenanted with you when ye came out of Egypt, so my spirit remaineth among you: fear ye not.' God remembers his covenant and keeps his ancient promises. When the people came out of Egypt the Lord was with them by his Spirit: hence he spoke to them by Moses, and through Moses he guided and judged and taught them.

The Lord was also with his people in the fiery cloudy pillar which was conspicuous in the midst of the camp. His presence was their glory and their defence. This is a type of the presence of the Spirit with the Church. At the present day, if we hold the truth of God, if we live in obedience to his holy commands, if we are spiritually-minded, if we cry to God in believing prayer, if we have faith in his covenant and in his Son, the Holy Spirit abides among us. The Holy Spirit descended on the Church at Pentecost, and he has never gone back again: there is no record of the Spirit's return to heaven. He will abide with the true Church evermore. This is our hope for the present struggle. The Spirit of God remains with us.

*The Holy Spirit helps existing ministries* To what end, my brethren, is the Spirit with us? Let us think of this, that we may be encouraged at this time. The Spirit of God remaineth among you *to aid and assist the ministry which he has already given.* Oh, that all of us who profess to preach the gospel would learn to speak in complete dependence on the direction of the Holy Spirit, not daring to utter our own words.

Do you not know the difference between the power which comes from human oratory and that which comes through the divine energy which speaks so to the heart that people cannot resist it? We have forgotten this too much. It would be better to speak six words in the power of the Holy Spirit than to preach seventy years of sermons without the Spirit.

*The Holy Spirit raises up other useful people* This same Spirit who of old gave to his Church eminent teachers can raise up other and more useful people. The other day, a brother from Wales told me about the great men he remembered: he said that he had never heard anyone like Christmas Evans, who surpassed all men when he was in the *hwyl.* I asked him if he knew another Welsh minister who preached like Christmas Evans. 'No,' he said, 'we have no such man in Wales in our days.' So in England we have neither Wesley nor Whitefield, nor any of their order; yet, as with God is with the residue of the Spirit, he can fetch out from some chimney-corner another Christmas Evans, or find in our Sunday school another George Whitefield, who will declare the gospel with the Holy Spirit sent down from heaven. Let us never fear for the future, or despair for the present, since the Spirit of God remains with us.

'Let us never fear for the future, or despair for the present, since the Spirit of God remains with us.'

148

When our Lord ascended on high he led captivity captive, and received gifts from men. He then gave apostles, teachers, preachers and evangelists, and he can do the same again. Let us fall back upon the eternal God, and never be discouraged for an instant.

*The Holy Spirit gives the whole Church various ministries* Nor is this all. Since the Holy Spirit is with us, he can move the whole Church to exercise its varied ministries. This is one of the things we want very much – that every member of the Church should recognise that he is ordained for service. Everyone in Christ, man or woman, has some testimony to bear, some warning to give, some deed to do in the name of the holy child Jesus; and if the Spirit of God is poured out on our young men and young women, each one will be aroused to energetic service.

If the Spirit is with us, there will come multitudinous conversions. We cannot get at 'the lapsed masses', as they are pedantically called. We cannot stir the crass infidelity of the present age: no, we cannot, but the Holy Spirit can. All things are possible with God.

If you walk down to our bridges at a particular time in the day you will see barges and boats lying in the mud; and all the king's horses and all the king's men cannot stir them. Wait until the tide comes in, and they will walk the water like things of life. The living flood accomplishes at once what no mortals can do. And so today our churches cannot stir. What shall we do? Oh, that the Holy Spirit would come with a floodtide of his benign influences, as he will if we will but believe in him; as he must if we will but cry to him; as he will if we will cease to grieve him. Everything will be just as the saints desire when the Lord of the saints is with us. The hope of the continuing increase of the Church lies in the remaining of the Spirit with us. The hope of the salvation of London lies in the wonder-working Spirit. Let us bow our heads and worship the omnipotent Spirit who designs to work in us, by us and with us.

'The hope of the salvation of London lies in the wonder-working Spirit.'

## Encouragement further applied

It is at the beginning of every gracious purpose that men have
most fear, even as these people had who had newly begun to
build. When first the Holy Spirit begins to strive with a man
and lead him to Jesus, he is apt to say, 'I cannot; I dare not; it
is impossible. How can I believe and live?' Now I want to
speak to some of you here who are willing to find Christ, and
to encourage you by the truth that the Spirit lives to help you. I
would even like to speak to those who are *not* anxious to be
saved.

I remember that Dr Payson, an exceedingly earnest and
useful man of God, once did a strange thing. He had been
holding inquiry meetings with all sorts of people, and great
numbers had been saved. At last, one Sunday he announced
that he would hold a meeting on Monday night for those
people who did not desire to be saved; and, strange to say,
some twenty people came who did not wish to repent or
believe. He spoke to them and said, 'I am sure that if a little
film, thin as the web of the gossamer, were let down by God
from heaven to each one of you, you would not push it away
from you. Although it were almost invisible, you would value
even the slightest connection between you and heaven. Now,
your coming to meet me tonight is a little link with God. I
want it to increase in strength until you are joined to the Lord
for ever.' He spoke to them most tenderly, and God blessed
those people who did not desire to be saved, so that before the
meeting was over they were of another mind. The film had
become a thicker thread, and it grew and grew until the Lord
Christ held them by it for ever.

Dear friends, the fact that you are in the Tabernacle this
morning is like that filmy thread: do not put it away. Here is
your comfort, the Holy Spirit still works with the preaching of
the Word. While the heavenly wind blows softly on you open
wide every window. You have not felt that you wanted it; but
that is the sure proof that you need it; for he who does not
know his need of Christ is most in need. Open wide your heart
that the Spirit may teach you your need; above all, breathe the
prayer that he would help you this morning to look to the

Lord Jesus Christ, for 'there is life in a look at the Crucified One – there is life at this moment for you'.

**'The final perseverance of saints is the result of the final perseverance of the Holy Spirit.'**

'Oh,' you say, 'if I began I should not keep on.' No; if *you* began perhaps you would not; but if *he* begins with you *he* will keep on. The final perseverance of saints is the result of the final perseverance of the Holy Spirit. He perseveres to bless, and we persevere in receiving the blessing. If he begins, you have begun with a divine power that neither faints nor grows weary.

# A brand plucked from the fire

'And the LORD said unto Satan, the LORD rebuke thee, O Satan; even the LORD that hath chosen Jerusalem rebuke thee: is not this a brand plucked out of the fire?' Zechariah 3:2

Suggested by a firebrand falling on the hearth.

### Remarks on the wording of the text

'Brand' – saints by nature like other 'brands'
'Out of the fire' – not away from it – to show the great danger
'Plucked' – by mighty grace of omnipotence

### Instances of plucking from the burning

(a) The narrow escapes saints have had from death, before conversion
(b) The old age of some
(c) The natural depravity of the heart
(d) Evil habits into which they had fallen
(e) Temptations and trials after conversion

(f)  The spirituality of the law
(g)  The immense price of our ransom

## How can I tell if I am one?

(a)  Can you remember the plucking?
(b)  Do you hate the fire?
(c)  Do you love other plucked brands?
(d)  Do you love to adore divine free grace?

(Preached at Waterbeach when Spurgeon was eighteen years old, his four hundred and twelfth sermon.)

# Independence of Christianity

'Not by might, nor by power, but by my spirit, saith the Lord of hosts' Zechariah 4:6

## Introduction

My object will be to glorify God, by showing you, who love the Saviour, that the preservation and the triumph of the Church are both of them to be accomplished, not by might, nor by power, but by the Spirit of God, in order that all the honour might be to God, and none of it to man.

You will ask me whether there is any distinction to be drawn between these two words, 'not by might, nor by power'. I reply, yes. The best Hebrew scholars tell us that the 'might', in the first place, may be translated 'army'. The Septuagint translation of the Bible does so translate it. It signifies power *collectively* – the power of a number of men combined together. The second word, 'power', signifies the prowess of a single individual, so that I might paraphrase my text thus – 'Not by the combined might of men labouring to assist each other, nor by the separate might of any single hero, but by my Spirit, saith the Lord.'

## Not by might

The preservation and triumph of the Church cannot be accomplished by might – that is, not by collective might.

(a) Human armies
(b) Great corporations
(c) Large congregations

## Nor by power

Nor by power – that is, individual strength.

The greatest works that have been done have been done by the weak ones.

(a) Not by learning

'I would give up all my talents to preach like Bunyan the tinker.' John Owen

(b) Not by eloquence

## By the Spirit of God

I was thinking yesterday, my friends, what a magnificent change would come over the face of Christendom if God would suddenly pour out his Spirit as he did on the day of Pentecost. We want the Holy Spirit, and then whatever faults there may be in our organisation, they can never materially impede the progress of Christianity, when once the Spirit of the Lord God is in our midst.

# Mourning at the cross

'And I will pour upon the house of David, and upon the
inhabitants of Jerusalem, the spirit of grace and of supplications: and they shall look upon me whom they have pierced,
and they shall mourn for him, as one mourneth for his only
son, and shall be in bitterness for him, as one that is in
bitterness for his firstborn' Zechariah 12:10

## Godly sorrow is always a creation of the Holy Spirit

My subject is evangelical sorrow, godly sorrow for sin. There
never was any real godly sorrow, such as works repentance
acceptable to God, except that which results from the Holy
Spirit's work within the soul. 'I will pour upon the house of
David, and upon the inhabitants of Jerusalem, the spirit of
grace and supplications . . . and they shall mourn.'

(a) True, godly repentance is not produced by mere con-
    science
(b) It is not the product of mere terror
(c) It can never be produced in the soul by any outward
    machinery
(d) Genuine mourning for sin comes as a gift of divine grace
(e) This work of grace is always accompanied by prayer
(f) True repentance is continuous in a Christian

## Godly sorrow is brought about by looking to Christ

Where there is this acceptable mourning for sin it is caused by
looking to Christ. 'They shall look upon me whom they have
pierced.' What is the inference from that fact? Why, that
repentance is not a preparation for looking to Christ. Do
you see that? The looking is put first, and the mourning
afterwards. Yet I know what many of you have thought.
You have said to yourselves, 'We must mourn for sin, and
then look to Christ to pardon it.' That is not God's order, and

we must always be careful to keep all the truths in the order in which he has put them. Remember, sinner, that there will never be a tear of acceptable repentance in your eye until you have first looked to Jesus Christ.

**Remember, sinner, that there will never be a tear of acceptable repentance in your eye until you have first looked to Jesus Christ.**

(a) Looking to Christ, we see how sin hates purity
(b) Looking to Jesus Christ on the cross, we see sin's ingratitude to love
(c) The cross of Christ shows us man's abhorrence of God
(d) As we look to Christ we see that our guilt was so great that only an infinite sacrifice could atone for it

## Godly sorrow for sin is the chief of sorrows

Whenever godly sorrow for sin comes into the heart, it is not a sham sorrow but a very real one. Our text says, 'They shall mourn for him, as one mourneth for his only son, and shall be in bitterness for him, as one that is in bitterness for his firstborn.' The death of an only child causes special sorrow. Such is the kind of grief that a true Christian feels concerning his sin.

## Godly repentance does not itself cleanse us from sin

Are you startled by that statement? Then read Zechariah 13:1, 'In that day there shall be a fountain opened to the house of David and to the inhabitants of Jerusalem for sin and for uncleanness.' Now, dear friends, if mourning for sin took the sin away, there would no need for the cleansing fountain. For, although the mourning was so real and so bitter, it did not take away the mourners' sin. Toplady was right when he sang:

> Could my zeal no respite know,
> Could my tears for ever flow,
> All for sin could not atone:
> Thou must save, and thou alone.

155

But while godly repentance does not take away sin, wherever it is present it is a proof that sin is taken away. If you have repented of your sin, and have believed in Jesus, then you have been cleansed in the open fountain, and that same blood, which has cleansed you from guilt, will yet prove that it can also cleanse you from the power of sin.

# NEW TESTAMENT

# Jesus

'And she shall bring forth a son, and thou shalt call his name
JESUS: for he shall save his people from their sins' Matthew
1:21

## Introduction

Bernard of Clairvaux has delightfully said that the name of
Jesus is honey in the mouth, melody in the ear and joy in the
heart. I rejoice in that expression on my own account, for it
gives me my share of the delight, and leads me to hope that,
while I am speaking, the sweetness of the precious name of
Jesus may fill my own mouth. Here also is a portion for you
who are listening: it is melody in the ear. If my voice should be
harsh and my words discordant, you will still have music of
the choicest order, for the name itself is essential melody, and
my whole sermon will ring with its silver note. May both
speaker and hearer join in the third word of Bernard's
sentence, and may we all find it to be joy in our hearts, a
jubilee within our souls. Jesus is the way to God, therefore we
will preach him; he is the truth, therefore will we hear of him;
he is the life, therefore shall our hearts rejoice in him.

So inexpressibly fragrant is the name of Jesus that it imparts
a delicious perfume to everything which comes in connection
with it. Our thoughts will turn to the first use of the name in
connection with our Lord, when the child who was yet to be
born was named Jesus. Here we find everything suggestive of
comfort. The person to whom that name was first revealed was
Joseph, a carpenter, a humble man, a working man, unknown
and undistinguished save by the justice of his character. It is
not, therefore, a title to be monopolised by the ears of princes,

sages, priests, warriors or men of wealth. It is a name to be made a household word among common people. He is the people's Christ, for of old it was said of him, 'I have exalted one chosen out of the people.'

There is consolation in the messenger who made known the name to Joseph, for it was the angel of the Lord who, in the visions of the night, whispered that charming name into his ear; and henceforth angels are in league with men, and gather to one standard, moved by the same watchword as ourselves – the name of Jesus. Did God send the name by an angel, and did the angel delight to come with it? Then is there a bond of sympathy between us and angelic spirits, and we are come this day not only 'to the general assembly and church of the firstborn' but 'to an innumerable company of angels', by whom that name is regarded with reverent love.

I shall ask for the exercise of your patience while I consider six things in reference to this transporting name. It is an ointment poured out, and its scent is varied so as to contain the essence of all fragrance.

## A name divinely ordered and expounded

According to the text, the angel brought a message from the Lord, and said, 'Thou shalt call his name Jesus.' The name is the highest, brightest and noblest of names; it is the glory of our Lord to be a Saviour. To the best that was ever born of woman God has given the best name that any son could bear.

JESUS is *the most appropriate name* that our Lord could receive. Of this we are quite certain, for the Father knew all about him, and could name him well. He knows much more about the Lord Jesus Christ than all saints and angels put together, for 'No man knoweth the Son but the Father'. When we plead the name of Jesus before God, we bring him back his own Word, and appeal to him by his own act and deed. He is not a Saviour of our own setting up, but God the everlasting Father has set him forth as our deliverer and Saviour.

It is a name which the Holy Spirit explains, for he tells us the reason for the name of Jesus – 'for he shall save his people from their sins'. 'Saviour' is the meaning of the name, but it has a fuller sense hidden within, for in its Hebrew form it means 'the salvation of the Lord', or 'the Lord of salvation', or 'the Saviour'. The angel interprets it 'he shall save', and the word for 'he' is very emphatic. According to many scholars, the divine name, the incommensurable title of the Most High, is contained in Joshua, the Hebrew form of Jesus, so that in full the word means 'Jehovah Saviour', and in brief it signifies 'Saviour'. It is given to our Lord because 'he saves' – not according to any temporary and common salvation, from enemies and troubles, but he saves from spiritual enemies, and specially from sins. Joshua of old was a saviour, Gideon was a saviour, David was a saviour; but the title is given to our Lord above all others because he is a Saviour in a sense in which no one else is or can be – he saves his people from their sins. The Jews were looking for a Saviour; they expected one who would break the Roman yoke and save them from being under bondage to a foreign power, but our divine Lord came not for such a purpose: he came to be a Saviour of a more spiritual sort, and to break quite another yoke, by saving his people from their sin.

Moreover, in addition to expounding this name, the Holy Spirit, through the evangelist Matthew, has been pleased to refer us to the synonym of it, and so to give us its meaning by comparison. Let me read you the next verses. 'Now all this was done, that it might be fulfilled which was spoken of the Lord by the prophet, saying, Behold, a virgin shall be with child, and shall bring forth a son, and they shall call his name Emmanuel, which being interpreted is, God with us.' If when our Lord was born and named Jesus the old prophecy which said that he would be called Emmanuel was fulfilled, it follows that the name Jesus bears a meaning tantamount to that of Emmanuel, and that its virtual meaning is 'God with us'. Indeed, brothers, he is Jesus, the Saviour, because he is Emmanuel, God with us; and as soon as he was born, and so became Emmanuel, the incarnate God, he became by that very fact Jesus, the Saviour. By coming down from heaven into the earth, and taking upon himself our nature, he bridged the otherwise bridgeless gap between God and man; by suffering in that human nature and imparting through his divine nature an infinite efficacy to those sufferings, he removed that which would have destroyed us, and brought us everlasting life and salvation. Our Saviour is *God*, and therefore able; he is God *with us*, and therefore pitiful; he is divine and therefore infinitely wise; but he is human, and therefore full of compassion.

This, then, is our first head; this charming name of Jesus lets us know the very heart of God in reference to his Son: why he sent him, what he meant him to be and to do, and in what manner he would glorify him.

## A name given by man

Although this name was thus chosen by God, our Lord was actually called by the name of Jesus by man. 'She [Mary] shall bring forth a son, and thou [Joseph] shalt call his name JESUS.' The God of heaven by his angel appoints the child's name, but his reputed father must announce it. Those who are taught by God joyfully recognise that Christ is salvation, and without a question give him the well-beloved name of Jesus, the Saviour.

Here note that the name Jesus, Saviour, was given to our Lord by two simple hearts as soon as ever he was revealed to them. They only needed to be told who he was, and what he had come for, how he was born and what was the object of his incarnation, and they at once accepted the divine message, and named the babe by the name of Jesus. And, brethren, all of us to whom Christ is revealed at all call him Jesus the Saviour. There are many who think they know our Lord, but since they only speak of him as a prophet, a teacher or a leader, and do not care for him as a Saviour, we are clear that they are in ignorance as to his chief character. They do not know his first name, his personal name. The Holy Spirit cannot have revealed Christ to any man if that man remains ignorant of his saving power. He who does not know him as Jesus the Saviour, does not know him at all. Certain anti-Christian Christians are craftily extolling Christ that they may smite Jesus: I mean that they cry up Jesus as Messiah, sent by God, to exhibit a grand example and supply a pure code of morals, but they cannot endure Jesus as a Saviour, redeeming us by his blood, and by his death delivering us from sin. I am not sure that they follow his example of holy living, but they are very loud in extolling it, and all with the purpose of drawing off men's thoughts from the chief character and main object of our Lord's sojourn among us, namely, the deliverance of his people from sin. If men knew our Lord they would call him Jesus the Saviour, and regard him not merely as a good man, a great teacher, a noble exemplar, but as the Saviour of sinners.

## A name identifying our Lord with his people

'Thou shalt call his name JESUS', for that name declares his relation to his people. It is to them that he is a Saviour. He would not be Jesus if he did not have a people: he could not be, for there could be no Saviour if there were no sinners. His name has no meaning apart from his people.

'He shall save his people.' It does not say God's people, for then it would have been understood as meaning only the Jews – or it would have been supposed to refer to some good and holy people who belonged to God, apart from the Mediator. 'He shall save *his* people' – those who are his own, and personally belong to him. These are evidently a very special people, a people set apart as Christ's own treasure; they are a people that belong to God incarnate – Emmanuel's people. These he saves. Who are they but his elect, whom his Father gave him before the earth was? Who are they but those whose names are engraved on the palms of his hands, and written on his heart? Who are they but the numbered sheep that will be required at his hands by the great Father, that he should render them back, saying, 'I have kept those whom thou hast given me, for they are thine.'

'He shall save his people.' Do you not see that this name of Jesus is an election name after all? It has a special bearing upon a chosen people; it has a ring of sovereignty about it, and is all the sweeter because of this to those who see in their own salvation an exhibition of distinguishing grace.

163

## A name which indicates his main work

Why do men write lives of Christ who know nothing about his main business and object? There is no knowing our Lord, if he is not known as a Saviour; for he is that or nothing. Those who fall short of his salvation do not even know his name; how, then, should they know his person? His name is not called Jesus because he is our exemplar, though indeed he is perfection itself, and we long to tread in his footsteps; but his name is called Jesus because he has come to save that which is lost. He is Christ, too, or the anointed, but then he is Christ Jesus; that is to say, it is as a Saviour that he is anointed. He is nothing if not a Saviour.

Now, Jesus saves his people from sin: for, first, he does it by taking all the sins of his people upon himself. Do you think that a strong expression? It is warranted by the Scriptures. 'The Lord hath laid on him the iniquity of us all' (Isaiah 53:6). Christ's shoulders bore the guilt of his people, and because he took their load his people are free, and have henceforth no burden of sin to weigh them down. He saves his people through his personal substitution, by standing in their stead and suffering in their place. There is no other way of salvation but by his vicarious sufferings and death.

Then he saves them by bearing the penalty due to their sin. 'The chastisement of our peace was upon him, and with his stripes we are healed.' 'He was made a curse for us.' 'Christ also hath suffered for us.' He died, 'the just for the unjust, to bring us to God'. He bore the wrath of God which was due to us. He has taken the sin and paid the penalty, and now cavillers come in and falsely say that we teach that a man is to believe the dogma of atonement and then he is saved, and may live as he likes. They know better; they know that they misrepresent us, for we always teach that this great work of substitution and penalty-bearing by Christ works in the person who partakes of its benefits, love to God, gratitude to Christ, and consequent hatred of all sin; *and this change of heart is the very core and essence of salvation.* This is how Christ saves his people from their sin – by rescuing them, by the force of his love, out of the power, tyranny and dominion of sins, which hitherto had the mastery over them.

## A name justified by facts

Many a child has had a grand name, and his life has contradicted it. I recollect a grave on which there is the name of a child, 'Sacred to the memory of Methuselah Coney, who died aged six months'. Many other names are equally inappropriate, and are proved to be so in the course of years. But this Jesus is a Saviour, a true Jesus. He bears a name which he well deserves. Come to the Christ and see there the many that once rioted in sin, and rolled in the mire, but they are washed, but they are sanctified, and now they rejoice in holiness. Who purified them? Who but Jesus? He that saves his people from their sin has saved them. When he comes from heaven, it will be seen that he has saved his Church, his people, from their sins.

## Christ's personal name for ever

It is the name his father and mother gave him – the child Jesus. We also belong to his family; for he that believes in him is his father, and mother, and sister, and brother, and that most dear and familiar name by which he was known at home is ever in our mouths. He is the Lord, and we worship him; but he is Jesus, and we love him. It is the name which moves our affections and fires our souls. Jesus is his death name – 'Jesus of Nazareth, King of the Jews' was written on his cross. That is his resurrection name. That is his gospel name, which we preach. It is the name which Peter preached to the Gentiles when he said, 'This is Jesus of Nazareth by whom is preached to you the remission of sins.' And this, beloved, is his heaven name. They sing to him there as Jesus. See how it concludes the Bible. Read the Revelation, and read its songs, and see how they worship Jesus the Lamb of God. Let us go and tell of his name; let us continually meditate upon it; let us love it henceforth and for ever. Amen.

# The star and the wise men

'Now when Jesus was born in Bethlehem of Judea in the days of Herod the king, behold, there came wise men from the east to Jerusalem, saying, Where is he that is born King of the Jews? for we have seen his star in the east, and are come to worship him.

When they had heard the king, they departed; and, lo, the star, which they saw in the east, went before them, till it came and stood over where the young child was. When they saw the star, they rejoiced with exceeding great joy' Matthew 2:1–2, 9–10

## Introduction

See the glory of our Lord Jesus Christ, even in his state of humiliation.

## Let us gather light from this star

(a) If ever men should fail to preach the gospel, God can conduct souls to his Son by a star

Remember that Omnipotence
Has servants everywhere.

(b) Star-preaching is all about Christ
(c) Star-preaching leads to Christ
(d) The star stopped at Jesus

## Let us gather wisdom from the wise men

(a) They practically used the teaching of the star
(b) They persevered in their search after him
(c) 'They rejoiced with exceeding great joy'
(d) They entered in
(e) They worshipped

**Let us act as wise men under the light of our star**

(a) There is light for you in your particular vocation
(b) What is there better to do in this life than seek after Christ?
(c) Do we see more in Jesus than in other people?
(d) What shall I render unto the Lord?

# Christ receives sinners

'And it came to pass, as Jesus sat at meat in the house, behold, many publicans and sinners came and sat down with him and his disciples' Matthew 9:10

**Illustrations of the way Christ receives sinners**

(a) Zacchaeus
(b) Matthew
(c) Anointed by a woman who was a sinner
(d) The dying thief on the cross
(e) Saul the persecutor

**How is it that Christ is so willing to come down to poor sinners, and save them?**

(a) Because he has such deep affection for sinners
(b) He sees in you the purchase of his precious blood
(c) Christ views the sinner, not as he is in himself, but as he is in the purpose of redemption

**The practical lesson**

Beware of self-righteousness.

Dean Trench, quoting from a Persian moralist, tells one of his old fables about Jesus. Of course, it is only a fable; but it

167

contains the very spirit of the truth about which I have been preaching.

When Christ, according to this fable, was travelling through a certain region, he stayed in a hermit's cave. It so happened that there was, living in the neighbouring town, a young man whose vices were so great that, according to common report, the devil himself did not dare to associate with him lest he should become worse than he was before. This young man, hearing that the Saviour who could pardon sin was in the hermit's cave, went to him. Falling down on his knees, he made confession of his guilt, and acknowledged that he was utterly unworthy of mercy, but entreated Christ, in the love of his gracious heart, to forgive him for the past, and make him a new man for the future.

The monk who lived in the same cave said to the young man, 'Get you gone; you are not worthy to be in such a holy spot as this'; and, turning to the Saviour, he said, 'Lord, in the other world, appoint me a place as far away as possible from this wretch.'

The Saviour answered, 'Your prayer is heard; you are self-righteous, so I appoint you your place in hell; this man is penitent, and seeks mercy at my hands; I appoint him his place in heaven. Thus both of you shall have your heart's desire.'

There is the very essence of justification by faith in that old fable.

# Come to Jesus

'Come unto me, all ye that labour and are heavy laden, and I will give you rest' Matthew 11:28

### Introduction

One is struck with the personality of this text. There are two persons in it, 'ye' and 'me' – that is to say, the labouring one and the tender Saviour who entreats him to come that he may find rest. It is most important, if we wish to see the way of peace clearly, to understand that we must each one come personally to Jesus for rest – 'come unto me, all ye that labour' – and that coming on our part must be to a personal Christ. In effect he says, 'Come yourselves to me. Come not through sponsors, nor through men whom you choose to call your priests, not through the petitions of ministers and teachers, but come yourselves, for yourselves.' The quarrel is between you and God, and this quarrel can only be made up by your approaching the Lord through a Mediator; it would be folly for you to ask another to come to the Mediator for you: you must trust in him yourself. Personal faith is indispensable to salvation.

I want at this time to set forth the glory of the Lord Jesus Christ, who sends this pressing personal invitation to every labouring and heavy-laden one in this place. I wish that I knew how to preach. I have tried to do so for thirty years or so, but I am only now beginning to learn the art. Oh that one knew how to set forth Christ so that men perceived his beauty, and fell in love with him at first sight! Oh, Spirit of God, make it so *now*. If men knew the grandeur of his gospel – the joy, the peace, the happiness which comes of being a Christian, they would run to him.

### The value of the boon

*Rest of the heart is worth more than all California* To be at peace – to be no more tossed up and down in the soul – to be secure, peaceful, joyful, happy, is worth mountains of diamonds. Oh rare peace which comes from the Prince of peace!

*It is practically helpful in all the affairs of life* Other things being equal, there is nobody so fit to run the race of life as the man who is unloaded of his cares and enjoys peace of mind. I commend to you in this busy London the precious boon of my text called 'rest', because it is not only a preparation for the world to come, but for the life that now is.

169

## It is rest for man's entire spiritual being

*Conscience* Conscience troubles us till Jesus speaks it into rest.

*Mind* Minds are tossed about like ships at sea, or birds caught in a fierce gale. Thousands of us can say, 'We know whom we have believed, and are persuaded that he is able to keep that which we have committed to him'; therefore we cannot leave the gospel. No new doctrines, no novelties, no scepticism, no fresh information can disturb us now. Having found rest of intellect in the doctrine of Jesus, there we will stay till death and heaven, or the second advent, solves all riddles.

*Heart* Here is rest and remedy for heart palpitations and the anguish of the breast. Let a man love Jesus and he will crave no other love, for this will fill his soul to the brim.

## The largeness of the Saviour's heart

Only a generous spirit would say, 'Come to me, all you that are downcast – all you that are desponding – all you that are broken-hearted.' Yet that is exactly what the text says. Christ courts the company of the sorrowful, and invites those who are ill at ease to approach him.

*He says, 'Come at once!'* There is a notion in some people's minds that they cannot believe in Christ till they are better. Christ does not want your betterness. You had better come just as you are. If you cannot come *with* a broken heart, come *for* a broken heart. If you cannot come *with* faith, come *for* faith.

*He promises this rest to all who come to him* He says, 'Him that cometh to me I will in no wise cast out.' Each heavy-laden one must and shall find rest if he will come to Jesus, or else the Redeemer's promise is not true.

## The blessedness of his power

Our Lord Jesus is able to give peace to all that labour and are heavy laden. He is conscious that within himself there resides a power which will be able to give peace to every conscience. Notice there is no limiting clause. There are desperate cases, but no one is too far gone for Jesus. You may have read the story of John Bunyan in *Grace Abounding*. Was there ever a poor wretch that was dragged about by the devil more than John was? For five years and more he could not call his soul his own. He did not dare to sleep, because he was afraid he would wake up in hell; and all day long he was troubled and fretted and worried with this and that and the other. I am sure such a case as that would have been given up by men; but when Jesus took it in hand John Bunyan found perfect rest; and his blessed *Pilgrim's Progress* remains a proof of the joy of heart which the poor tinker found when he came to rest in Christ. Jesus is able to give rest. He is willing to cause joy. Doubt no more.

## The simplicity of this invitation

What is the way of salvation? If any minister replies, 'I should want a week or two to explain it to you,' he does not know the way of salvation; because the way of salvation which we need must suit a dying man, an illiterate man and a guilty man, or else it will be unavailing in many cases.

Our Lord Jesus Christ proves how willing he is to save sinners by making the method of grace so easy. He says, 'Come to me.' 'Well,' says someone, 'how am I to come?' Come anyhow. If you can run, come running; if you can walk, come walking; if you can creep, come creeping; if you can only limp, come limping – come anyhow, so long as you come to Jesus.

## The unselfishness of the Lord Jesus Christ

'Come unto me,' says he, 'and I will *give* you.' That is the gospel. '*I* will give *you*.' You say, 'Lord, I cannot give you anything.' He does not want anything. Not what you give to God, but what he gives to you, will be your salvation. Will you come and have it? It lies open before you. Jesus wants nothing of you. Suppose you were to become Christ's disciples, and serve him with all your might throughout your life – in what way would that enrich *him*? He has died for you; how can you ever pay him for that? He lives in heaven to plead for you, and he loves you; how can you ever reward him for that? See, then, how the unselfishness of his character comes out in his inviting to come to himself those who cannot benefit him, but must be pensioners on his bounty.

## Conclusion

If we are on the right track now, which is believing, loving, fearing, serving, honouring God, we shall go on loving, fearing, serving, honouring God for ever and ever. 'Come,' says Christ, 'to me.' What will Jesus say at the judgment day to those who thus come? Why, he will say, 'Come' – 'Come, ye blessed of my Father. Keep on coming. Come, and inherit the kingdom prepared for you from before the foundation of the world.' Ah, my hearers, you will prize this coming when death and eternity are near you.

# Sweet comfort for feeble saints

'A bruised reed shall he not break, and smoking flax shall he not quench, till he send forth judgment unto victory' Matthew 12:20

## Introduction

Our text seems full of gentleness; it seems to have been steeped in love; and I hope I may be able to show you something of the immense sympathy and the mighty tenderness of Jesus.

### Mortal frailty

The bruised reed is an emblem of a sinner in the first stage of his conviction. The smoking flax is a backsliding Christian.

(a) This encouragement is for weak people
(b) This encouragement is for people who are regarded as worthless
(c) This encouragement is for people who are regarded as offensive
(d) You may yet be of some service

### Divine compassion

(a) The little saint is just as much God's elect as the great saint
(b) The salvation of great saints often depends on the salvation of little ones.

### Certain victory

'Until he bringeth forth judgment unto victory.' This victory applies to all age groups: the elderly, the middle-aged and the young.

# Feeble faith appealing to a strong Saviour

'And straightway the father of the child cried out, and said with tears, Lord, I believe; help thou mine unbelief' Mark 9:24

### The supposed difficulty and the real difficulty

(a) He thought that the difficulty lay in the case of his child

(b) He thought that the difficulty lay with Jesus Christ himself

## The tearful discovery

(a) He discovered that he did not believe
(b) He was distressed at his discovery

## The sensible appeal

'Lord, I believe; help thou mine unbelief.'

(a) He prayed to One whom he believed could help him
(b) Nobody other than Jesus can help us to get rid of unbelief

# Unbelievers upbraided

'He . . . upbraided them with their unbelief' Mark 16:14

## Your unbelief is an evil in itself

(a) Think how you would feel if others disbelieved you
(b) The sin of your unbelief may be measured by the excellence of the Person whom you mistrust
(c) Remember the relationship in which Jesus Christ stands to you
(d) Consider how many times some of us have doubted our Lord
(e) Some of these actions have been repetitions of former ones
(f) Often our unbelief has come in the teeth of our own assurance to the contrary
(g) Although you do not trust the Lord as you should, you do trust your fellow-creatures

**The many evils which come out of unbelief to those of us who love the Lord**

(a) Unbelief is so cruel to Christ, and grieves his Holy Spirit so much
(b) Remember how much unrest unbelief has given you
(c) Remember how much you lose, in other things, besides unhappiness
(d) Unbelief weakens us for all practical purposes
(e) Unbelief has a very injurious effect on other Christians
(f) Unbelief in Christians influences the unconverted

# Who loves Christ most?

'There was a certain creditor which had two debtors: the one owed five hundred pence, and the other fifty. And when they had nothing to pay, he frankly forgave them both. Tell me therefore, which of them will love him most? Simon answered and said, I suppose that he, to whom he forgave most. And he said unto him, Thou hast rightly judged' Luke 7:41–3

## Introduction

When we commence the Christian life, it is very natural that we should say to ourselves, 'We do not wish to be second-rate Christians, much less prove to be like the Laodiceans, neither cold nor hot, or, like those of whom the apostle John wrote, "They went out from us, but they were not of us."' I like to see the holy ambition of the young convert who desires to bring forth much fruit to the glory of God, to love Christ much, and manifest that love by every possible act of devotion to him.

## We must all be saved in the same way

(a) Both parties were in debt

(b)  Neither of them could meet their debts

(c)  The creditor freely forgave them both

## It will increase our love for Christ if we have a deep sense of our own sinfulness

'Which of them will love him most?' 'I suppose that he, to whom he forgave most.'

(a)  Anyone who has been forgiven very great open sin ought to have the greatest motive for loving Christ

(b)  You may love Christ much if you have a very deep sense of sin

(c)  Many Christians have a deeper sense of their sin years after their conversion

(d)  You must often feel the spirituality of the law of God

(e)  Endeavour more and more to appreciate the excellency of God

(f)  Cultivate a consciousness of sin's tendency

(g)  Have a sense of divine love

(h)  Have a realisation of what Jesus Christ is to us

## If we possess a burning love for Christ this will lead us to show our love very much as this woman did

(a)  By desiring to be near him

(b)  By imitating the boldness of her confession

(c)  By imitating her deep humility

(d)  By imitating her penitence

(f)  By imitating her self-denying service

# Anxiety, ambition, indecision

'Neither be ye of doubtful mind' Luke 12:29

## Introduction

The chief concern of a man should be to see that his own soul is right in the sight of God. Solomon said, 'Keep thy heart with all diligence; for out of it are the issues of life.'

The word 'doubtful' means so much that I do not expect to be able to tell you all that it means, but shall rather give you a few practical thoughts concerning it.

## Children of God, be not anxious

Be not tossed up and down by your outward circumstances. If God prospers you, do not ride high, as the vessel does when the tide lifts it up.

Our Saviour's injunction means, 'Do not be anxious about your temporal affairs.'

Have you – you who are in the habit of worrying and fretting – ever made any profit by doing so?

'I cannot help fretting.' Do you not think that the Lord can help you?

'I feel that I must be doing something.' That 'doing' will be your undoing unless you consider what God would have you do.

'I just cannot help being anxious.' What is the difference between you and the man of the world?

'I am anxious about God's work.' And what are you doing, good friend, to bring about a good result? Are you agonising before the Lord in prayer, or is your anxiety just confined to yourself?

## 'Be not ambitious'

This is another possible meaning of the text.

177

(a) Some aim at amassing great wealth
(b) Some aim at high positions
(c) Some are over-ambitious in the service of God

### 'Be ye not of irresolute mind, without decision of character'

This is a third possible meaning of the text.

Some people are time-servers. John Bunyan in *Pilgrim's Progress* describes such people: Mr By-ends and Mr Fair-speech. Every Christian should say, 'By the grace of God, my mind is made up to him, cost what it may.'

### 'Do not be at sea about your personal salvation'

This is the fourth possible meaning of the text.

(a) Some people who are not saved imagine that they are
(b) Some people think that doubts are necessary for a child of God

# A sabbath miracle

'And he was teaching in one of the synagogues on the sabbath. And, behold, there was a woman which had a spirit of infirmity eighteen years, and was bowed together, and could in no wise lift up herself. And when Jesus saw her, he called her to him, and said unto her, Woman, thou art loosed from thine infirmity. And he laid his hands on her: and immediately she was made straight, and glorified God' Luke 13:10–13

### Christ's compassion was aroused

(a) Not by her prayers
(b) Not by any description which she gave of her condition

## Jesus issued a command

'He called her to him.'

   (a) Evidence of Christ's great grace
   (b) Given directly and personally to her
   (c) A call which was promptly obeyed

## Christ's power was manifested

   (a) The Word of the Lord has power
   (b) Christ laid his hands on her
   (c) The woman was healed immediately
   (d) The woman's cure was complete

## Christ's power brought glory to God

'She . . . glorified God.'

# The Redeemer's tears over sinners

'And when he [Jesus] was come near, he beheld the city, and wept over it' Luke 19:41

## Introduction

Jesus had a triumphant entrance into Jerusalem; he rode not on the forbidden horse of Egypt, but on the noble ass of Palestine; all around were shouting, palm branches were waving, clothes were spread on the ass and on the ground, while the whole city was stirred. 'Tis a man riding on the ass, and in triumph, too, and yet this triumphant man weeps – he is looking on a fair and beautiful city, and yet he weeps.

    There were pleasing associations connected with it; there, Abraham offered Isaac; there, David danced before the ark,

179

and dwelt in solemn state. Through its streets Solomon once rode in regal splendour; there Josiah held his great Passover. Once, happy feet ransomed from Babylon had trod its stones; thither the tribes went up every year in joyful procession; but these are not in his mind, for, see, he weeps.

He wept at the grave of Lazarus, but then he lost a friend; but now 'tis for a city flourishing, blooming, gorgeous with a temple surpassing all edifices on earth.

## He wept at the remembrance of what she had been

(a) A city abounding with privileges, but having not at all made use of them

(b) A city to whom prophets had been sent, but she had spilt their blood, and disregarded all

(c) A city of the highest order and degree about to be brought down to the lowest depths

## What she then was

(a) A city filled with those whom he had benefited, and those same persons remaining most ungrateful

(b) He knew her state of sinfulness, and wept at the remembrance that she was a sink of sin – cruel, bloody, vile hypocrites there

(c) A city he had lived and preached in

(d) A city given over – condemned

## What she would be

(a) She was to be stripped of all her privileges

(b) Utterly ruined and destroyed

Now let Jesus stand up, and weep over Waterbeach, and over this congregation.

You have been distinguished for sin; yes, many here, and your sin is aggravated by your many privileges. You are now many, yes, most of you, dead in trespasses and sins, and some especially vile.

You have long resisted divine calls – you will yet go on in sin, and many of you will be damned. Weep, oh preacher! Weep. Weep. Weep – men and women.

Now let Jesus stand up, and weep over you one by one.

(a)  Over the open reprobate, despisers, drunkards
(b)  Over the unconverted many-year hearer
(c)  Over the hopeful young, who yet will go aside
(d)  Over convinced sinners wiping their tears away
(e)  Over many feast-goers, who go despite warnings
(f)   Over old men, on the brink of hell
(g)  Over hypocrites, deceiving their own souls
(h)  Over those who are given up and let alone
(i)   Over laughing hearers

Weep one by one. Oh, that mine eyes were fountains of tears.

(Sermon preached at Waterbeach.)

# The dying thief in a new light

'But the other answering rebuked him, saying, Dost not thou fear God, seeing that thou are in the same condemnation? And we indeed justly; for we receive the due reward of our deeds: but this man hath done nothing amiss. And he said unto Jesus, Lord, remember me when thou comest into thy kingdom' Luke 23:40–2

### Introduction

A great many people, whenever they hear the conversion of the dying thief, remember that he was saved in the very moment of death, and they dwell on that fact, and that alone. He has always been quoted as a case of salvation at the eleventh hour; and so, indeed, he is. The cross of Christ avails even for a man hanging on a gibbet, and drawing near to his last hour.

But that is not everything that the story teaches us. I do not think, dear friends, that the only speciality about the thief is the lateness of his repentance.

## The means of his conversion

*The sight of our great Lord and Saviour* There was, to begin with, our Saviour's wonderful behaviour on the way to the cross. Never had a cross been carried by a Cross-bearer of his form and fashion. When the thief heard that mysterious Sufferer say so solemnly, 'Daughters of Jerusalem, weep not for me, but weep for yourselves, and for your children,' he must have been struck with wonder.

When the thief saw the Saviour surrounded by the Roman soldiery – saw the executioners bring out the hammers and the nails, and lay him down on his back, and drive the nails into his hands and feet – this crucified criminal was startled and astonished as he heard him say, 'Father, forgive them; for they know not what they do.'

'As the thief looked at Christ on the cross, he felt in his soul, "It must be He. Could there be another so God-like, so divine?" '

And when the central cross was lifted up, that thief, hanging on his own cross, looked around, and I suppose he could see Pilate's inscription written in Hebrew, Greek and Latin – 'Jesus of Nazareth, the King of the Jews'. If so, that writing was his little Bible, his New Testament, and he interpreted it by what he knew of the Old Testament. Then he would remember the words of the prophet Isaiah, 'The chastisement of our peace was upon him.' 'Why,' he would say to himself, 'I never understood that passage in the prophet Isaiah before, but it must point to him! Can this be he who cried in the Psalms, "They pierced my hands and my feet"?' As he looked at him again, he felt in his soul, 'It must be He. Could there be another so God-like, so divine?'

*The dying thief learned the gospel from the lips of Christ's enemies* They said, 'He saved others.' 'Ah,' he thought, 'did he save others? Why should he not save *me*?'

*The thief must have begun to look at Jesus again* Surely what won him most must have been to *look at Jesus again*, as he was hanging upon the cruel tree. Possibly nothing about the physical person of Christ would be attractive to him, for his appearance was more marred than that of any man, and his form more disfigured than the sons of men; but yet there must have been in that blessed face a singular charm. As I conceive the face of Christ it was very different from anything that any painter has yet been able to place upon his canvas. It was all sorrow, yet all love; all meekness, yet all resolution; all wisdom, yet all simplicity.

## The faith of the dying thief

I think it was a very singular faith that this thief exerted towards our Lord Jesus Christ. I greatly question whether the equal and the parallel of the dying thief's faith will be readily found outside the Scriptures, or even in the Scriptures.

'I greatly question whether the equal and the parallel of the dying thief's faith will be readily found outside the Scriptures, or even in the Scriptures.'

*He believed in Christ when he saw him dying the death of a criminal* The thief saw Christ die under circumstances of the greatest personal shame. You have never understood what it was to be crucified. None of you could do that, for the sight has never been seen in England in our day. This dying thief leads us in the matter of faith, for what he saw of the circumstances of the Saviour was calculated to contradict rather than help his confidence, for he saw our Lord in the very extremity of agony and death, and yet he believed in him as the King shortly to come into his kingdom.

*All the disciples had forsaken Christ, and fled* John might have been lingering at a little distance, and holy women may have stood farther off; but no one was present bravely to champion the dying Christ. After our Lord was nailed to the tree, the first to bear witness for him was this thief. The centurion bore witness afterwards, when Jesus expired; but this thief was a lone confessor, holding on to the Saviour when nobody would say 'Amen' to what he said. Brethren, the dying robber exhibited marvellous faith, and I beg you to think of this next time you speak of him.

*He himself was in extreme torture* Remember, he was crucified. It was a crucified man trusting in a crucified Christ. Oh, when the whole frame is racked with pain, when the tenderest nerves are tortured, when the body is hung up to die by we know not what length of torment, then to forget the present and live in the future is a grand achievement of faith!

*He saw so much* He saw the future world. He did not say, 'Lord, let me sit at thy right hand' or 'Let me share the dainties of thy palace.' He only said, 'Remember me.' 'Think of me.' 'Cast an eye my way.' I see deep humility in his prayer.

## The result of his faith while he was here below

I have heard people say, 'Well, you see, the dying thief was converted; but then he was not baptised. He never went to communion, and never joined the Church.' He could not do either; and that which God himself renders impossible to us he does not demand of us. The poor man was nailed to the cross; how could he be baptised? But he did a great deal more than that; for if he could not carry out the outward signs, he most manifestly exhibited the things which they signified, which, in his condition, was better still.

*The dying thief confessed the Lord Jesus Christ* That is the essence of baptism. He confessed Christ. Did he not acknowledge him to his fellow-thief?

*He rebuked his fellow-sinner* He answered the ribaldry with which the other criminal assailed our Lord, saying, 'Dost not thou fear God, seeing thou art in the same condemnation? And we indeed justly; for we receive the due reward of our deeds: but this man hath done nothing wrong.' Our 'other men's sins' make up a great item in our personal guilt unless we rebuke them as we have opportunity. This our Lord expects us to do. The dying thief did it, and he did it with all his heart.

*The dying thief made a full confession of his guilt* He said to him who hanged with him, 'Dost not thou fear God, seeing thou art in the same condemnation? *And we indeed justly*.' Not many words, but what a world of meaning was in them – 'we indeed justly'. 'You and I are dying for our crimes,' said he, 'and we deserve to die.'

*The dying thief defends his Lord manfully* He says, 'We indeed justly, but this man hath done nothing amiss.' When all other voices were silent, one suffering penitent spoke out words which mean, 'This man is perfectly innocent.'

*His prayer is directed to Jesus* Here is another mark of this man's faith. He prayed, 'Lord, remember me when thou comest into thy kingdom.' True faith is always praying faith.

**'True faith is always praying faith.'**

*He adores and worships Jesus* 'Lord, remember me when thou comest into thy kingdom.' I think that there was about his prayer a worship equal to the eternal hallelujahs of cherubim and seraphim.

## Our Lord's promise to him about the future

There was something very special about the dying thief when our Lord said to him, 'To day shalt thou be with me in paradise.' He only asked the Lord to remember him, but he received this surprising answer: 'To day shalt thou be with me in paradise.' Dying thief, you were favoured above many, 'to be with Christ, which is far better', and to be with him soon!

## Conclusion

Why is it that our Lord does not thus emparadise all of us at once? It is because there is something for us to do on earth. My brethren, are you doing it?

# The Holy Spirit compared to the wind

'The wind bloweth where it listeth, and thou hearest the sound thereof, but canst not tell whence it cometh, and whither it goeth: so is every one that is born of the Spirit' John 3:8

## Introduction

Our Saviour draws a parallel between the wind and the Holy Spirit. In Hebrew and Greek the same word is used for wind and spirit. 'The wind,' said our Saviour, 'bloweth', and the same word would have been used if he had intended to say, 'The Spirit bloweth where he listeth.'

### How the Holy Spirit may be compared with the wind

*Mystery* The work of the Spirit is a mystery. Nicodemus asked Jesus, 'How can these things be?' The Holy Spirit's person and work cannot be understood by man's mind.

*Divinity* Our Saviour uses the simile of the wind for the Spirit to teach about the Holy Spirit's divinity. 'Ye must be born again from above', for human regenerations are a lie.

*Sovereignty* 'The wind bloweth where it listeth.' Sinner, God can give you the Holy Spirit if he will; but if he should say, 'Let him alone,' your fate is sealed.

*Varied methods*
1  Observe the different *force* of the wind. To some of us he came like a 'rushing mighty wind'. Read the conversions of John Bunyan and Martin Luther.

To others the Holy Spirit comes so gently, they cannot tell when first the Spirit of God came.
2  Observe the different *directions* of the wind. In the days of Wesley and Whitefield, there was very little of the divine Spirit anywhere, except among the Methodists. I am sure they have no monopoly now.

Sometimes the wind blows from the pulpit, or the Sunday school or from an individual believer.

*Varied qualities* There is the east wind of the Spirit with its denunciations; there is the north wind convicting the world of 'sin, of righteousness, of judgment'; there is the south wind, blowing softly on poor troubled spirits. Yet 'all these worketh the self-same Spirit'.

*Duration* The Spirit of God does not always work with us. He does as he pleases. He comes, and he goes.

## The parallel between the Holy Spirit and the effects of the wind

(a)  A great wrecker (of false hopes and carnal confidences)
(b)  A great leveller
(c)  A purifier
(d)  A trier of the nature of things
(e)  A developer of character

## Conclusion

It is a blessed thing to wait on God, watching for his hand and in quiet contentment leaving all to him.

# Immeasurable love

'For God so loved the world, that he gave his only begotten Son, that whosoever believeth in him should not perish, but have everlasting life' John 3:16

## Introduction

I will keep to the one point of setting forth the love of God. I want to make you see how great that love is.

## The divine gift

'God so loved the world, *that he gave his only begotten Son.*' Men who love much will give much, and you may usually measure the truth of love by its self-denials and sacrifices.

*What this gift was* Think of the sacred person whom the great Father gave in order to demonstrate his love to men. It was his only-begotten Son – his beloved Son, in whom he was well pleased. Judge, you fathers, how you love your sons: could you give them to die for your enemy?

*How he gave his Son* If you desire to see God's love you must consider *how* he gave his Son. He sent him to a manger, united him with a perfect manhood, which first took the form of an infant. There he slept, where horned oxen fed!

The Lord God sent the heir of all things to toil in a carpenter's shop: to drive the nail, and push the plane, and use the saw. He sent him down among the scribes and Pharisees, whose cunning eyes watched him and whose cruel tongues scourged him with base slanders. At length he gave him up to death – a felon's death, the death of the crucified.

Remember that our Lord Jesus Christ died what his countrymen considered to be an accursed death. To the Romans it was the death of a condemned slave, a death which had all the elements of pain, disgrace and scorn mingled in it to the uttermost. 'But God commendeth his love towards us, in that, while we were yet sinners, Christ died for us.' Oh, wondrous stretch of love, that Jesus Christ should die!

*When God gave his Son* There is love in the time. 'God so loved the world that he gave his only begotten Son.' But when did he do that? In his eternal purpose he did this from before the foundation of the world.

## The divine plan of salvation

Note the love of God in the plan of salvation. He has put it thus: 'that whosoever believeth on him should not perish, but have everlasting life'. The way of salvation is extremely simple to understand, and exceedingly easy to practise, when once the heart is made willing and obedient. So, what is it to believe in Jesus?

*To give your firm and cordial assent to the truth* Accept that God did send his Son, born of a woman, to stand in the place of guilty men and bear the punishment of our transgressions.

*Accept this for yourself* Jesus offered an atonement, and that atonement becomes yours when you accept it by putting your trust in him.

*Personal trust* One thing more is necessary; and this is personal trust. First comes assent to the truth, then acceptance of that truth for yourself, and then a simple trusting of yourself wholly to Christ, as a Substitute. The essence of faith is trust, reliance, dependence.

## The divine choice of the people to whom salvation comes

They are described in these words – 'whosoever believeth in him'. There is in the text a word which has no limit – 'God so loved the world'; but then comes in the descriptive limit, which

I beg you to notice with care: 'He gave his only begotten Son *that whosoever believeth in him* should not perish.'

God did not love the world that any man who does not believe in Christ shall be saved; neither did God so give his Son that any man shall be saved who refuses to believe in him. See how it is put – 'God so loved the world, that he gave his only begotten Son, that whosoever believeth in him should not perish.' Here is the compass of the love: while every unbeliever is excluded, every believer is included.

## The divine deliverance

This is implied in the words, 'that whosoever believeth in him should *not perish*'. I understand that word to mean that whoever believes in the Lord Jesus Christ shall not perish, though he is ready to perish. His sins would cause him to perish, but he shall never perish.

What is it to perish? It is to lose all hope in Christ, all trust in God, all light in life, all peace in death, all joy, all bliss, all union with God. This shall never happen to you if you believe in Christ.

## The possession

The last commendation of God's love lies in the *positive* – in the possession. God gives to every person who believes in Christ everlasting life. As long as there is a God, the believer shall not only exist, but live.

# The source

'The woman saith unto him, Sir, thou hast nothing to draw with, and the well is deep: from whence then hast thou that living water?' John 4:11

## What led the woman to ask her question?

She asked, 'From whence then hast thou that living water?'
Jesus Christ had told her that, had she known him, she would
have asked from him and he would have given her living
water. They were both next to Jacob's well. The woman
understood the figure, though she did not at first understand
its spiritual meaning. Its spiritual meaning is this. Jesus Christ
has grace in himself, grace to give to sinners, grace to give to
those who ask him for it.

## Our Saviour's answers to the woman's question

Her question was, 'From whence then hast thou that living
water?' Our Saviour shows the woman how he has this living
water.

(a) He has it in his very nature
(b) He has it by divine appointment
(c) He has it by the anointing which he received from the
Holy Spirit
(d) He has it because (we now know) his redeeming work is
finished
(e) It is the reward which the Father promised him for his
mediatorial work
(f) Because of his intercession at his Father's right hand in
glory

## The inferences to be drawn from this truth

(a) Christ is still able to bless the children of men
(b) Christ needs nothing from us
(c) The living water is not exhausted at this present time
(d) We should all drink this living water, which Christ so
freely gives

# In no wise cast out

'All that the Father giveth me shall come to me; and him that
cometh to me I will in no wise cast out' John 6:37

Upon reading this verse, one feels inclined to break out with
the angelic song, 'Behold, I bring you good tidings of great
joy.'
Here are two sets of doctrines, the high and the low joined;
surely, this passage will suit all, from the 'Hyper' down to the
Primitive.

## The positive eternal 'shall'

'All that the Father giveth me shall come to me.' These words
may be regarded as:

(a)  A prophecy of our Lord, the Prophet of his people
(b)  A solemn oath of God the Son
(c)  A triumphant boast of Jesus the Conqueror
(d)  A challenge to death and hell

In these words, he speaks like one:

(a)  Who knows the number of his people: 'all'
(b)  Who regards past and present as one: 'giveth'
(c)  Who is convinced of his own power to perform what he
has promised

But this is of no comfort unless we can see:

(a)  That he has given us the Holy Spirit
(b)  That we have given ourselves to him

If we have done so, then let us glory in these blessed words,
and sing them aloud: 'All that the Father giveth me shall come
to me.'

## The negative eternal 'will'

'And him that cometh to me I will in no wise cast out.'

*Notice here the Speaker, our Lord Jesus Christ* The Father has never spoken thus in his absolute character; it would be an insult to try to go to him except through Christ, when he has made his Son the only medium of access to him.

*Notice the character addressed* Not the Jew who comes, not the king or rich man who comes, not the good man who comes, not the young or old, but 'him that cometh', whosoever he may be.

*Notice the words of Jesus* 'I will in no wise case out.' It is very strong in the original; Christ means, 'I will not, not, not,' or, 'I will never, never, never cast out any who come to me.' Christ will not cast them out:

(a) Because of their great sins
(b) Because of their long delays
(c) Because of their trying other saviours
(d) Because of the hardness of their hearts
(e) Because of their little faith
(f) Because of their poor and dull prayers
(g) Because everyone else passes them by

When they are once in, they are in for ever. Christ will not cast them out:

(a) Because of their unbelief
(b) Because of their old corruptions
(c) Because of their backslidings

Read, write, print, shout – 'him that cometh to me I will in no wise cast out.'

What is it to come to Christ? People do not know what it is; they fancy it is to reform themselves, to be moral, honest, good, upright, etc., etc. But it is to trust, to believe in Jesus.

'Believe on the Lord Jesus Christ, and thou shalt be saved.'

Great Saviour, I thank thee for this text; help thou me so to preach from it that many may come to thee, and find eternal life!

# The search-warrant

'But there are some of you that believe not' John 6:64

## Some people's unbelief is secret

    (a) Even in the ministry, there are some who do not have faith

    (b) There are some, in other offices of the Church, who do not have faith

    (c) Secret unbelief may be true of others who are engaged in works of piety

    (d) Secret unbelief may be true of church members in general

## Those who are known to us as unbelievers

    (a) 'We have no faith, but we are keen to have it'

    (b) The despairing ones

    (c) The careless and thoughtless

# A mournful defection

'Will ye also go away?' John 6:67

## Why do others go?

(a) They cannot bear our Lord's teaching
(b) They desert for the sake of gain
(c) They are terrified of persecution
(d) They forsake true religion out of sheer levity
(e) They are tempted away by evil companions
(f) They leave Christ for the sake of sensual enjoyment
(g) Considerable numbers gradually grow cold
(h) Some turn away because of a change of circumstances
(i) Some forsake Christ when they become rich
(j) Unsound doctrine induces many to apostatise
(k) Some turn away through sheer laziness

## What happens to those who turn away?

(a) They are not happy
(b) Those who prove traitors to a profession they once made are the hardest people in the world to impress.
(c) Many of them go away to die in blank despair.

## Why should we not turn away as they have?

Were we left to ourselves, I cannot think of any reason why we should not go as they have gone. Nor, indeed, could I tell you why the best man here should not be the worst before tomorrow morning if the grace of God left him. John Bradford, you know, as he saw the poor criminals taken away to Tyburn to be executed, used to say. 'There goes John Bradford but for the grace of God.'

**'There goes John Bradford but for the grace of God.'**

(a) Have a real foundation on Christ to begin with
(b) Be schooled in humility, and keep very low before the Lord
(c) Shun the company which has led other people away

# The indwelling and outflowing of the Holy Spirit

'He that believeth on me, as the scripture hath said, out of his belly shall flow rivers of living water. (But this spake he of the Spirit, which they that believe on him should receive: for the Holy Ghost was not yet given; because that Jesus was not yet glorified)' John 7:38–9

## The work of the Spirit is intimately connected with the work of Christ

(a) The Holy Spirit was not given until Jesus had been glorified
(b) The Holy Spirit was given after the ascent of our Lord to his glory, partly to make that ascent the more renowned
(c) The Holy Spirit was sent at this time as an evidence of our divine Master's acceptance
(d) The Holy Spirit's work is to bear witness to Jesus Christ
(e) It is by the gospel of Jesus Christ that the Spirit of God works in the hearts of men
(f) The Holy Spirit's work is to make us like Jesus Christ
(g) It is for the glory of Jesus that the Spirit of God works

## The operations of the Holy Spirit are of incomparable value

The Spirit of God abiding in his Church is better than Jesus Christ's earthly ministry. The work of the Holy Spirit is a truer

196

work, a deeper work, a surer work, and will more effectually achieve the purposes of God than even would the enthusiasm to which we should be stirred by the bodily presence of our well-beloved Saviour.

### These operations are of marvellous power

(a) An inward work
(b) A life-giving work
(c) An abundant work
(d) A spontaneous work
(e) A perpetual work

### These operations of the Spirit of God are easily to be obtained by the Lord's children

(a) Through believing in Jesus
(b) Through prayer

### Conclusion

Ask God to make you all that the Spirit of God can make you, not only a satisfied believer who has drunk for himself, but a useful believer, who overflows the neighbourhood with blessing.

# 'Though he were dead'

'Martha saith unto him, I know that he shall rise again in the resurrection at the last day. Jesus said unto her, I am the resurrection, and the life: he that believeth in me, though he were dead, yet shall he live: And whosoever liveth and believeth in me shall never die. Believest thou this?' John 11:24–6

## Introduction

Martha is a very accurate type of a class of anxious believers.

(a) She set a practical bound to the Saviour's words
(b) She put the words of Jesus on the shelf
(c) She put the promise in the remote distance
(d) She made the promise unreal and impersonal

## View the text as a stream of comfort to Martha and other bereaved people

(a) The presence of Jesus Christ means life and resurrection
(b) When Jesus comes the dead shall live
(c) When Jesus comes, living believers will not die
Paul said, 'We shall not all sleep, but we will be changed.'
(d) Even now the dead in Christ are alive
(e) Even now the living in Christ do not die

No longer is it death to die.

## View it as a great spring of comfort for all believers

(a) The Lord Jesus Christ is the life of his people
(b) Faith is the only channel by which we can draw from Jesus our life
(c) To the reception of Christ by faith there is no limit
(d) There is no limit to this power
(e) 'Whosoever liveth and believeth in me shall never die'

# Precepts and promises

'If any man serve me, let him follow me; and where I am, there shall also my servant be: if any man serve me, him will my Father honour' John 12:26

## A sentence of precept

'If any man serve me, let him follow me.'

- (a) If you become Christ's servant you must obey him
- (b) Your service will be most like our Lord's when you do as closely as you can what Christ did
  You will become a marked man.
  It will mean being put in the ground to die.
- (c) If you want to serve Christ, follow him

## A precept and a promise

Now I turn to the second clause in my text, which seems to me to be both a precept and a promise.

*A precept* 'Where I am, there *let* my servant be.' Wherever Jesus was, and is, there you are to be, if you are really his servant.

*A promise* 'Where I am, there *shall* also my servant be.' When we die we shall be in good company.

## A sentence which is altogether a promise

'If any man serve me, him will my Father honour.'

- (a) God will honour us by setting his seal on our work
- (b) God will honour you in your opponent's sight
- (c) The best honour God will give his people will be in heaven

# A blessed gospel chain

'Jesus answered and said unto him, If a man love me, he will keep my words: and my Father will love him, and we will come unto him, and make our abode with him' John 14:23

### The first link: Loving Christ

'If a man love me.'

- (a) Some only pretend to love him
- (b) Some are only Christ's disciples in name
- (c) If you do love Christ, remember that he must have loved you first

### The second link: Keeping Christ's words

'If any man love me,' says Christ, 'he will keep my words.'

- (a) By treasuring them, and prizing them
- (b) Find your way into the inner meaning of his words
- (c) Keep his words in practice

### The third link: A high privilege and great joy

'He will keep my words: and *my Father will love him.*' What wonderful words these are: 'My Father will love him'!

### The fourth link: 'We will come unto him'

This is a singular use of the plural pronoun: '*We* will come unto him.' It means:

- (a) Distance removed
- (b) Honour conferred
- (c) Knowledge increased
- (d) Assistance brought

**'And make our abode with him'**

(a) What knowledge of one another is implied here
(b) A sacred friendship
(c) The complete acceptance of the man before God
(d) Do nothing to make them leave you even for a moment

# The Comforter

'But the Comforter, which is the Holy Ghost, whom the Father will send in my name, he shall teach you all things, and bring all things to your remembrance, whatsoever I have said unto you' John 14:26

## Introduction

'Comforter' is also translated 'Paraclete', meaning monitor or instructor or teacher. No one learns anything correctly, unless he is taught by the Spirit.

'Comforter' is also translated 'Advocate'. The Holy Spirit is our Advocate, who makes intercession for us, with groanings that cannot be uttered.

## The Comforter

The Holy Spirit's characteristics:

(a) The Holy Spirit is a loving Comforter
(b) The Holy Spirit is a faithful Comforter
(c) The Holy Spirit is a wise Comforter
(d) The Holy Spirit is a safe Comforter
(e) The Holy Spirit is an active Comforter

## The comfort

(a) Beware of claims of 'new' revelations
   The canon of revelation is closed.
(b) The Holy Spirit comforts by telling us old things over again
(c) Look to Calvary
(d) Chastisement is for your good

## Who are comforted people?

If you have received one blessing from God, you will receive all other blessings too. Whom he calls, them he justifies; whom he justifies, them he sanctifies; and whom he sanctifies, them he also glorifies.

## Conclusion

What do you know of the Comforter?

# The mission of the Holy Spirit

'And when he is come, he will reprove the world of sin, and of righteousness, and of judgment: Of sin, because they believe not on me; Of righteousness, because I go to my Father, and ye see me no more; Of judgment, because the prince of this world is judged' John 16:8–11

## The Holy Spirit's threefold conviction of people

The apostles had a stern task in front of them. They were to go to all nations and proclaim the gospel to everyone, starting in Jerusalem. Remember that only two or three years previously they were simple fishermen – men of little or no education, men of no rank or standing. They were told by their Lord that they would be brought before rulers and kings for his sake, and that they would be persecuted wherever they went. They were to proclaim the gospel in the teeth of the imperial power of Rome and the ancient wisdom of Greece and the fierce cruelties of barbaric lands, and to set up the kingdom of peace and righteousness.

At the very moment when they were about to receive their commission, they were also to lose the physical presence of their great Leader. While he was with them they were not afraid. But now that he was about to leave this world and go to the Father they would be like orphans. Here was a sad case. Work given, and power withdrawn: a battle beginning, and the conquering general leaving.

How good it was for these disciples that our Lord could tell them that his going away would be to their advantage and not to their disadvantage. For after he left them the Spirit of God would come to be an Advocate for them and with them, and by his power they would be able to silence all their enemies and achieve their mission.

We will observe how the Holy Spirit acted as their Advocate. To my mind this passage is a compendium of all the work of God's Spirit. In it was seen, first, the Spirit of God going with the preaching of the gospel to reprove people of their sin; second, to convince people of sin, and to lead them to repentance towards God and faith in our Lord Jesus Christ; and, third, the ultimate result of the Holy Spirit's work will be to convict people of being guilty of the most terrible sin, of having opposed perfect righteousness. We shall try to see the meaning of the passage through these three windows.

## To reprove people

First, we believe that a promise is made here to Christ's servants, that when they go and preach the gospel the Holy Spirit will be with them to reprove people. By this is meant not so much to save them as to silence them. When Christ's minister stands up to plead his Master's cause, another

Advocate appears in court, whose pleadings would make it hard for people to resist the truth.

*About sin* Observe how this reproof was given with regard to sin. On the day of Pentecost the disciples spoke in different tongues, as the Spirit gave them utterance. People from all over the world heard their own native languages being spoken. When Peter stood up to preach and told the Jews that they had crucified the Holy One, signs and wonders performed by the Spirit in the name of Jesus were a witness which they could not refute. The fact that the Spirit of God had given these uneducated men the gift of tongues was evidence that Jesus of Nazareth, about whom they spoke, was no impostor.

The Lord Jesus Christ had promised the outpouring of the Spirit. When, therefore, that mark of the true Messiah rested on Jesus of Nazareth through the coming of the Holy Spirit and the working of miracles, people were reproved for having refused to believe in Jesus. The evidence was brought home to them that they had with wicked hands crucified the Lord of glory and so they stood reproved.

All the subsequent miracles went on to prove the same thing; for when the apostles performed miracles the world was reproved of sin because it did not believe in Christ. It was not that a few disciples testified to the sin of the race, but the Holy Spirit himself made people tremble on account of his powerful deeds which witnessed to the Lord Jesus. Do you not see the wonderful power with which the first disciples were thus armed? It needed all the wilfulness of that stiff-necked generation to resist the Holy Spirit and refuse to bow before him whom they had pierced.

*About righteousness* The working of the Holy Spirit with the apostles and their immediate followers was also a great rebuke to the world about righteousness. Jesus was gone. His divine example no longer stood out like a clear light reproving the darkness, but the Holy Spirit attested to that righteousness, and compelled them to feel that Jesus was the Holy One and that his cause was righteous. The teaching of the apostles, sealed by the Holy Spirit, made the world see what righteousness was as they had never seen it before.

If people continued to sin it would be against light and knowledge, for they knew what righteousness was. God was with the preachers of a new righteousness, and by various signs and wonders he attested to the gospel. Today, we are the covenanted servants of a Lord whose righteousness was declared to people by the personal witness of God the Holy Spirit.

*About judgment* At this time people felt that a judgment had come; that somehow the life and the death of Jesus of Nazareth had caused a crisis in the world's history and condemned the way of the ungodly. The thought flashed on humanity, more clearly than ever before, that there would be a day of judgment. People heard and felt the truth of the warning that God would judge the world by the man Jesus Christ. The Holy Spirit had reproved men and women through the prospect of judgment.

People who despise the witness of the Holy Spirit are profane. Let them beware in case they sin against the Holy Spirit and can never be forgiven.

## To convince people

The Holy Spirit would accompany the preaching of the Word to convince people of three great truths. This would be a saving Word: they were to be so convinced that they would repent of sin, accept righteousness and yield themselves to the judgment of the Lord. Here is a map of the work of the Spirit in the hearts of those who are ordained to eternal life. Those three effects are all necessary, and each one is most important for true conversion.

*To convince people about sin* First, the Holy Spirit came to convince people about sin. The fashionable theology is: 'Convince people about the goodness of God: show them the universal Fatherhood and assure them of unlimited mercy.' But the way of the Spirit of God is very different.

He comes to convince people about sin, to make them feel that they are guilty, very guilty – so guilty that they are lost, and ruined, and undone. The Holy Spirit comes to remind them not only of God's loveliness but of their own unloveliness. The Holy Spirit does not come to make sinners comfortable in their sins, but to make them grieve over their sins.

**'The Holy Spirit comes to remind them not only of God's loveliness but of their own unloveliness.'**

Flowers fill the fields when the grass is green. But then a burning wind comes from the desert, and the flowers fall down. What makes the beauty and excellence of human righteousness wither like green grass? Isaiah says it is 'because the Spirit of God blows on it'. There is a withering work of the Spirit of God which we must experience or we will never know his quickening and restoring power. This withering is a most necessary experience, and just now needs to be greatly insisted on. Today we have so many built up who were never pulled down; so many filled who were never emptied; so many exalted who were never humbled. I remind you earnestly that the Holy Spirit must convince us of sin, or we cannot be saved.

Note that the Spirit of God comes to convince people about sin, because they will never be convinced about sin apart from his divine advocacy. A natural conscience touched by God's Spirit may do a good deal to reveal a person's faults; it may make him uneasy, and may bring about a reformation of life; but it is only the Spirit of God who will so convince a person about sin that will end in repentance, self-despair and faith in Jesus. It is not easy, brethren, to explain this. But this I know, that the extent of sin is never known until the Spirit of God reveals the secret rooms of the heart's wickedness. We do a thousand things that we do not realise are sinful until God's Spirit enlightens us and pleads the need for holiness in us. The fact that we not only sin but are by nature sinful is one which our pride kicks against, and we do not learn about it until God's Spirit teaches us about it.

The Holy Spirit dwells on one particular point: 'of sin, because they believe not on me'. No one sees the sin of unbelief except by the Spirit's light. People think, 'Unbelief is a matter of very little consequence; I can set that right at any time.' But the Holy Spirit makes a person see that not to believe in Christ is the crowning, damning sin.

*To convince people about righteousness* The next work of the Spirit is to convince people about righteousness. In terms of the gospel this means showing them that they have no righteousness of their own, and no way of creating righteousness. Thus, the Holy Spirit leads them to value the righteousness of God which is on all who believe, this righteousness which covers sin and makes people acceptable with God.

Let me now draw your attention to a great wonder. In human law, if a person is convicted of wrong-doing, the next step is judgment. A young man is caught embezzling money. He is taken to court and convicted of the crime and found guilty. What follows next? Why, judgment is pronounced, and he must bear the penalty. But note how our gracious God inserts an additional process. He does convict of sin, so you would expect the next step to be judgment; but no, the Lord introduces a hitherto unknown middle term, as he convinces about 'righteousness'. Be amazed at this. The Lord takes a person, even when he is sinful and conscious of that sin, and makes him righteous on the spot by putting away his sin, and justifying him by the righteousness of faith, a righteousness which comes to him by the worthiness of Another who has bought righteousness for him. Can that be? Brethren, this seems to be so impossible that it needs the Spirit of God to convince people about it.

All my labours in preaching are in vain until the Spirit makes God's righteousness plain. Many people hear the good news, but they do not receive the truth, for they are not convinced about it. They need to be persuaded about it before they will embrace it, and that kind of persuasion is not in my power. Did I hear someone say, 'I cannot see this way of righteousness?' I reply, 'No, and you never will until the Spirit of God convinces you about it.'

Dear people of God, pray hard that the Spirit of God may even now convince unbelievers that the only true righteousness for mortal humans is that which comes not by the works of the law but by the hearing of faith.

*To convince people about judgment* Now comes a third point: the Spirit of God is to convince people about judgment. To whom is this judgment committed? 'The Father hath committed all judgment unto the Son' (John 5:22). The Spirit of God is needed to convince our unbelieving hearts that this is the case. We need to be convinced about judgment. We need to be convinced that we have been judged and condemned. The day of judgment is not a thing to be dreaded by a believer. We have stood our trial, and have been acquitted. Our representative has borne the penalty of our sin. There is now no curse for us: there can be none: heaven, earth, hell cannot find a curse for those whom God has blessed, since the Lord Jesus 'was made a curse for us'. May the Spirit of God come on you afresh, my dearly beloved, and make you confident and joyful in him who is the Lord our righteousness, by whom evil has been judged once for all!

## To convict people

Last of all, let us read our text by translating it 'convict'. 'The Spirit of God will convict the world of sin, of righteousness, and of judgment.' There is the world. It stands a prisoner at the bar, and the charge is that it is and has been full of sin. Everyone agrees, 'He is a villain if ever there was one.' Now hear the Spirit of God. The Spirit came into the world to make everyone know that Jesus is the Christ. But what did the wicked world do with Christ? They nailed him to a cross. By this the world is condemned. The world's guilt is proved beyond doubt. The wrath of God abides on it.

What happens after this? The trial is regarded from another point of view. Up to this day the world is trying to defeat God's cause. But the Spirit of God, through his teaching, proves that the gospel is full of righteousness. By sanctifying people through the gospel the Holy Spirit proves that the gospel is righteous. The Holy Spirit makes the world know that Christ is righteous by flashing into its face the fact that Christ has gone – gone up to glory, at the right hand of God – and this could not have happened if he had not been the righteous One.

When the world sees Jesus enthroned, and everyone looks at the Son of Man in the clouds of heaven, what conviction will seize every mind! Then the Spirit of God will make everyone see the judgment. Oh, how the Spirit of God will convict everyone at that last day when they hear the Judge say, 'Come, ye blessed of my Father,' and 'Depart, ye cursed, into everlasting fire.'

Christian friends, will you be convinced by the Holy Spirit now, or will you wait till then? Will it be the conviction of grace or the conviction of wrath? The Spirit still bears witness with us who preach the gospel: will you yield to that gospel, and believe it now? Or will you wait until the blaze of the last tremendous day? O Spirit of God, make us sane and wise, for Christ Jesus' sake. Amen.

# The Holy Spirit – the great Teacher

'Howbeit when he, the Spirit of truth, is come, he will guide you into all truth: for he shall not speak of himself; but whatsoever he shall hear, that shall he speak: and he will shew you things to come' John 16:13

### An attainment mentioned

A knowledge of all truth.

(a) Nature itself (sanctified by grace) gives us a strong desire to know all truth

(b) A knowledge of all truth is essential for our comfort

(c) The knowledge of all truth is very desirable for the usefulness which it will give us in the world at large

## A difficulty suggested

We require a guide to conduct us into all truth.

(a) Because of the great intricacy of truth itself
(b) Because of the invidiousness of error
(c) Because we are prone to go astray

## A person provided

God himself, the Spirit of truth.

(a) He is ever-present
(b) The Spirit can guide us into truth

## A method suggested

'He shall guide you into all truth.'

(a) The Holy Spirit guides into all truth by suggesting it
(b) The Holy Spirit leads us by direction
    You were brought to see Jesus Christ crucified not by a new idea suggested, but by direction given to your thoughts.
(c) The Holy Spirit guides into all truth by illumination. He illumines the Bible

## An evidence

How may I know whether I am enlightened by the Spirit's influence?

(a) By the constant unity of his testimony
    He guides us into all *truth*.
(b) By its universality
    He guides us into *all* truth.

**Practical inferences**

(a) With reference to the ignorant Christian
He can be instructed.
(b) How to deal with people who do not understand the truth
Do not be angry with them, pray for them, 'Lord, open his eyes . . .'
(c) To those who are indifferent to the Spirit of truth
Only the truth can save you.

# The Ascension practically considered

'And while they looked steadfastly toward heaven as he went up, behold, two men stood by them in white apparel; Which also said, Ye men of Galilee, why stand ye gazing up into heaven? this same Jesus, which is taken up from you into heaven, shall so come in like manner as ye have seen him go into heaven' Acts 1:10–11

## A gentle chiding

'Ye men of Galilee, why stand ye gazing up into heaven?'

(a) Note that what these saintly men were doing seems at first sight to be quite right
(b) What they did was not after all justifiable
(c) What they did we are apt to imitate

## The cheering description of our Lord

'This same Jesus . . .'

(a) A description from those who knew him
(b) Jesus is still gone, but he still exists

(c) Jesus means a Saviour

(d) He who is to come will be the same Jesus that went up into heaven

## The practical truth

'This same Jesus, which is taken up from you into heaven, shall so come in like manner as ye have seen him go into heaven.'

(a) Jesus is gone into heaven

(b) Jesus will come again

(c) He is coming in a like manner as he departed

(d) Be ready to meet your coming Lord

# Wind and fire at Pentecost

'And suddenly there came a sound from heaven as of a rushing mighty wind, and it filled all the house where they were sitting. And there appeared unto them cloven tongues like as of fire, and it sat upon each of them. And they were all filled with the Holy Ghost, and began to speak with other tongues, as the Spirit gave them utterance' Acts 2:2–4

## Introduction

From the descent of the Holy Spirit at the beginning we may learn something about his work today. Remember at the outset that whatever the Holy Spirit was at the first that he is now, for as God he remains the same – whatever he did then he is able still to do, for his power is by no means diminished. Although we may not expect, and need not desire, the miracles which came with the gift of the Holy Spirit, so far as they were physical, yet we may both desire and expect that which was intended and symbolised by them, and we may reckon to see the like spiritual wonders performed among us today.

May God grant that the meditation of this morning may increase our faith in the Holy Spirit, and inflame our desires towards him, so that we may look to see him fulfilling his mission among people as at the beginning.

## The instructive symbols

First, I call your attention to the instructive symbols of the Holy Spirit, which were made prominent at Pentecost. They were two. There was the sound as of a rushing mighty wind, and there were cloven tongues as it were of fire.

*The wind* This first symbol is an emblem of deity, and therefore an appropriate symbol of the Holy Spirit. In the Old Testament God often revealed himself under the emblem of breath or wind. Indeed, the Hebrew word for 'spirit' and 'wind' is the same.

The meaning of the symbol is that as breath, air, wind, is the very life of man, so is the Spirit of God the life of the spiritual man. By God's Spirit we are brought to life in the first place; by him we are subsequently kept alive; by him is the inner life nurtured and increased and perfected. The breath of the nostrils of the man of God is the Spirit of God.

The holy breath was not only intended to quicken them, but to invigorate them. They took in great draughts of heavenly life and they felt animated and aroused.

Doubtless this wind was intended to show the irresistible power of the Holy Spirit. The air appears to be feeble, but once it moves you feel a sense of life among you. It can quickly become a storm or a tornado. Nothing is more potent than the wind when it is thoroughly roused, and so, although the Spirit of God is despised by men, once he works with the fullness of his power you will see what he can do.

*Fire* Fire is also a frequent symbol of deity. Abraham saw a burning lamp, and Moses beheld a burning bush. The intention of this symbol was to show the disciples that the Holy Spirit would illuminate them, as fire gives light. 'He shall lead you into all truth.' After Pentecost they were not to be uneducated children but teachers in Israel, instructors of the nations whom they were to make Christ's disciples. Hence the Spirit of light was upon them.

But fire does more than give light: it inflames. The flames which sat on each person showed them that they were to be ablaze with love, intense with zeal, burning with self-sacrifice.

The fire signified inspiration. God was about to make them speak under a divine influence, to speak as the Spirit of God gave them utterance.

Now put these symbols together; only mind out what you are doing. Wind and fire together! Remember the fire in the old city of London. When the flames started it was impossible to put them out because the wind fanned the flame, and the buildings gave way before the fire-torrent. O God, send us the Holy Spirit in this fashion: give us both the breath of spiritual life and the fire of unconquerable zeal, until nation after nation yields to the sway of Jesus.

## The immediate effects

These symbols were not sent in vain. There were two immediate effects:

*Filling* 'It filled all the house where they were sitting.' It did not merely fill the house, but the men – 'They were all filled with the Holy Ghost.' When they stood up to speak even those who mocked them in the crowd noticed this, for they said, 'These men are full,' and though they added 'with new wine', they evidently detected a singular fullness about them. We are poor, empty things by nature, and useless while we remain so: we need to be filled with the Holy Spirit. Where the Spirit of God is truly at work he first fills and then gives utterance; that is his way. Oh that you and I were at this moment filled with the Holy Spirit.

> 'Where the Spirit of God is truly at work he first fills and then gives utterance; that is his way.'

*Utterance* As soon as God's Spirit filled them they began to speak. It seems to me that they began to speak before the people had come together. They could not help it; the inner forces demanded expression, and they had to speak. So when God's Spirit really comes on a person, he does not wait until he has collected an audience of the size he wants, but he seizes the next opportunity. He speaks to one person, he speaks to two, he speaks to three, to anybody. He must speak, for he is full.

When God's Spirit fills a person he speaks in order to be understood. The crowd spoke different languages, and these Spirit-taught men spoke to them in the language of the country in which they were born. This is one of the signs of the Spirit's utterance. If my friend talks in a Latinised style to a company of costermongers, I am sure that the Holy Spirit has nothing to do with him.

The crowd not only understood, but they felt. The preachers were speaking flame, and the fire dropped into the hearts of men until they were amazed and confounded.

## The most prominent subject

The Holy Spirit being thus at work, what was the most prominent subject which these full men began to preach about with words of fire? Suppose that the Holy Spirit should work mightily in the Church, what would our ministers preach about? 'We do hear them speak in our own tongues the wonderful works of God.' Their subject would be the wonderful works of God. Oh, that this might be to my dying day my only topic – 'The wonderful works of God'.

*Redemption* Peter's sermon was an example of how they spoke about redemption, that wonderful work of God. He told the people that Jesus was the Son of God, that they had crucified and slain him, but that he had come to redeem men and that there was salvation through his precious blood. He preached redemption.

*Regeneration* There was no concealing the work of the Holy

Spirit in that primitive ministry. It was brought to the front. Peter said, 'Ye shall receive the Holy Ghost.' The preachers at Pentecost told of the Spirit's work by the Spirit's power: conversion, repentance, renewal, faith, holiness, and such things were freely spoken of and ascribed to the real author, the divine Spirit.

*Remission* This was the point that Peter pushed home to them, that on repentance they should receive forgiveness of sins.

These are the doctrines which the Holy Spirit will revive in the midst of the land when he works mightily – redemption, regeneration, remission.

## The glorious results

*Deep feeling* The result of the Spirit coming as wind and fire, filling and giving utterance, was, first, in the hearers' deep feeling. There was never, perhaps, in the world such a feeling excited by the language of mortal man as that which was aroused in the crowds in Jerusalem on that day. Our ministry has failed, and has not the divine seal on it, unless it makes men tremble, makes them sad, and then, later, brings them to Christ, and causes them to rejoice.

*Earnest enquiry* 'They were pricked in their heart, and said unto Peter and to the rest of the apostles, Men and brethren, what shall we do?' Emotion is of itself but a poor result unless it leads to practical action.

*Reception of the Word* We are told that they gladly received the Word, and they received it in two senses. First, Peter told them to repent, and they did so. They also believed in Jesus whom they had killed, and accepted him as their Saviour there and then, without hesitating.

*They were baptised* But what next? Why, they were baptised directly. Having repented and believed, the next step was to confess of their faith; and they did not postpone that act for a single day; why should they?

*Great steadfastness* Furthermore, there was not merely this immediate confession, but as a result of the Spirit of God there was great steadfastness. 'They continued steadfastly in the apostles' doctrine.' We have had plenty of revivals of the human sort, and their results have been sadly disappointing. But where the Spirit of God is really at work the converts stand. They are well rooted and grounded, and hence they are not carried about by every wind of doctrine, but they continue steadfast in the apostolic truth.

*Abundant worship of God* They were steadfast not only in teaching, but in breaking of bread, and in prayer, and in fellowship.

*Striking generosity* Funds were not hard to raise: liberality overflowed its banks, for believers poured all that they had into the common fund. Then was it indeed seen to be true that the silver and the gold are the Lord's.

*Continual gladness* 'They did eat their meat with gladness.' They were full of gladness, and that gladness showed itself in *praising God.* I have no doubt they broke out now and then in the services with shouts of, 'Glory! Hallelujah!' I should not be surprised if all propriety was thrown to the winds. They were so glad, so exhilarated that they were ready to leap for joy.

*A daily increase* 'The Lord added to the church daily such as should be saved.' Conversion was going on perpetually; additions to the Church were not events which happened once a year, but they were everyday matters, 'so mightily grew the word of God and prevailed'. O Spirit of God, you are ready to work with us today even as you did then. We beseech you, work at once.

# Bonds which could not hold

'Whom God hath raised up, having loosed the pains of death: because it was not possible that he should be holden of it' Acts 2:24

## It was not possible that the bonds of death should hold our Lord

(a)  Christ had in himself the inherent power to die, and to live again
(b)  The dignity of his person made it impossible for death to hold him
(c)  Because his redeeming work was done
(d)  He had his Father's promise that he would not stay in the tomb
(e)  The perpetuity of his office

## As Christ could not be held by the bonds of death, Christ could not be held by any other bonds

(a)  Old-established error could not hold Christ
(b)  The wisdom of this world was defeated
(c)  The bonds of ignorance were broken
(d)  Wealth, rank, fashion and prestige avail nothing

## As Christ could not be held by the bonds of death, it is not possible to keep in bondage anything that belongs to him

(a)  Those struggling to get to Christ are helped
(b)  A child of God in great trouble is assisted
(c)  Death knows his power must yield to Christ

# The first Christian sermon

'Therefore let all the house of Israel know assuredly, that God hath made that same Jesus, whom ye have crucified, both Lord and Christ. Now when they heard this, they were pricked in their heart, and said unto Peter and to the rest of the apostles, Men and brethren, what shall we do?' Acts 2:36–7

## Introduction

This was the first public preaching of the gospel after our Lord was taken up into glory. It was thus a very memorable sermon, a kind of firstfruits of the great harvest of gospel testimony. It is very encouraging to those who are engaged in preaching that the first sermon should have been so successful. Three thousand made up a grand take of fish at that first cast of the net. We are serving a great and growing cause in the way chosen by God, and we hope in the future to see still grander results produced by that same undying and unchanging power which helped Peter to preach such a heart-piercing sermon.

## Their evil behaviour towards the Lord Jesus

(a) Blaspheming the name of Jesus
(b) Neglecting the Lord Jesus
(c) Rejection of the Lord Jesus
(d) Forsaking of the Lord Jesus

## The exaltation God gave to the Lord Jesus

(a) Our Lord enjoys infinite happiness
(b) Our Lord sits in infinite majesty
(c) Our Lord is exalted to the place of power
(d) Our Lord is seated as our Judge
(e) Our Lord is Head over all things in his Church

**The result of knowing for certain about Christ's death and exaltation**

(a) Peter's hearers felt a mortal sting
(b) They were stirred to love Christ
(c) They showed obedient faith

# Christ's people – imitators of him

'Now when they saw the boldness of Peter and John, and perceived that they were unlearned and ignorant men, they marvelled; and they took knowledge of them, that they had been with Jesus' Acts 4:13

## Introduction

I urge you to imitate Jesus Christ, our heavenly pattern, that men may perceive that you are disciples of the holy Son of God.

## What a believer should be

(a) Be like Christ in your boldness
(b) Be like Christ in your love
(c) Be like Christ in your sincere humility
(d) Be like Christ in your holiness

## When should Christians be like this?

There is an idea abroad that people ought to be very religious on Sundays, but that it does not matter what they are on Mondays.

(a) Imitate Christ in public
(b) Imitate Christ in church

(c) Imitate Christ in your home
(d) Imitate Christ in secret

## Why should Christians imitate Christ?

(a) For their own sake
(b) For Christ's sake

## How can I imitate Christ?

(a) You must know Christ as your Redeemer before you can follow him as your Exemplar
(b) Seek more of the Spirit of God, for this is the way to become Christ-like

# The work of the Holy Spirit

'While Peter yet spake these words, the Holy Ghost fell on all them which heard the word' Acts 10:44

## Introduction

In creation all three divine persons took their share.
In salvation all three persons of the Godhead were involved.

## The method of the Holy Spirit's operation

We can explain what the Spirit does, but how he does it no man must pretend to know.

(a) The Holy Spirit awakens the mental powers
(b) The Holy Spirit gives powers which people did not have before

### The absolute necessity of the Holy Spirit's work in conversion

- (a) The preacher should be under the influence of the Spirit
- (b) The Spirit of God must fall on the hearers of the gospel
- (c) Man cannot be converted by physical means
- (d) Man cannot be converted by moral argument
- (e) Only God can accomplish conversion
- (f) Man cannot save himself

### What must be done at this time to bring down the Spirit on our churches

- (a) Look to the Holy Spirit and not to instrumentality [the means]
- (b) Honour the Holy Spirit – especially by praying

# The church at Antioch

'And it came to pass, that a whole year they assembled themselves with the church, and taught much people. And the disciples were called Christians first in Antioch' Acts 11:26

### Introduction

Kings are wont to chronicle their wars; mighty men expect to be made to live after death in the historic page; but though these matters have a certain amount of interest, what is it compared with the interest attaching to this inspired book of the Acts of the Apostles? The history of England is not so important as this one part of the Bible. It is a book of martyrs – Stephen, James and many more. It is a book of voyages and travels of thrilling and permanent interest. It is volume one of *The Christian Times*. It is a book of debates, speeches, addresses and sermons.

The church at Antioch has a history so interesting that I only pray that I may be helped to make it so, as I give:

## A brief sketch of the history of the church in Antioch

Certain saints, driven by persecution from Jerusalem, fled to Antioch, and commenced there their labours of love. Their names are not mentioned, but God knows them, and they now receive their reward. Let my name perish, but let Christ's name last for ever.

The Lord's hand helped them, and many believed and turned to the Lord. These were so pious that the church in Jerusalem heard of it, and for their further edification sent down Barnabas to work among them. He was full of faith and the Holy Spirit, and under him the church grew so great that he went after Paul to assist him.

The saints at Antioch were a generous people; and by God's grace continuing to increase, they soon had five pastors, and the Holy Spirit put it into their minds to send out, as missionaries elsewhere, two who became eminently successful. Thus, Antioch became a mother-church to many surrounding parts. Paul and Barnabas used to return there, after their laborious missionary tours. They anchored at Antioch, as in a haven of refuge.

*The gospel does not always make slow progress* Let us note that the gospel is not of necessity a slowly progressing affair. The first preachers were very successful, for it seems that in about two years the church at Antioch was firmly established. That church grew amazingly, then why should not ours, and why should not all others grow in similar fashion? The conversion of the world will not always go on at snail-pace, and we ought to pray that it may not in this place. O God, grant it!

*The principal elements of success remain the same* Let us notice the principal elements of success in this case, believing them to be the same in all. There were things from God, the ministers and the people.

1   The ministers: God – in Providence – shielded this Gentile

223

Jerusalem from persecution, and gave peace to the people. He sent them faithful ministers, and with those ministers he sent his Spirit.

The ministers preached the Lord Jesus. Barnabas was a good, kind, faithful, Spirit-filled man. Paul also was a mighty preacher of the Word.

2   The people: The people must have had much grace, a close cleaving to God and to one another, liberality and readiness to assist any work of faith, and abundance of what the Bible commentator Jewel called 'all prayer'.

## The title first gained by this church at Antioch – 'Christians'

Perhaps the name was given as a designation by the Gentiles, gladly adopted by the disciples and sanctioned by divine authority. They had hitherto styled themselves 'disciples', 'the faithful', 'the elect', 'brethren'. The Jews called them Nazarenes, Galileans, etc. The sect was so small that, doubtless, among the masses of the heathen it was nondescript; but in Antioch the talent, the zeal, the number, the influence and (in some cases) the wealth of the members of the new church made it necessary that it should have a name. The name given is a good one: Christians.

*Unity* This intimates that there was much unity among the disciples, so that one name would apply to all. Blessed time when this unity shall return, and we shall be all gathered in one!

*Centred on Christ* This name shows that the conversation, singing, worship and preaching of these men and women must have been much about Christ; or else how would the common people know their name?

*Christ's example* This name 'Christians' shows that their life and conduct must have been according to the example of Christ; otherwise, the more knowing members of the community would have denied their right to the title.

'But I also am called a Christian.' How honourable a name!

Manaen, the foster-brother of Herod, was more honoured in hearing this name than by his connection with an earthly prince. Paul, at one time a learned doctor in the pharisaic school, owns this name of Christian as his highest title. Surely, 'tis a title which an angel might almost covet. But what does this name show?

*A believer in Christ's divine mission* That I am a believer in the divine mission of Jesus. A believer in his official name, 'Christ'. Let me then take care to trust in him most implicitly, and never by my doubts dishonour him.

*An imitator* That I am a professed imitator of the holy, harmless, undefiled, loving, generous Jesus; let me then really be so in all things.

*A lover of Jesus* That I am a lover of Jesus; then let my conversation and talk and meditation be concerning him.

A Christian is one who is anointed to be God's priest, to offer continual prayer and praise in the name of Jesus. Bearing the one name which the glorious army of martyrs, the great apostles of Christ and the saints in all ages have borne, may we honour the name of Jesus, and on our shoulder bear the cross of Jesus!

# Christ put on

'But put ye on the Lord Jesus Christ, and make not provision for the flesh, to fulfil the lusts thereof' Romans 13:14

## Introduction

Christ must be in us before he can be on us. Grace puts Christ within, and enables us to put on Christ without. Christ must be in the heart by faith, before he can be in the life by holiness.

This text is about everyday practical life, and to these it must refer. It is not justification but sanctification that we have here. You are every day continually more and more to wear as the dress of your lives the character of your Lord.

## Where are we to go for our daily dress?

Beloved, there is but one answer to all questions as to our necessities. We go to the Lord Jesus Christ for everything. 'Put ye on the Lord Jesus Christ.' To us, 'Christ is all'. He 'of God is made unto us wisdom, and righteousness, and sanctification, and redemption' (1 Corinthians 1:30). Having begun with Jesus, you are to go on with him, even to the end, 'for ye are complete in him', fully equipped in him.

(a) Christ is our example
(b) Christ is our stimulus
(c) Christ is our strength
(d) In Christ we have perfection
(e) Christ is for each individual believer
'Put *thou* on the Lord Jesus Christ.'

## What is this daily dress?

The Lord Jesus Christ is to be put on.

*The sacred dress is described here in three words*
1   Put him on as *Lord*. Call him your Master and Lord, and you do well.
2   Then put on *Jesus*. Jesus means Saviour: in every part be covered by him in that blessed capacity.
3   Then put on *Christ*. You know that Christ signifies 'anointed'. Now, our Lord is anointed as Prophet, Priest and King, and as such we put him on.

What a splendid thing it is to put on Christ as the anointed *Prophet*, and to accept his teaching as our creed!

Put him on also as your *Priest*. Notwithstanding your sins, your unworthiness, your defilement, go to the altar of the

Lord by him who, as Priest, has taken away your sin, clothed you with his merit and made you acceptable to God.

Our Lord Jesus is also anointed to be *King*. Oh, put him on in all his imperial majesty, by yielding your every wish and thought to his sway!

*Note the description given in Colossians 3:12* 'Put on therefore, as the elect of God, holy and beloved, bowels of mercies, kindness, humbleness of mind, meekness, longsuffering.' I will take you to the wardrobe for a minute, and ask you to look over the items of our dress. You are to *put on* the whole armour of God. In true religion everything is designed for practical use. We keep no clothes in the drawer; we have to put on all that is provided.

Notice that these choice things come in pairs.

1 'Mercy and kindness.' I am to be merciful, as tender-hearted, as kind, as sympathetic, as loving to my fellow-man as Christ himself was.

2 'Humbleness of mind, meekness.' These choice garments are not so much esteemed as they should be. The cloth of one called Proud-of-heart is very fashionable, and the trimmings of Mr Masterful are much in request. Permit me to say to any dear brother who has not a very tender nature, who is naturally hard and rasping, 'Put on the Lord Jesus Christ', my brother, and make not provision for that unfeeling nature of yours. Endeavour to be lowly in mind, that you may be gentle in spirit.

3 'Longsuffering and forbearance.' Some men have no patience with others: how can they expect God to have patience with them? Put on the Lord Jesus Christ, and bear and forbear.

4 'Forgiving one another, if any man have a quarrel against any; even as Christ forgave you, so also do ye' (Colossians 3:13). Is not this heavenly teaching? Put it into practice.

5 'And above all these things put on charity, which is the bond of perfectness' (Colossians 3:14). Love is the belt which gathers up the other clothes, and keeps all the other graces well braced and in their right places. Put on love. What a golden belt.

*Practical ways of 'putting on the Lord Jesus Christ'*

(a) Put on the Lord Jesus Christ for daily wear
(b) If you have put on something of Christ, put on more of Christ
(c) Put on the Lord in every time of trial

## How we are to act towards evil in this dress

The text says, 'Put ye on the Lord Jesus Christ, and make not provision for the flesh, to fulfil the lusts thereof.' By 'the flesh' is here meant the evil part of us, which is so greatly aided by the appetites and desires of the body.

**'I fear we have all very much of the flesh about us, and therefore we need to be on our guard against it.'**

When a man puts on Christ, has he still the flesh about him? Alas, it is even so. I hear some brethren say that they have no remaining corruptions. When a man tells me he is perfect, I hear what he has to say, but I quietly think within myself that, if he had been so, he would not have felt it necessary to spread the information. Brethen, I fear we have all very much of the flesh about us, and therefore we need to be on our guard against it. What does the apostle say? 'Make not provision for the flesh.' By this he means several things.

(a) Give no tolerance to it
(b) Give sin no time
(c) Provide no food for it

## Why should we hasten to put on Christ?

A moment is all that remains. It is dark. Here is armour made of solid light; let us put on this attire at once; then the night will be light about us, and others beholding us will glorify God and ask for the same raiment.

# The power of the Holy Spirit

'Through the power of the Holy Ghost' Romans 15:13

## Introduction

Power is the special and peculiar prerogative of God, and God alone. 'Twice have I heard this: that power belongeth unto God' Psalm 62:11. God is God: and power belongs to him. If he delegates part of it to his creatures, it is still his power.

This exclusive prerogative of God is found in each of the three persons of the glorious Trinity. The Father has power: for by his word were the heavens made, and all the host of them; by his strength all things stand, and through him they fulfil their destiny. The Son has power: for like the Father, he is the Creator of all things; 'Without him was not anything made that was made', and 'by him all things consist'. And the Holy Spirit has power. It is about the power of the Holy Spirit that I wish now to speak.

## The Holy Spirit's outward and visible displays

First, then, we view the power of the Spirit in his outward and visible displays. The power of the Spirit has not been dormant; he has exerted himself. We look at three works which reveal his power: creation works, resurrection works and witness works.

*Creation works* Though not very frequently in Scripture, yet sometimes creation is ascribed to the Holy Spirit, as well as to the Father and the Son; see Job 26:13. Also, in Genesis 1 you see more particularly set out that peculiar work of power on the universe which was put forth by the Holy Spirit. There you will see what was his special work. Genesis 1:2 says, 'And the earth was without form, and void; and darkness was upon the face of the deep. And the Spirit of God moved upon the face of the waters.' When the Spirit came, stretching out his broad wings, the different parts of matter came into their places, and it was no longer 'without form, and void'.

But there was one particular instance of creation in which the Holy Spirit was more especially concerned – the formation of the body of our Lord Jesus Christ. Though our Lord Jesus Christ was born of a woman and made in the likeness of sinful flesh, yet the power which begat him was entirely in God the Holy Spirit – as the Scriptures express it, 'The power of the Highest shall overshadow thee.'

*Resurrection works* The resurrection of Christ is sometimes ascribed to himself: as he willingly gave up his life he had power to take it again. Sometimes the resurrection of Christ is ascribed to God the Father: 'Him hath God the Father exalted.' But the Scriptures also say that Jesus Christ was raised by the Holy Spirit; see 1 Peter 3:18. Romans 8:11 says, 'But if the Spirit of him that raised up Jesus from the dead dwell in you, he that raised up Christ from the dead shall also quicken your mortal bodies by his Spirit that dwelleth in you.'

*Witness works* When Jesus Christ raised the dead, healed the leper and expelled demons it was done by the power of the Spirit. The Spirit dwelt in Jesus without measure, and by that power all those miracles were worked. These were attestation works.

After Jesus Christ had gone the Holy Spirit affirmed their ministry through such miraculous deeds as Peter raising Dorcas, and as the Holy Spirit breathed life into Eutychus, 'mighty signs and wonders were done by the Holy Ghost, and many believed thereby.' Who will doubt the power of the Holy Spirit after that?

## The inner and spiritual power of the Holy Spirit

What I have already spoken of may be seen; what I am about to speak of must be felt, and no one will understand what I say with truth unless he has felt it.

*The heart* The Holy Spirit has a power over men's hearts. Now men's hearts are very hard to affect. The Spirit alone has power over man's heart. If anyone thinks that a minister can convert the soul, I wish he would try. He will soon find 'It is not by might nor by power, but by my Spirit, saith the Lord.' We cannot reach the soul, but the Holy Spirit can. He can give a sense of blood-bought pardon that will dissolve a heart of stone.

*The will* But if there is one thing more stubborn than the heart it is the will. 'My lord Will-be-will', as Bunyan calls him in his *Holy War*, is a fellow who will not easily be bent. I find the old proverb very true, 'One man can bring a horse to the water, but a hundred cannot make him drink.' I do not think any man has power over his fellow-creature's will, but the Spirit of God has. 'I will make them willing in the day of my power.'

*The imagination* There is one thing more which I think is rather worse than the will, and that is the imagination. Those who have a fair share of imagination know what a difficult thing it is to control. You cannot restrain it. My imagination will sometimes take me over the gates of iron, across that infinite unknown, to the very gates of pearl, and discover the blessed glorified.

> 'These thoughts will come; and when I feel in the holiest frame, the most devoted to God, and the most earnest in prayer, it often happens that that is the very time when the plagues break out the worst.'

But if it is potent one way it is another; for my imagination has taken me down to the vilest sewers of earth. It has given me thoughts so dreadful that, while I could not avoid them, yet I was thoroughly horrified at them. These thoughts will come; and when I feel in the holiest frame, the most devoted to God, and the most earnest in prayer, it often happens that that is the very time when the plagues break out the worst. But I rejoice and think of one thing, that I can cry out when this imagination comes upon me. If a Christian cries out, there is hope. Can you chain your imagination? No; but the power of the

Holy Spirit can. Ah, it will do it, and it does do it at last; it does it even on earth.

## The future and desired effects

But the last thing was the future and desired effects; for after all, though the Holy Spirit has done so much, he cannot say, 'It is finished.' He has more to do yet. What, then, has the Holy Spirit to do?

*Perfect us in holiness* There are two kinds of perfection which a Christian needs – one is the perfection of justification in the person of Jesus; and the other is the perfection of sanctification worked in him by the Holy Spirit. At present corruption still rests even in the hearts of the regenerate. At present there are still lusts and evil imaginations. But, oh my soul rejoices to know that the day is coming when God will finish the work he has begun; and he will present my soul, not only perfect in Christ, but perfect in the Spirit, without spot or blemish, or any such thing.

*Usher in the latter-day glory* In a few more years – I know not when, I know not how – the Holy Spirit will be poured out in a far different style from the present. Perhaps there will be no miraculous gifts – for they will not be required; but yet there will be such a miraculous amount of holiness, such an extraordinary fervour of prayer, such a real communion with God and so much vital religion, and such a spread of the doctrines of the cross, that everyone will see that the Spirit is poured out like water, and the rains are descending from above. For that let us pray: let us continually labour for it, and seek it of God.

*The general resurrection* We have reason to believe from Scripture that the resurrection of the dead, whilst it will be effected by God's voice and his Word (the Son) it will also be brought about by the Spirit. That same power which raised Jesus Christ from the dead will also give life to your mortal bodies. The power of the resurrection is perhaps one of the finest proofs of the works of the Spirit. When the wind of the Holy Spirit comes dry bones live and stand up on their feet as an exceeding great army.

## Conclusion

We must now have a moment or two for practical inference. The Spirit is very powerful, Christian! What do you infer from that fact? Why, that you never need distrust God's power to carry you to heaven. The power of the Holy Spirit is your bulwark, and all his omnipotence defends you. For the power of the Spirit is our power.

Again, Christians, if this is the power of the Spirit, *why do you doubt anything*? Do not doubt the power of the Spirit to raise you up. Then go out and labour with this conviction, that the power of the Holy Spirit is able to do anything. Go to your Sunday school; go to your tract distribution; go to your missionary enterprise; go to your preaching in your home, with the conviction that the power of the Spirit is our great help.

# The God of peace

'Now the God of peace be with you all. Amen' Romans 15:33

## The title

Mars among the heathen was called the god of war. But our God Jehovah styles himself not the God of war, but the God of peace.

If you consider the Trinity of his persons you will see that in each – Father, Son, and Holy Spirit – the title is apt, 'the God of peace'.

There is *God the everlasting Father*: he is the God of peace, for he from all eternity planned the great covenant of peace.

There is *Jesus Christ*, who is also the God of peace. For 'he is our peace who hath made both one, and hath broken down the middle wall of partition between us'. He makes peace between God and man.

So is the *Holy Spirit* the God of peace. In dark chaotic souls he is the God of peace.

(a) God is the God of peace because he created nothing but peace
(b) God is the God of peace because he restores peace
(c) God is the God of peace because he preserves peace
(d) God is the God of peace because he will perfect peace at the end

## The benediction

'The God of peace be with you all.' I am not about to address you concerning that inward peace which rests in the heart. But I wish to address you as a church, and exhort you to peace.

(a) There are enemies of peace always lurking in all societies
(b) Ambition can be an enemy of peace
(c) Anger can be an enemy of peace
(d) Envy can be an enemy of peace
(e) Pride can be an enemy of peace

## Conclusion

Here, then, are our five great enemies. I would I could see the execution of them all. Continual bickering and jealousy have brought disgrace on the holy name of Christ. He has been wounded in the house of his friends. Brethren, again I say, for the gospel's sake, for the truth's sake, that we may laugh at our enemies and rejoice with joy unimaginable, let us love one another.

# Christ crucified

'But we preach Christ crucified, unto the Jews a stumbling-block, and unto the Greeks foolishness; but unto them which are called, both Jews and Greeks, Christ the power of God, and the wisdom of God' 1 Corinthians 1:23–4

### A gospel rejected

    (a) To the Jew the gospel is a stumblingblock
    (b) To the Greek the gospel is foolishness

### A gospel triumphant

Unto us who are called, both Jews and Greeks, it is the power of God, and the wisdom of God.

I received a note this week asking me to explain that word 'called', because in one passage it says, 'Many are called but few are chosen', while in another it appears that all who are called must be chosen. Now, let me observe that there are two calls. As my old friend John Bunyan says, 'The hen has two calls, the common cluck, which she gives daily and hourly, and the special one which she means for her little chickens.'

### A gospel admired

    (a) The gospel is to the true believer a thing of power
    (b) The gospel is to the true believer a thing of wisdom

# Preach the gospel

'For though I preach the gospel, I have nothing to glory of; for necessity is laid upon me; yea, woe is unto me, if I preach not the gospel' 1 Corinthians 9:16

## What is it to preach the gospel?

   (a) To state every doctrine contained in God's Word, and to give every truth its proper prominence
   (b) To exalt Jesus Christ
   (c) To preach to all types of people
   (d) To preach to the heart

## Why should ministers not take the glory?

   (a) Because they should be very conscious of their own imperfections
   (b) All our gifts are borrowed
   (c) They should feel their constant dependence on the Holy Spirit

## What is that necessity that is laid upon us to preach the gospel?

   (a) Much of it springs from the call itself
   (b) The sad destitution of this poor fallen world

# A warning to the presumptuous

'Let him that thinketh he standeth take heed lest he fall'
1 Corinthians 10:12

### The character of the presumptuous

This is the man who thinks that he stands.

    (a) Worldly prosperity
    (b) Light thoughts about sin
    (c) Low thoughts about the value of religion
    (d) Ignorance of what we are, and where we stand
    (e) Pride: pride of talent, and pride of grace

### The danger the presumptuous is in

He may fall. I must now show you why a man who thinks he stands is more exposed to the danger of falling than any other.

    (a) Such a man in the middle of temptation will be sure to be careless
    (b) He will not keep out of the way of temptation
    (c) He will not use the means of grace
    (d) God's Spirit always leaves the proud

### Counsel for the presumptuous

'Let him take heed.'

    (a) Take heed because so many have fallen
    (b) A fall greatly damages Christ's cause

# Comfort for tried believers

'There hath no temptation taken you but such as is common to man: but God is faithful, who will not suffer you to be tempted above that ye are able; but will with the temptation also make a way to escape, that ye may be able to bear it' 1 Corinthians 10:13

## We have not been tried in any very unusual way

You may think, my dear brethren and sisters, that you have been tried more than others; but it is only your lack of knowledge of the trials of others which leads you to imagine that your own are unique.

(a) Are you tempted to lust after evil things?
(b) Are you tempted to commit fornication?
(c) Are you tempted 'to tempt Christ'?
(d) Are you tempted to murmur?

## 'God is faithful'

'But' – oh, that blessed 'but' – '*but* God is faithful'! God is faithful to all his promises. He will never leave you or forsake you.

## God's power

The third comfort for a tried and tempted believer arises from God's power, for Paul says, 'God is faithful, who will not suffer you to be tempted above that ye are able.' God, then, has power to limit temptation.

## God's judgment

God knows just how much you have to bear, so leave yourself in his hands.

**God has something in store to go with our temptations**

Even with the temptation to sin, the Lord often sends, to the tempted soul, such a revelation of the sinfulness of sin and of the beauty of holiness that the poison of the temptation is quite neutralised.

**God makes a way of escape**

'He will with the temptation also make a way to escape, that ye may be able to bear it.' I will read that over again: 'He will with the temptation also make a way to escape' – that you may get out of it? Oh, no! – that you may not endure it? Oh, no! – '*that ye may be able to bear it*'. That is a curious way to escape, is it not?

# The right observance of the Lord's supper

'For I have received of the Lord that which also I delivered unto you, That the Lord Jesus the same night in which he was betrayed took bread: and when he had given thanks, he brake it, and said, Take, eat: this is my body, which is broken for you: this do in remembrance of me. After the same manner also he took the cup, when he had supped, saying, This cup is the new testament in my blood: this do ye, as oft as ye drink it, in remembrance of me. For as often as ye eat this bread, and drink this cup, ye do shew the Lord's death till he come' 1 Corinthians 11:23–6

**The form of the Lord's Supper**

   (a) Begin with thanksgiving
   (b) Break the bread
   (c) 'He took the cup'
   (d) To be observed in remembrance of Christ

### The importance of the Lord's Supper

(a) It was revealed by the Lord himself
(b) This supper was commanded by the Lord
(c) This supper was instituted by Christ himself, and he himself first set the example for its observance
(d) He established it on a very special occasion
(e) The special personal motive with which it was instituted
(f) It is to be observed 'till he come'

### In what spirit ought we to come to this table?

(a) In the spirit of deep humility
(b) Very thankfully
(c) With great thoughtfulness
(d) With great receptiveness

### The great lessons which this supper incidentally teaches

(a) Jesus is for us
(b) His blood has sealed his covenant
(c) Believers feed on Christ himself
(d) The way to remember Christ is to feed on him again and again

# Fencing the table

'But let a man examine himself, and so let him eat of that bread, and drink of that cup' 1 Corinthians 11:28

### The necessity for this examination

(a) Many have profaned the Lord's table
(b) The purpose of this ordinance requires that we should be in a fit condition for its observance

(c) If we do not come in the correct way, we shall incur very severe penalties

(d) We must be aware that some among us take part of the Lord's Supper unworthily

## The person who is to perform this examination

'Let a man examine *himself.*' Let no one say, 'I was examined by the proper officers of the church, before I was admitted into church membership, so I do not need further examination.' Rather, pray the words of David, 'Search me, O God, and know my heart.'

## What are the vital points in this examination?

(a) Examine yourselves about your knowledge
(b) Examine yourselves about your faith
(c) Examine yourselves about your repentance
(d) Examine yourselves about your love
(e) Examine yourselves about your obedience

## The spirit in which, after this self-examination, we ought to come to the communion

(a) In the spirit of holy wonder
(b) With a sense of self-abasement
(c) In a spirit of strong spiritual thirst
(d) With a believing hope
(e) You will still trust in your Lord and not depend on outward signs

# Consolation proportionate to spiritual suffering

'For as the sufferings of Christ abound in us, so our consolation also aboundeth by Christ' 2 Corinthians 1:5

## Expect suffering

'The sufferings in Christ abound in us.'

(a) Look upward
The martyrs fought before they reigned.
(b) Look downward
There are hell and its lions against thee. Satan is the foe beneath your feet.
(c) Look around you
You are in the world, in a land of enemies not of friends.
(d) Look inside yourself

## The distinction to be noticed

Our sufferings are said to be the sufferings *of Christ*. Suffering in itself is not an evidence of Christianity. Our troubles are 'the trials of Christ' if we suffer for Christ's sake.

## A proportion to be experienced

As the sufferings of Christ abound, *so* our consolations abound.

(a) Trials make room for consolation
(b) Trouble exercises our graces
(c) Trouble brings us closer to God

**The person to be honoured**

'So our consolation aboundeth by Christ.' Christ will come to you and never fail you in your future troubles, in your present troubles, even if they make you despair.

# Spiritual liberty

'Where the Spirit of the Lord is, there is liberty' 2 Corinthians 3:17

**What are we freed from?**

(a) Freedom from the slavery of sin
(b) Freedom from the penalty of sin
(c) Freedom from the guilt of sin
(d) Freedom from the dominion of sin
(e) Freedom from the slavish fear of law
(f) Freedom from the fear of death

**What are we freed for?**

(a) You are free to all that is in the Bible
(b) You are free to the throne of grace
(c) You are free to enter the heavenly city

# Substitution

'For he hath made him to be sin for us, who knew no sin;
that we might be made the righteousness of God in him'
2 Corinthians 5:21

## The doctrine

There are three people mentioned here. '*He* [that is, God] hath
made *him* [that is, Christ] who knew no sin, to be sin for *us*
[sinners] that we might be made the righteousness of God in
him.' Before we can understand the plan of salvation it is
necessary to know something about the three people.

*Three people*
1   God. The God of Scripture is a *sovereign* God.
         God is a God of *infinite justice*
         God is a God of *grace*
2   The Son of God. Christ knew no sin. He was pure, perfect,
spotless; like his own divinity, without spot or blemish, or any
such thing. This gracious Person is he who is spoken of in the
text.
3   The sinner. Will you turn your eyes within you, and look
for him, each one of you?

*The scene* I must now introduce you to a scene of a great
exchange which is made according to the text. The third
person whom we introduced is *the prisoner at the bar*. As a
sinner, God has called him before him; he is about to be tried
for life or death. God is gracious, and he desires to save him;
God is just, and he must punish him.

**'My Son, the pure and perfect shall stand in your place,
and be accounted guilty; and you, the guilty, will stand
in my Son's place and be accounted righteous!'**

There is no hope for you. How then shall the prisoner at the bar escape? Is there any possibility? Oh, how did heaven wonder! God showed how he might be just, and yet be gracious! I think I have seen silence in the courts of heaven when Almighty God said, 'Sinner, I must and will punish you on account of sin. My justice says, "Smite," but my love stays my hand and says, "Spare, spare the sinner." Oh, sinner, my heart has devised it; my Son, the pure and perfect shall stand in your place, and be accounted guilty; and you, the guilty, will stand in my Son's place and be accounted righteous!'

*The consequences of this great substitution* Christ was made sin; we are made the righteousness of God. This man is pure in himself, but he has made himself impure by taking his people's sin. Guilt is imputed to him.

## What is the use of this doctrine?

Turn to the Scriptures and you will see. 'Now, then, we are ambassadors for God, as though God did beseech you by us; we pray you in Christ's stead to be reconciled to God, for' – and here is our grand argument – 'he hath made him to be sin for us, who knew no sin.' I beseech you now be reconciled to God.

## The enjoyment of this doctrine

Are you a mourning Christian? Dry your tears. Are you weeping because of your sin? Do not weep for fear of punishment. Look to your perfect Lord, and remember, you are complete in him, you are in God's sight as perfect as if you had never sinned.

# Our manifesto

'But I certify you, brethren, that the gospel which was
preached of me is not after man' Galatians 1:11

[Preached to an assembly of ministers of the gospel, 25th April
1890.]

### Paul's gospel was not received from men

In a certain sense we received the gospel from men as we were
called by God's grace through parental influence, or through a
Sunday school teacher, or by the ministry of the Word, or by
the reading of a godly book, or by some other agency. But in
Paul's case none of these were used. He was distinctly called by
the Lord Jesus Christ himself speaking to him from heaven,
and revealing himself in his own light. It was necessary that
Paul should not be indebted to Peter, or James, or John, so
that he might truly say, 'I neither received it of man, neither
was I taught it, but by the revelation of Jesus Christ.' Yet we
can say this in another sense. We have also received the gospel
in a way beyond the power of man to convey it to us.

(a)  None of us have received the gospel by birthright
(b)  None of us have received the gospel because of the
     teaching of any man, or group of men
(c)  We have received the truth personally by its revelation
     to our own souls by the Spirit of the Lord

How sweetly the Spirit has taught us *in meditation!*
   How often the Lord taught his servants his own truth *in the
school of tribulation!*
   We have learned the truth of the gospel *in the field of
sacrifice and service with our Lord.*
   Some of us have received the gospel through *the wonderful
unction that has gone with it at times to our souls.*

246

## To us the truth itself is not after man

(a) Our gospel is beyond the reach of human thought
(b) Our gospel is immutable, and nothing that man pro-
    duces can be so called
(c) Our gospel is opposed to human pride
(d) Our gospel does not give sin any quarter
(e) Our gospel is so suitable for the poor and illiterate
(f) Men do not take to it

We are sure that the gospel we have preached is not after men,
because *men do not take to it*. My dear brethren, do not make it
tasteful to carnal minds. Learn, then, that if you take Christ
out of Christianity, Christianity is dead. If you remove grace
out of the gospel, the gospel is gone. If the people do not like
the doctrine of grace, give them all the more of it.

'If you take Christ out of Christianity, Christianity is
dead.
If you remove grace out of the gospel, the gospel is
gone.'

## Practical conclusions

(a) Let us continue to receive truth by the divinely ap-
    pointed channel of faith
(b) Expect opposition if you receive the truth from the
    Lord
(c) If you do not receive the truth except through the power
    of the Holy Spirit of God, you cannot expect others to
    do so
(d) If these things come to us from God, we can safely rest
    our all upon them

Let craft and criticism, priestcraft and rationalism, do their
best, or their worst! The Word of the Lord endures for ever,
and even that Word which by the gospel is preached to men!

# Adoption

'Having predestinated us unto the adoption of children by Jesus Christ to himself, according to the good pleasure of his will' Ephesians 1:5

## Introduction

Meaning of the term. Common among Romans. Two instances in Scripture: Moses and Esther. Adoption differs from justification and regeneration.

## The sense in which believers are sons of God

Not as Jesus. More so than creatures.

*In some things spiritual adoption agrees with civil*
  (a) In name and thing
  (b) To an inheritance
  (c) Voluntary on the part of the adopter
  (d) Taking the adopter's name
  (e) Received into the family
  (f) Considered as children: food, protection, clothing, education
  (g) Under the control of the Father

*In some things they disagree*
  (a) Civil adoption requires the consent of the adopted
  (b) Civil adoption was intended to provide for childless people
  (c) In civil adoption, the adopted had something to recommend him
  (d) The nature of a son could not be given
  (e) The children did not inherit till their father's death
  (f) The Pontifex might make it void

## The cause of adoption

(a) The Person
   God. Father. Son. Spirit.
(b) The motive
   Free grace, not works.

## The object of it

Elect sinners, not angels. All believers. Not all men, but justified men.

## The excellency of it

(a) It is an act of surprising grace (1 John 3:1)
   Consider the people.
(b) It exceeds all others
(c) It makes men honourable
(d) It brings people into the highest relations
(e) It includes all things
(f) It is immutable and everlasting

## The effects of it

(a) Share in the love, pity and care of God
(b) Access with boldness
(c) Conformity to the image of Jesus
(d) The Holy Spirit
(e) Heirship
   Encouragement. Appeal to saints and sinners.

# Spiritual resurrection

'And you hath he quickened, who were dead in trespasses and sins' Ephesians 2:1

## Introduction

The general doctrine is that every man that is born into the world is dead spiritually, and that spiritual life must be given by the Holy Spirit, and can be obtained from no other source. That general doctrine I shall illustrate in rather a singular way. You remember that our Saviour raised three dead people. The first was a young girl, *the daughter of Jairus*, who, when she lay on her bed dead, rose up to life at the single utterance of Christ, '*Talitha cumi*!' The second was the case of *the widow's son*, who was on his bier, about to be carried to his tomb; and Jesus raised him up to life by saying, 'Young man, I say unto thee, arise.' The third was *Lazarus*, who was not on his bed or in his bier, but in his tomb; but, notwithstanding that, the Lord Jesus Christ, by the voice of his omnipotence, crying, 'Lazarus, come forth,' brought him out of the tomb.

I shall use these three facts as illustrations for this text.

## The different states of men, though they are all dead

Men by nature are all dead.

*Jairus' daughter* She lies on her bed, and seems as if she were alive. Her beauty lingers. She is still caressed by her mother. She has no grave clothes on her yet. Her death was confined to her room.

So it is with the young woman or the young man I now describe. His sin is as yet a secret thing, kept to himself. As yet he only sins in his heart. Alas, my brother; alas, my sister, that you who in your outward behaviour are so good should yet have sins in the chamber of your heart, and death in the

250

secrecy of your being, which is as true a death as that of the grossest sinner, though not so thoroughly manifested.

*The widow's son* He is not more dead than the other, but he is further gone. Come, now, and stop the bier; you cannot look at him! So it is with some young men I have here. They are not who they were in childhood, their corruption is breaking out and people are shrinking away from them. You are not quite avoided; you are still received among the people of God, yet there is a coldness that manifests that they understand that you are not a living one.

The young girl was wrapped in the clothes of life, but this young man was wrapped in the clothes of death. So many of you have begun to form habits that are evil; you know that already the screw of the devil is tightening on your finger.

The young girl's death was in her room, but the young man's death was in the city gates. In the first case I described the sin was secret. But, young man, your sin is not. You have gone so far that your habits are openly wicked; you have dared to sin in the face of God's sun.

Oh, Lord Jesus, touch the bier today. Stop some young man in his evil habits, and say to him, 'Arise!'

*Lazarus* Lazarus was dead and buried. I cannot take you to see Lazarus in his grave. Stand away from him. His corpse reeks. There is no beauty there. I must not attempt to describe the spectacle. Nor dare I tell the character of some men present here. I should be ashamed to tell the things which some of you have done. The last stage of death, the last stage of corruption, oh, how hideous; but the last stage of sin, hideous far more!

> 'The last stage of death, the last stage of corruption, oh, how hideous; but the last stage of sin, hideous far more!'

Yet the rotten Lazarus may come out of his tomb, as well as the slumbering maiden from her bed. The last, the most corrupt, the most desperately abominable, may yet be quickened; and he may join in exclaiming, 'And I have been quickened, though I was dead in trespasses and sins.'

## The different means of grace used for raising the dead

These three people were all quickened, and they were all quickened by the same person, that is, by Jesus. But they were all quickened in a different way.

*Jairus' daughter* When she was brought to life, it is said, 'Jesus took her by the hand and said, Maiden, arise.' It was a still small voice. Now, usually, when God converts young people in the first stage of sin, he does it in a gentle manner. There is just the sweet breathing of the Spirit. They perhaps scarcely think it is a true conversion; but true it is, if they are brought to life.

*The widow's son* Christ did not do the same thing with the young man that he did with the daughter of Jairus. No; the first thing he did was, he put his hand, not on him, mark you, but *on the bier*; 'and they that bare it stood still', and, after that, without touching the young man, he said in a louder voice, 'Young man, I say unto thee, arise!' Note the difference: the young girl's new life was given to her secretly. The young man's was given more publicly.

*Lazarus* Now comes the worst case. Notice the preparations Christ made for Lazarus. He wept, groaned in his spirit, said, 'Take away the stone', and prayed, 'I know that thou hearest me always.' And then, 'Jesus cried with a loud voice, Lazarus, come forth!' Jesus spoke to all these three people. It was his word that saved all of them; but in the case of Lazarus, he cried to him in a loud voice.

A still small voice will not do for some; it must be a loud crashing voice. John Bunyan was one of those rotten ones. What strong means were used in his case! Terrible dreams, fearful convulsions, awful shakings to and fro – all had to be employed to make him live. Yet some of you think, when God is terrifying you, that really he does not love you. It is not so: you were so dead that it needed a loud voice to arrest your ears.

252

### The subsequent experience of people brought to life

*Jairus' daughter* Christ said to her, 'Give her meat.' Young people need instruction to build them up in the faith.

*The widow's son* Jesus gave the young man to his mother. Endeavour as much as possible to be found in the company of the righteous; for, as you were carried before to your grave by bad companions, you need to be led to heaven by good ones.

*Lazarus* Jesus commanded, 'Loose him, and let him go.' When a man is far gone into sin, Christ does this for him – he breaks off his evil habits.

# Faith: What is it? How can it be obtained?

'By grace are ye saved through faith' Ephesians 2:8

### Introduction

I mean to dwell upon that expression 'through faith'. I call attention, however, first of all, to the fountain head of our salvation, which is the grace of God. 'By grace are ye saved.' Faith is the channel. Grace is the fountain and the stream. Faith is the aqueduct along which the flood of mercy flows down to refresh the thirsty sons of men.

### Faith, what is it?

What is this faith concerning which it is said, 'By grace ye are saved *through faith*'? Faith is the simplest of all mental acts, and perhaps, because of its simplicity, it is the more difficult to explain.

*It is made up of three things – knowledge, belief and trust*

1   *Knowledge* comes first. 'How shall they believe in him of whom they have not heard?' A measure of knowledge is essential to faith; hence the importance of knowledge. Faith begins with knowledge, hence the value of being taught in divine truth; for to know Christ is eternal life.

2   Then the mind goes on to *believe* that these things are true. The soul believes that God is, and that he hears the cries of sincere hearts; that the gospel is from God; that justification by faith is the grand truth that God has revealed in these last days by his Spirit more clearly than before.

3   So far you have made a considerable advance towards faith; but one more ingredient is absolutely necessary to complete saving faith, and that ingredient is *trust*. Commit yourself to the merciful God. Faith ventures its all on the truth of God.

*Faith is believing that Christ is what he is said to be, that he will do what he has promised to do, and expecting this of him* The Scriptures speak of Jesus Christ as being God, God in human flesh. We are most firmly to believe that it is so. Faith believes that Christ will do what he has promised; that if he has promised to cast out no one who comes to him, it is certain that he will not cast us out, if we come to him.

*Illustrations commonly used to explain faith*
  (a)  Clinging to Christ
  (b)  Following Christ's lead
  (c)  Learning from a master
  (d)  Faith which grows out of love
  (e)  Faith realises the presence of the living God and Saviour
  (f)  A firm faith arises out of assured knowledge
  (g)  Faith commits our soul and all its eternal interests into the Saviour's keeping. Have faith in God, and then hear Jesus say, 'Ye believe in God, believe also in me.'

## Why is faith selected as the channel of salvation?

'By grace ye are saved *through faith.*'

*There is a natural adaptation in faith to be used as the receiver* Faith which receives Christ is as simple an act as when your child receives an apple from you, because you hold it out, and promise to give him the apple if he comes for it.

*Faith gives all the glory to God* God has selected faith to receive the unimaginable gift of his grace, because it cannot take to itself any credit, but must adore the gracious God who is the Giver of all good.

*Faith is a sure method, linking man with God* When man confides in God, there is a point of union between them. Faith unites us to God.

*Faith touches the springs of action* When we believe in Christ, and the heart possesses God, then we are saved from sin, and are moved to repentance, holiness, zeal, prayer, consecration and every other gracious thing.

*Faith has the power of working by love* Faith touches the secret springs of the affections, and draws the heart towards God.

*Faith creates peace and joy* He who has faith rests and is tranquil, glad and joyous; and this is a preparation for heaven.

## How can we obtain and increase faith?

The shortest way to understand faith is to believe at once what we know to be true. The gospel command is clear: 'Believe in the Lord Jesus Christ, and thou shalt be saved.'

   (a) If you have difficulty, take it before God in prayer
       Tell the great Father exactly what it is that puzzles you, and beg him by his Holy Spirit to solve the question.
   (b) Listen very frequently and earnestly to what you are commanded to believe

(c)  Consider the testimony of others
(d)  Note the authority upon which you are commanded to believe
(e)  Think over what it is that you have to believe
(f)  Think on the person of Jesus Christ
(g)  Submit yourself to God!

# Grieving the Holy Spirit

'And grieve not the Holy Spirit of God, whereby ye are sealed unto the day of redemption' Ephesians 4:30

## Introduction

There is something very touching in this admonition, 'Grieve not the Holy Spirit of God.' It does not say, 'Do not make him angry.' A more delicate and tender term is used – 'Grieve him not.' The Holy Spirit of God's emotion is here described, in human language, as being that of grief. Is it not a tender and touching thing that the Holy Spirit should direct his servant Paul to say to us, 'Grieve not the Holy Spirit', do not excite his loving anger, do not vex him, do not cause him to mourn? He is a dove; do not cause him to mourn, because you have treated him harshly and ungratefully.

## The love of the Holy Spirit

The few words I have to say about the love of the Holy Spirit will help to stir you up not to grieve the Holy Spirit. For when we are persuaded that another person loves us, we find at once a very potent reason why we should not grieve him. The love of the Spirit – how can I explain this? Surely it needs a singer to sing it, for love is only to be spoken about in words of song. The love of the Spirit – let me tell you about his early love for us. He loved us without beginning. In the eternal covenant of

256

grace, he was one of the parties in the divine plan by which we are saved. All that can be said about the love of the Father, or the love of the Son, may be said about the love of the Spirit – it is eternal, it is infinite, it is sovereign, it is everlasting; it is a love that cannot be dissolved, which cannot be lessened, a love which cannot be removed from those who are its objects.

Permit me, however, to refer you to his acts, rather than to his attributes. Let me tell you about the love of the Spirit to you and to me.

*When we were unregenerate* Oh, but let us blush to tell it – how often have we turned against him. When we were in a state of being unregenerate, how often we resisted him. We quenched the Spirit. He engaged with us, but we fought against him. But blessed be his dear name, and let him have everlasting songs for it, he would not let us go. We did not want to be saved, but he desired to save us. We sought to thrust ourselves into the fire, but he sought to pluck us from the burning flames. We would throw ourselves over the precipice, but he fought to hold on to us. He would not let us destroy our souls. How we ill-treated him! We ignored his counsel. We scoffed at him; we scorned him and we despised the ordinances which would lead us to Christ. How we tugged at that holy cord which was gently drawing us to Jesus and his cross! I am certain that as you recall your rebellion against the Holy Spirit you must be stirred to love him.

*In our conversion* Ah, then, in that happy moment, dear to the memory, was it not the Holy Spirit who guided you to Jesus? Do you remember the love of the Spirit, when, after you were brought alive, he took you aside and showed you Jesus on the tree? Who was it that opened your blind eye to see a dying Saviour? Who was it that opened your deaf ear to hear the voice of pardoning love? Who opened your clasped and palsied hand to receive the tokens of a Saviour's grace? Who was it that broke your hard heart and made a way for the Saviour to enter and live there? Oh, it was the precious Spirit, that self-same Spirit, whom you had rejected, whom in previous days you had resisted! What a mercy it was that he did not say, 'I will swear in my wrath that they shall not enter into my rest, for they have vexed me, and I will take my everlasting flight from them'; or thus, 'Ephraim is joined unto idols, I will let him alone!'

*Teaching us about the kingdom* Since that time, my brethren, how sweetly has the Spirit proved his love to you and to me. It is not only in his first strivings, and then his divine quickenings; but in all the sequel, how much have we owed to his instruction! We have been dull scholars with the Word before us, plain and simple, so that he that runs may read, and he that reads may understand, yet how small a portion of his Word has our memory retained – how little progress have we made in the school of God's grace! We are but learners yet, unstable, weak and apt to slide, but what a blessed instructor we have had! Has he not led us into many a truth, and taken the things of Christ and applied them to us? Oh, when I think how stupid I have been, I wonder that he has not given me up. When I think what a stupid person I have been, when he would have taught me about the kingdom of God, I marvel that he should have had such patience with me. Is it a wonder that Jesus should become a baby? Is it not an equal wonder that the Spirit of the living God should become a teacher of babies? It is a marvel that Jesus should lie in a manger; is it not an equal marvel that the Holy Spirit should become an usher in the sacred school, to teach fools and make them wise? It was condescension that brought the Saviour to the cross, but is it not equal condescension that brings the mighty Spirit of grace down to live with stubborn, unruly wild asses' colts, to teach them the mystery of the kingdom, and make them know the wonders of a Saviour's love?

*Helping us in our praying* But also remember that he assists us in our praying, when we do not know what to pray for, when 'we ourselves groan within ourselves', then the Spirit himself makes intercession for us with groanings which cannot be uttered – groans as we should groan, but more audibly, so that our prayer, which otherwise would have been silent, reaches the ears of Christ, and is then presented before his Father's face.

To help our infirmities is a mighty instance of love. When God overcomes infirmity altogether, or removes it, there is something very noble and grand and sublime in the deed; when he permits the infirmity to remain and yet works with the infirmity, this is tender compassion indeed. When the Saviour heals the lame man you see his Godhead, but when he walks with the lame man, limping though his walk is, then you see a manifestation of love almost unequalled. Except for Christ bearing our infirmities and sins on the tree, I know of no greater or more tender instance of divine love than when it is written: 'Likewise the Spirit also helpeth our infirmities.' Oh, how much you owe to the Spirit when you have been on your knees in prayer! You know, my brethren, what it is to be dull and lifeless there; to groan for a word, and yet the very wish is languid; to long to have desires, and yet all the desire you have is a desire that you may be able to desire. Oh, have you not sometimes, when your desires have kindled, longed to get a grip at the promise by the hand of faith? 'Oh,' you have said, 'if I could but plead the promise, all my necessities would be removed, and all my sorrows would be allayed,' but, alas, the promise was beyond your reach. If you touched it with the tip of your finger, you could not grasp it as you desired, you could not plead it, and therefore you came away without the blessing. But when the Spirit has helped our infirmities how have we prayed! Why, there have been times when you and I have so grasped the knocker of the gate of mercy, and have let it fall with such tremendous force, that it seemed as if the very gate itself did shake and totter; there have been seasons when we have laid hold on the angel, have overcome heaven by prayer, have declared we would not let Jehovah himself go except he should bless us. We have, and we say it without blasphemy, moved the arm that moves the world. We have brought down upon us the eyes that look upon the universe. All this we have done, not by our own strength, but by the might and by the power of the Spirit; and seeing he has so sweetly enabled us, though we have so often forgotten to thank him; seeing that he has so graciously assisted us, though we have often taken all the glory to ourselves instead of giving it to him, must we not admire his love, and must it not be a fearful sin indeed to grieve the Holy Spirit by whom we are sealed?

*Helping us to persevere* Oh, my friends, when I think how often you and I have let the devil in, I wonder the Spirit has not withdrawn from us. The final perseverance of the saints is one of the greatest miracles on record; in fact, it is the sum total of miracles. The perseverance of a saint for a single day is a multitude of miracles of mercy. When you consider that the Spirit is of purer eyes than to behold iniquity, and yet he dwells in the heart where sin often intrudes, a heart out of which come blasphemies and murders and all manner of evil thoughts, what if sometimes he is grieved, and retires and leaves us to ourselves for a season? It is a marvel that he is there at all, for he must be daily grieved with these evil guests, these false traitors, these base intruders who thrust themselves into that little temple which he had honoured with his presence, the temple of the heart of man.

I am afraid, dear friends, we are too much in the habit of talking about the love of Jesus, without thinking about the love of the Holy Spirit. Now I would not wish to exalt one person of the Trinity above another, but I do feel this, that because Jesus Christ was a man, bone of our bone and flesh of our flesh, and therefore there was something tangible in him that can be seen with the eyes and handled with the hands, therefore we more readily think of him, and fix our love on him, than we do on the Spirit. But why should it be? Let us love Jesus with all our hearts, and let us love the Holy Spirit too. Let us have songs for him, gratitude for him. We do not forget Christ's cross; let us not forget the Spirit's work. We do not forget what Jesus has done for us; let us always remember what the Spirit does in us. Why, you talk of the love and grace and tenderness and faithfulness of Christ; why do you not say the same of the Spirit? Was ever love like his, that he should visit us? Was ever mercy like his, that he should bear with our ill manners, though constantly repeated by us? Was ever faithfulness like his, that multitudes of sins cannot drive him away? Was ever power like his, that overcometh all our iniquities, and yet leads us safely on, though hosts of foes within and without would rob us of our Christian life?

> Oh, the love of the Spirit I sing,
> By whom is redemption applied.
> And unto his name be glory for ever and ever.

## It is by the Holy Spirit that we are sealed

This brings me to my second point. Here we have another reason why we should not grieve the Spirit. It is by the Holy Spirit that we are sealed. 'By whom we are sealed unto the day of redemption.' The Spirit himself is expressed as a seal, even as he himself is directly said to be the pledge of our inheritance. The sealing, I think, has a three-fold meaning.

*A sealing of attestation* It is a sealing of attestation or confirmation. I want to know whether I am truly a child of God. The Spirit himself also bears witness with my spirit that I am born of God. I have the writings, the title-deeds of the inheritance that is to come – I want to know whether those are valid, whether they are true, or whether they are mere counterfeits written out by that old scribe of hell, Master Presumption and Carnal Security. How am I to know? I look for the seal. After we have believed on the Son of God, the Father seals us as his children, by the gift of the Holy Spirit. 'Now he which . . . hath anointed us, is God; who also hath sealed us, and given the earnest of the Spirit in our hearts' (2 Cor. 1:21–2). No faith is genuine which does not bear the seal of the Spirit. No love, no hope can ever save us, unless it is sealed with the Spirit of God, for whatever does not have the Spirit of God on it is spurious. Faith that is unsealed may be a poison, it may be presumption; but faith that is sealed by the Spirit is true, real, genuine faith. Never be content, my dear hearers, unless you are sealed, unless you are sure, by the inner witness and testimony of the Holy Spirit, that you have been born again to a living hope by the resurrection of Jesus Christ from the dead. It is possible for a person to know infallibly that he is certain of heaven. He may not only hope so, but he may know it beyond a doubt, and he may know it in this way: by being able with the eye of faith to see the seal, the broad stamp of the Holy Spirit set on his own character and experience. It is a seal of attestation.

*A sealing of appropriation* In the next place, it is a sealing of appropriation. When people put their mark on an article, it is to show that it is their own. The farmer brands his tools so that they may not be stolen. They are his. The shepherd marks his sheep that they may be recognised as belonging to his flock. The king himself puts his broad arrow on everything that is his property. So the Holy Spirit puts the broad arm of God on the hearts of all his people. He seals us. 'Thou shalt be mine,' saith the Lord, 'in the day when I make up my jewels.' And then the Spirit puts God's seal on us to signify that we are God's reserved inheritance – his special people, the portion in which his soul delights.

*A sealing of preservation* But, again, by sealing is meant preservation. People seal up what they want to preserve, and when a document is sealed it becomes valid henceforth. Now, it is by the Spirit of God that the Christian is sealed, that he is kept, he is preserved, sealed unto the day of redemption – sealed until Christ comes fully to redeem the bodies of his saints by raising them from the dead, and fully to redeem the world by purging it from sin, and making it a kingdom unto himself in righteousness. We shall hold on our way; we shall be saved. The chosen seed cannot be lost, they must be brought home at last, but how? By the sealing of the Spirit. Apart from that they perish; they are undone. When the last general fire is alight, everything that has not been sealed by the Spirit will be burned up. But the people who have the seal on their forehead will be preserved. They shall be safe, 'amid the wreck of matter, and the crash of worlds'. Their spirits, mounting above the flames, shall dwell with Christ eternally, and with that same seal on their forehead on Mount Zion, they shall sing the everlasting song of gratitude and praise. I say this is the second reason why we should love the Spirit and why we should not grieve him.

## The grieving of the Spirit

I come now to the third part of my discourse, namely, the grieving of the Spirit. How may we grieve him? What will be the sad result of grieving him? If we have grieved him, how may we bring him back again?

How may we grieve the Spirit? I am now, please note, speaking about those who love the Lord Jesus Christ. The Spirit of God is in your heart, and it is very, very easy indeed to grieve him. Sin is as easy as it is wicked. You may grieve him by impure thoughts. He cannot bear sin. If you indulge in lascivious expressions, or if even you allow imagination to dwell on any lascivious act, or if your heart goes after covetousness, if you set your heart on anything that is evil, the Spirit of God will be grieved, for thus I hear him speaking of himself, 'I love this man, I want to have his heart, and yet he is entertaining these filthy lusts. His thoughts, instead of running after me, and after Christ, and after the Father, are running after the temptations that are in the world through lust.' And then the Spirit is grieved. He sorrows in his soul because he knows what sorrow these things must bring to our souls.

*By outward acts of sin* We grieve him even more if we indulge in outward acts of sin. Then he is sometimes so grieved that he takes his flight for a season, for the dove will not dwell in our hearts if we take loathsome carrion in there. The dove is a clean being, and we must not strew the place which the dove frequents with filth and mire; if we do he will fly elsewhere. If we commit sin, if we openly bring disgrace on our religion, if we tempt others to sin by our example, it is not long before the Holy Spirit will begin to grieve.

*By neglect of prayer* Again, if we neglect prayer, if our closet door is cobwebbed, if we forget to read the Scriptures, if the pages of our Bible are almost stuck together through neglect, if we never seek to do any good in the world, if we live merely for ourselves and not for Christ, then the Holy Spirit will be grieved, for he says, 'They have forsaken me, they have left the fountain of waters, they have hewn unto themselves broken cisterns.' I think I now see the Spirit of God grieving when you are sitting down to read a novel and there is your Bible unread. Perhaps you take down some travel book, and you forget that you have got a more precious book of travels in the Acts of the Apostles, and in the story of your blessed Lord and Master. You have not time for prayer, but the Spirit sees you very active about worldly things, and having many hours to spare for relaxation and amusement.

*By our love of the world* And then he is grieved because he sees that you love worldly things more than you love him. His spirit is grieved within him; take care that he does not go away from you, for it will be a pitiful thing for you if he leaves you to yourself. Again, ingratitude tends to grieve him. Nothing cuts a person to the heart more than, after having done his utmost for another, he turns round and repays him with ingratitude and insult. If we do not want to be thanked, at least we do love to know that there is thankfulness in the heart on which we have conferred a boon, and when the Holy Spirit looks into our soul and sees little love for Christ, no gratitude towards him for all he has done for us, then he is grieved.

*By unbelief* Again, the Holy Spirit is exceedingly grieved by our unbelief. When we distrust the promise he has given and applied, when we doubt the power or the affection of our blessed Lord, then the Spirit says within himself: 'They doubt my faithfulness; they distrust my power; they say Jesus is not able to save unto the uttermost.' Thus the Spirit is grieved again. Oh, I wish the Spirit had an advocate here this morning that could speak in better terms than I can. I have a theme that overwhelms me, I seem to grieve for him; but I cannot make you grieve, nor fully speak about how I feel. In my own soul I keep saying, 'Oh, this is just what you have done – you have grieved him.' Let me make a full and frank confession even before you all. I know that, too often, I as well as you have grieved the Holy Spirit. Much within us has made that sacred dove mourn, and the wonder is that he has not taken his flight from us and left us completely to ourselves.

## The effects of grieving the Spirit

Now suppose the Holy Spirit is grieved, what is the effect produced in us?

*He bears with us at first* When the Spirit is grieved, he bears with us to start with. He is grieved again and again, and again and again, and still he bears with it all. But at last the grief becomes so excessive that he says, 'I will suspend my work; I will go; I will leave life behind me, but my own actual presence I will take away.' And when the Spirit of God goes away from the soul and suspends all his work, what a miserable state we are in. He suspends his work; we read the Word, we cannot understand it; we go to our commentaries, they cannot tell us the meaning; we fall on our knees and ask to be taught, but we receive no answer, we learn nothing. He suspends his comfort; we used to dance, like David before the ark, and now we sit like Job in the ash-pit, and scrape our ulcers with a potsherd. There was a time when his candle shone around us, but now he is gone; he has left us in the blackness and darkness. Now, he takes from us all spiritual power. Once we could do all things; now we can do nothing. We could slay the Philistines, and lay them heap upon heap, but now Delilah can deceive us, and our eyes are put out and we are made to grind at the mill. We go preaching, and there is no pleasure in preaching, and no good follows it. We go distributing tracts and to our Sunday school, and we may as well have stayed at home. The machinery is there, but there is no love. There is the intention to do good, or perhaps not even that, but alas, there is not power to accomplish the intention. The Lord has withdrawn himself, his light, his joy, his comfort, his spiritual power, all are gone.

*All our graces flag* Then all our graces flag. Our graces are much like the hydrangea flower. When it has plenty of water it blooms, but as soon as moisture fails, the leaves drop down at once. And so when the Spirit goes away, faith shuts up its flowers; no perfume is exhaled. Then the fruit of our love begins to rot and drops from the tree; then the sweet buds of our hope become frostbitten, and they die. Oh, what a sad thing it is to lose the Spirit. Have you never, my brethren, been on your knees and been conscious that the Spirit of God was not with you, and what awful work it has been to groan and cry and sigh, and yet go away again, and no light to shine on the promises, not so much as a ray of light through the chink of the dungeon? All forsaken, forgotten and forlorn, you are almost driven to despair. You sing with Cowper:

> What peaceful hours I once enjoyed,
> How sweet their memory still!
> But they have left an aching void,
> The world can never fill.

> Return, thou sacred dove, return,
> Sweet messenger of rest,
> I hate the sins that made Thee mourn,
> And drove Thee from my breast.

> The dearest idol I have known,
> Whate'er that idol be,
> Help me to tear it from its throne,
> And worship only Thee.

*The spiritual decline of the nation* Ah, sad enough it is to have the Spirit taken away from us. But, my brethren, I am about to say something with the utmost charity which, perhaps, may look severe, but, nevertheless, I must say it. The churches of the present day are very much in the position of those who have grieved the Spirit of God; for the Spirit deals with churches just as he deals with individuals. In recent years how little has God wrought in the middle of his churches! Throughout England, at least some four or five years ago, an almost universal torpor had fallen on the visible body of Christ. There was a little action, but it was spasmodic; there was not real vitality. Oh, how few sinners were brought to Christ, how empty had our places of worship become; our prayer-meetings were dwindling to nothing, and our church meetings were mere matters of farce. You know very well that this is true of many London churches today, and some people do not mourn over this. They go up to their usual place, and the minister prays, and the people either sleep with their eyes or else with their hearts, and they go out, and there is never a soul saved. The pool of baptism is seldom stirred; but the saddest part of all is this: the churches are willing to have it so. They are not earnest to get a revival of religion. We have been doing something, the Church at large has been doing something. I will not just now put my finger on what the sin is, but there has been something done which has driven the Spirit of God from us. He is grieved, and he is gone.

*Unexpected revival* He is present with us here, I thank his name, he is still visible in our midst. He has not left us. Though we have been as unworthy as others, yet has he given us a long outpouring of his presence. These five years or more, we have had a revival which is not to be exceeded by any revival upon the face of the earth. Without cries and shoutings, without fallings down or swooning, steadily God adds to this church numbers upon numbers, so that your minister's heart is ready to break with the very joy when he thinks how manifestly the Spirit of God is with us.

But, brethren, we must not be content with this; we want to see the Spirit poured out on all churches. Look at the great gatherings that there were in St Paul's and Westminster Abbey and Exeter Hall and other places. How was it that no good was done, or so very little? I have watched with anxious eye, and I have never from that day forth heard but of one conversion, and that in St James's Hall, from all these services. Strange it seems. The blessing may have come in larger measure than we know, but not in so large a measure as we might have expected, if the Spirit of God had been present with all the ministers. Oh, would that we may live to see greater things than we have ever seen yet. Go home to your houses, humble yourselves before God, you members of Christ's Church, and cry aloud that he will visit his Church, and that he will open the windows of heaven and pour out his grace on his thirsty hill of Zion, that nations may be born in a day, that sinners may be saved in their thousands – that Zion may go into labour and bear many children.

Oh, there are signs and tokens of a coming revival. We have heard recently of a good work among the Ragged School boys of St Giles's, and our soul has been glad on account of that; and the news from Ireland comes to us like good tidings. Let us cry aloud to the Holy Spirit, who is certainly grieved with his Church, and let us purge our churches of everything that is contrary to his Word and to sound doctrine, and then the Spirit will return, and his power will be manifest.

## Conclusion

And now, in conclusion, there may be some present who have lost the visible presence of Christ with you; who have in fact so grieved the Spirit that he has gone. It is a mercy for you to know that the Spirit of God never leaves his people finally; he leaves them for chastisement, but not for damnation. He sometimes leaves them that they may get good by knowing their weakness, but he will not leave them finally to perish. Are you in a state of backsliding and coldness? Christian friend, do not stay a moment longer in this dangerous condition. Do not be at ease for a single second that the Holy Spirit is not with you. I plead with you to use every means through which that Spirit may be brought back to you.

Once more, let me tell you clearly what these means are. Search out for the sin that has grieved the Spirit, give it up, put that sin to death at once; repent with tears and sighs; continue in prayer, and never rest satisfied until the Holy Spirit has returned to you. Attend an earnest ministry, get much with earnest saints, but above all, be much in prayer to God, and let your daily cry be, 'Return, return, O Holy Spirit return, and live in my soul.'

Oh, I plead with you not to be content until that prayer is heard, for you have become weak as water, and faint and empty while the Spirit has been away from you. Oh, it may be there are some here today with whom the Spirit has been striving during the past week. Oh yield to him, resist him not; grieve him not, but yield to him. Is he saying to you now, 'Turn to Christ'? Listen to him, obey him, he moves you. Oh, I beseech you, do not despise him. Have you resisted him many times? Then take care you do not again, for there may come a last time when the Spirit may say, 'I will go unto my rest, I will not return to him, the ground is accursed, it shall be given up to barrenness.' Oh, hear the word of the gospel, before you separate, for the Spirit speaks effectively to you now in this short sentence: 'Repent and be converted, every one of you, that your sins may be blotted out when the times of refreshing shall come from the presence of the Lord.' Also, take this solemn sentence to heart: 'He that believeth in the Lord Jesus, and is baptised, shall be saved; but he that believeth not shall be damned.' May the Lord grant that we may not grieve the Holy Spirit. Amen.

# The good man's life and death

'For to me to live is Christ, and to die is gain' Philippians 1:21

### The life of a Christian

'For to me to live is Christ.'

- (a)  The life of a Christian derives its parentage from Christ
- (b)  The model of his life is Christ
- (c)  The end of his life is Christ

### The death of a Christian

'To die is gain.'

- (a)  We have more dear friends in glory than we have here
- (b)  We have more riches in heaven than we have here
- (c)  Means of grace are replaced by the Lord himself
- (d)  Our knowledge of God is increased: we shall see face to face

### Conclusion

This makes the Christian long to die and 'land us all in heaven'.

# 'Christ is all'

'Where there is neither Greek nor Jew, circumcision nor uncircumcision, Barbarian, Scythian, bond nor free: but Christ is all, and in all' Colossians 3:11

## What is obliterated in the new creation?

(a) All national distinctions
(b) Ceremonial distinctions are obliterated
(c) Social distinctions are gone from Christ's Church

## What takes its place in the new creation?

(a) Christ is all our culture
(b) Christ is all our revelation
(c) Christ is all our ritual
(d) Christ is all our simplicity
(e) Christ is all our natural traditions
(f) 'Christ is all' as our Master, if we are 'bond'
(g) Christ is our Magna Carta; yes, our liberty itself if we are 'free'

# Election

'But we are bound to give thanks always to God for you, brethren beloved of the Lord, because God hath from the beginning chosen you to salvation through sanctification of the Spirit and belief of the truth: Whereunto he called you by our gospel, to the obtaining of the glory of our Lord Jesus Christ' 2 Thessalonians 2:13–14

## The doctrine is true

*Anglican support*

Predestination to life is the everlasting purpose of God, whereby (before the foundations of the world were laid) he hath continually decreed by his counsel secret to us, to deliver from curse and damnation those whom he hath chosen in Christ out of mankind, and to bring them by Christ to everlasting salvation, as vessels made to honour. Wherefore they which be endued with so excellent a benefit of God be called according to God's purpose by his Spirit working in due season: they through grace obey the calling: they be justified freely: they be made sons of God by adoption: they be made like the image of his only-begotten Son Jesus Christ: they walk religiously in good works, and at length, by God's mercy, they attain to everlasting felicity.

> The Thirty-nine Articles. Article 17:
> Upon Predestination and Election

*Waldenses support*

That God saves from corruption and damnation those whom he has chosen from the foundation of the world, not for any disposition, faith, or holiness that he foresaw in them, but of his mere mercy in Christ Jesus his Son, passing by all the rest according to the irreprehensible reason of his own free-will and justice.

> One of the Articles of their faith,
> copied from an old book

*Baptist support*

By the decree of God, for the manifestation of his glory, some men and angels are predestined, or foreordained to eternal life through Jesus Christ, to the praise of his glorious grace; others being left to act in their sin to their just condemnation, to the praise of his glorious justice. These angels and men thus predestined and foreordained, are particularly unchangeably designed, and their number so certain and definite, that it cannot be either increased or diminished. Those of mankind that are predestined to life, God, before the foundation of the world was laid, according to his eternal and immutable purpose, and the secret counsel and good pleasure of his will, hath chosen in Christ unto everlasting glory, out of his mere free grace and love, without any other thing in the creature as a condition or cause moving him thereunto.

Baptist Confession, Article 3

As for these human authorities, I care not one rush for all three of them. I have only used them as a kind of confirmation to your faith, to show you that while I may be railed upon as a heretic and as a hyper-Calvinist, after all I am backed up by antiquity.

*God's Word* I have selected a few texts for you to read: Mark 13:20, 22, 27; Luke 18:7; John 15:16; Acts 13:48; Romans 8:29ff; all of Romans 9, especially verse 2; Romans 11:5, 7; 1 Corinthians 1:26–9; and 1 Thessalonians 5:9.

Methinks, my friends, that this overwhelming mass of Scripture testimony must stagger those who dare to laugh at this doctrine.

*'Is it not hard for God to choose some and leave others?'* In reply to this question, I will ask you one. Is there any one of you here this morning who wishes to be holy, who wishes to be regenerate, to leave off sin and walk in holiness? 'Yes, there is,' says someone, 'I do.' Then God has elected you. But another says, 'No; I don't want to be holy; I don't want to give up my lusts and my vices.' Why should you grumble, then, that God has not elected you? For if you were elected you would not like it, according to your own confession.

## Election is absolute

Election does not depend on what we are. The text says, 'God hath from the beginning chosen us unto salvation'; but our opponents say that God chooses people because they are good, that he chooses them on account of sundry works they have done.

Election, we are certain, is absolute, and altogether apart from the virtues which the saints have afterwards. Our only hope still hangs on grace as exhibited in the person of Jesus Christ.

'He will have mercy on whom he will have mercy'; he saves because he will save.

## This election is eternal

God has from the beginning chosen you to eternal life.

## The election is personal

Here again, our opponents have tried to overthrow election by telling us that it is an election of nations, and not of people. But here the apostle says, 'God hath from the beginning chosen you.' Scripture continually speaks of God's people one by one and speaks of them as having been the special subjects of election.

## Election produces good results

'He hath from the beginning chosen you unto sanctification of the spirit, and belief of the truth.'

Do not fancy that election excuses sin – do not dream of it – do not rock yourself in sweet complacency in the thought of your irresponsibility. You are chosen 'unto sanctification of the spirit, and belief of the truth'. You are responsible. We must give you both things. We must have divine sovereignty, and we must have man's responsibility.

> 'You are responsible. We must give you both things. We must have divine sovereignty, and we must have man's responsibility.'

Election is a most humbling doctrine which should also make a Christian fearless and bold.

273

# The minister's self-watch

'Take heed unto thyself, and unto the doctrine' 1 Timothy 4:16

Every workman knows the necessity of keeping his tools in a good state of repair, for 'if the iron be blunt, and he do not whet the edge, then must he put to more strength'. We are, in a certain sense, our own tools, and therefore must keep ourselves in order. It will be in vain for me to stock my library, or organise societies, or project schemes, if I neglect the culture of myself. The godly pastor M'Cheyne, writing to a ministerial friend who was travelling with a view to perfecting himself in the German tongue, wrote:

> I know you will apply hard to German, but do not forget the culture of the inner man – I mean of the heart. How diligently the cavalry officer keeps his sabre clean and sharp; every stain he rubs off with the greatest care. Remember you are God's sword, his instrument – I trust, a chosen vessel unto him to bear his name. In great measure, according to the purity and perfection of the instrument, will be the success. It is not great talents God blesses so much as likeness to Jesus. A holy minister is an awful weapon in the hand of God.

**A holy minister is an awful weapon in the hand of God.**

We may miss our mark, lose our end and aim and waste our time, through not possessing true vital force within ourselves, or not possessing it in such a degree that God could consistently bless us. Beware of being shoddy preachers.

## We must be saved men

    (a)  The unconverted minister is unhappy
    (b)  The unconverted minister is unserviceable
    (c)  The unconverted minister is dangerous
    (d)  The unconverted minister faces a terrible state hereafter

Richard Baxter, in his *Reformed Pastor,* writes:

> Take heed to yourselves lest you should be void of that
> saving grace of God which you offer to others, and be
> strangers to the effectual working of that Gospel which you
> preach; and lest, while you proclaim the necessity of a
> Saviour to the world, your hearts should neglect him,
> and you should miss of an interest in him and his saving
> benefits. Take heed to yourselves, lest you perish while you
> call upon others to take heed of perishing, and lest you
> famish while you prepare their food . . . Believe it, brethren,
> God never saved any man for being a preacher, nor because
> he was an able preacher; but because he was a justified,
> sanctified man, and consequently faithful in his Master's
> work. Take heed, therefore, to yourselves first, that you be
> that which you persuade others to be, and believe that which
> you persuade them daily to believe, and have heartily
> entertained that Christ and Spirit which you offer unto
> others.

## Our piety must be vigorous

Recollect, as ministers, that your whole life, your whole
pastoral life especially, will be affected by the vigour of your
piety. If your zeal grows dull, you will not pray well in the
pulpit; you will pray worse in the family, and worst in the
study alone. Your discourses will next betray your declension.
You may utter as well-chosen words and as fitly-ordained
sentences as before; but there will be a perceptible loss of
spiritual force.

*Our danger is greater than that of others* On the whole, no place
is so assailed with temptation as the ministry. The great enemy
of souls takes care to leave no stone unturned for the preacher's ruin. Baxter says:

> Take heed to yourselves, because the tempter will make his
> first and sharpest onset upon you. If you will be leaders
> against him, he will spare you no further than God restrai-

neth him. He breathes the greatest malice to those that are
engaged to do him the greatest mischief . . . Take heed,
therefore, brethren, for the enemy hath a special eye upon
you. You shall have his most subtle insinuations, and
incessant solicitations, and violent assaults. As wise and
learned as you are, take heed to yourselves lest he overwit
you. The devil is a greater scholar than you are, and a
nimbler disputant; he can 'transform himself into an angel
of light' to deceive. He will get within you and trip up your
heels before you are aware; he will play the juggler with you
undiscerned, and cheat you of your faith or innocency, and
you shall not know that you have lost it; nay, he will make
you believe it is multiplied or increased when it is lost . . . O
do not so far gratify Satan; do not make him so much sport;
suffer him not to use you as the Philistines did Samson –
first to deprive you of your strength, and then to put out
your eyes, and so to make you the matter of his triumph and
derision.

*Our work requires the highest degree of godliness* To face the
enemies of truth, to defend the bulwarks of the faith, to rule
well in the house of God, to comfort all that mourn, to edify
the saints, to guide the perplexed, to bear with the froward, to
win and nurse souls – all these and a thousand other works
beside are not for a Feeble-mind or a Ready-to-halt, but are
reserved for Great-heart whom the Lord has made strong for
himself. Seek then strength from the Strong One, wisdom from
the Wise One, in fact, all from the God of all.

## Our character must agree with our ministry

We have all heard the story of the man who preached so well
and lived so badly that when he was in the pulpit everybody
said he ought never to come out again, and when he was out of
it they all declared he never ought to enter it again. May the
Lord deliver us from the limitation of such a Janus. May we
never be priests of God at the altar, and sons of Belial outside
the tabernacle door; but on the contrary, may we, as the Bible
commentator Nazianzen says of Basil, 'thunder in our

doctrine, and lightning in our conversation'. We do not trust those persons who have two faces, nor will men believe in those whose verbal and practical testimonies are contradictory. As actions, according to the proverb, speak louder than words, so an ill life will effectually drown the voice of the most eloquent ministry. After all, our truest building must be performed with our hands; our characters must be more persuasive than our speech. Here I would not alone warn you of sins of commission, but of sins of omission. Too many preachers forget to serve God when they are out of the pulpit; their lives are negatively inconsistent. Abhor, dear brethren, the thought of being clockwork ministers who are not alive by abiding grace within, but are wound up by temporary influences; men who are only ministers for the time being, under the stress of the hour of ministering, but cease to be ministers when they descend the pulpit stairs. True ministers are always ministers. Too many preachers are like those sand-toys we buy for our children: you turn the box upside down, and the little acrobat revolves and revolves till the sand is all run down, and then he hangs motionless; so there are some who persevere in the ministrations of truth as long as there is an official necessity for their work, but after that, no pay, no paternoster; no salary, no sermon.

It is a horrible thing to be an inconsistent minister. Our Lord is said to have been like Moses, for this reason, that he was 'a prophet mighty in word and in deed'. The man of God should imitate his Master in this; he should be mighty both in the word of his doctrine and in the deed of his example, and mightiest, if possible, in the second. It is remarkable that the only church history we have is the *Acts* of the Apostles. The Holy Spirit has not preserved their sermons. They were very good ones, better than we shall ever preach, but still the Holy Spirit has only taken care of their acts. We have no books of the resolutions of the apostles; when we hold our church meetings we record our minutes and resolutions, but the Holy Spirit only puts down the acts. Our acts should be such as to bear recording, for recorded they will be. We must live as under the more immediate eye of God, and as in the blaze of the great all-revealing day.

# The form of sound words

'Hold fast the form of sound words, which thou hast heard of me, in faith and love which is in Christ Jesus' 2 Timothy 1:13

## Introduction

My incessant anxiety for you, dearly beloved, in the faith of Jesus Christ, is that I may be able, in the first place, to teach you what God's truth is; and then, that you should 'hold fast the form of sound words'; that whatever may occur in the future, you might stand firm as rocks, abiding in 'the faith which was once delivered unto the saints'.

## What is a 'form of sound words'?

  (a) 'Sound words' must be ones which exalt God and put down man
  (b) Judge soundness of doctrine by its general tenor: does it promote holiness?
  (c) 'Sound words' embrace God's being and nature
  (d) 'Sound words' teach about man as well as about God
  (e) A sound doctrine must have a right view of salvation, as being of the Lord only

## The necessity for holding fast this form of sound words

  (a) Keep it for your own sake
    It will make you grow. Remember: every deviation from truth is a sin; every error in doctrine almost inevitably leads to error in practice.
  (b) For the good of the Church
    This will promote strength in the Church.
  (c) For the sake of the world
    When men see the true gospel it will be sure to win them.

**Two dangers**

    (a) You will be tempted to give up because of open opposition

    (b) You will be tempted to give up through people who insidiously undermine every doctrine

**Two great holdfasts by which you are to hold fast the truth of the gospel**

Before I come to the two holdfasts may I say, Seek to understand the truth and pray yourselves into the truth.

*The first holdfast is faith* Believe the truth. Do not pretend to believe it, but believe it thoroughly.

*The second holdfast is love* Love Christ and love Christ's truth because it is Christ's truth, for Christ's sake, and if you love the truth you will not let it go.

# Good works

'Zealous of good works' Titus 2:14

**Introduction**

There are some who hear us preach and constantly declare that we are saved by grace through faith, and that not of ourselves, and that we could not preach a good sermon of exhortation to Christians to live in holiness. I reply, we will try and preach so as to lead the children of God to live in holiness. The children of God are a holy people – for this purpose were they born and brought into the world, that they should be holy. For this they were redeemed with blood, and made a peculiar people. God's end in election, and the end of all his purposes, is not answered until they become a people 'zealous of good works'.

## The nature of good works

There are many things called good works that are not so at all.

(a) Nothing is a good work unless it is done with a good motive
(b) Nothing is a good work until the blood of Christ is sprinkled on it

## Trace good works to their origin

Good works spring from union with Christ.

## The use of good works

(a) Good works are useful as evidences of grace
(b) Good works testify to other people about the truth of what we believe
(c) Good works are an adornment to a Christian

You will remember how a woman should adorn herself: 'Whose adorning let it not be that outward adorning of plaiting the hair, and of wearing of gold, or of putting on of apparel; but let it be the hidden man of the heart, in that which is not corruptible, even the ornament of a meek and quiet spirit' (1 Peter 3:3–4). The adornment in which we hope to enter heaven is the blood and righteousness of Jesus Christ; but the adornment of a Christian here below is his holiness, his piety, his consistency. I beseech you, brethren, 'adorn the doctrine of God our Saviour in all things'.

## The doctrine of free grace makes us 'zealous of good works'

The religion that we profess, and preach in this place is calculated to produce good works in the child of God.

# By faith Jericho fell

'By faith the walls of Jericho fell down, after they were compassed about seven days' Hebrews 11:30

## Introduction

Faith is the one grand essential in salvation. It must be inwrought, or else there will be no spiritual life at first. It is necessary ever after in numberless ways. We cannot have knowledge of gospel doctrines without faith, nor can we lay hold on the promises without it. The graces are all dependent on faith. He loves most who believes most. He will have most zeal who has most faith. Humility is produced by faith, and hope breathes through faith. In doing good to others, and particularly in combat with evil, let us have faith.

## Faith is the grace to which victory is given

1   The other graces are not decked with laurel, lest man should steal their crowns; but faith is too tall, man cannot reach its head. Faith has less to do with man and more to do with God than any of the other graces; for faith is looking away from self, and trusting the Eternal.
2   Faith gains the victory because she engages the arm of the Almighty on her behalf. She has power with him, and therefore she prevails.
3   That man is most able to bear with humility the joy of victory who endured the conflict by faith; he will give all the glory to God.
4   Other graces do wonders, but faith does impossibilities. She is the only grace that can act in certain places, and under certain circumstances. She is intended for this very purpose.

## Faith wins her victories in God's appointed way

1   She uses no means of her own contrivance; she waits upon God for guidance.

2  She neglects not his appointments; she is not presumptuous.

3  When she uses the means, she does not despise them. She ungirds the sword, she follows the ark, she hears the rams' horns.

4  She is laughed at for seeming folly; but in her turn she smiles.

5  She does her Maker's will, and she expects the blessing, but all in an orderly way. That is no faith at all which believes and does nothing. We may not expect to be saved by faith, unless that faith pushes us on to run in God's way. Whether we seek salvation, the good of our friends, the stopping of evil or the destruction of our corruptions, let us seek it in the divinely appointed way.

## Faith wins her victories in God's time

1  She goes round Jericho thirteen times; she expects the wall will come down at last, so round and round she goes.

2  She expects that, on the Lord's appointed day, her sins will all be overthrown, and she thinks her work well repaid when she knows this will happen. Therefore is she persevering in the conflict.

## Application

Now let us apply these thoughts:

*To the pulling down of Jericho in our own hearts* We want to slay all the old sinful inhabitants, but the lofty wall stands firm. Let us have faith. Let us follow the ark. Let us hear the sound of the trumpets, even though they are only rams' horns. Let us go round the wall all the seven days, that is all the week, all the days of our life. Let us inwardly groan, but not grumble with our lips; and soon, when the ordained day arrives, the walls will tremble, we shall shout, and our enemies will be gone.

*To the pulling down of Jericho in the world* Sin has strong and lofty towers. The Tower of Babel, idolatry, etc., let us yet believe that these will tumble to the earth. Let us continue our rounds as minister, Sunday school teachers and Christian workers. Keep the poor rams' horns going; do your duty, and one day Jesus shall reign universally.

*To the pulling down of Jericho in this village* Dagon stands fast here; but the ark of God is come. The trumpeters of God have long blown the trumpet; the rams' horns are still sounding a loud rough blast. Many are following the ark, but the time for the complete victory has not quite come. Keep on, brethren, and give a great shout, all at once, by faith, and down will come the mighty walls

The Lord help us to believe his Word, and then fulfil to us his promises! Amen, through JESUS.

# Holiness demanded

'Holiness, without which no man shall see the Lord' Hebrews 12:14

### What are the signs which indicate that you do not have holiness?

(a) Four groups of people who try to get on without holiness
The Pharisee; the moralist; the experimentalist; and the opinionist.
(b) That you look back on your past life without sorrow
(c) That you look forward to future indulgence of sensual appetites with a delightful anticipation
(d) That your holiness is not uniform
(e) That you delight in other people's sins

### 'Without holiness, no man shall see the Lord'

Sinner, it is a settled matter with God that no one shall see him without holiness.

### A plea

I plead, in the place of Christ, with those who are lovers of gain, that they may change their minds while there is still time.

# Conversion

'Brethen, if any of you do err from the truth, and one convert him; Let him know, that he which converteth a sinner from the error of his way shall save a soul from death, and shall hide a multitude of sins' James 5:19–20

### A principle involved: instrumentality

1   Instrumentality is not necessary with God: God can, if he pleases, convert souls without any instruments whatsoever.
2   Instrumentality is very honourable to God, and not dishonourable. It is as honourable to God to convert by means of Christians and others as it would be if he should effect it alone.
3   Usually God does use instruments. In ninety-nine cases out of a hundred, God is pleased to use the instrumentality of his ministering servants, of his Word, of Christian people, or some other means to bring us to the Saviour.
4   If God sees fit to make use of any of us for the conversion of others, we must not therefore be too sure that we are converted ourselves.
5   If God in his mercy does not make us useful to the conversion of sinners, we are not therefore to say we are sure we are not children of God.

6   God by using us as instruments confers upon us the highest honour which men can receive.

### The general point

'He who converteth the sinner from the error of his way shall save a soul from death, and shall hide a multitude of sins.' People have been converted through a single word spoken, through a letter written, through the example of true Christians, through reading godly books or simple tracts, as well as through hearing God's Word preached.

### The application

He who is the means of the conversion of a sinner does, under God, 'save a soul from death, and hide a multitude of sins'.

Particular attention should be paid to backsliders: 'Brethren, if any of you do err from the truth, and one convert him.' Alas, the poor backslider is often the most forgotten. A member of the Church had disgraced his profession; the Church excommunicated him, and he was accounted 'a heathen man and a publican'.

# Christ is precious

'Unto you therefore which believe he is precious' 1 Peter 2:7

This was the theme of the first sermon I ever preached; I hope it is my theme now, and ever shall be, living, dying and glorified.

This is one of the texts from which everyone imagines he could preach; but which, for that reason, is all the more difficult to preach from to your satisfaction. However, if the Good Spirit will apply to your hearts my few homely thoughts, your being satisfied will not matter.

## A precious people

Not so in themselves, but quite the reverse; yet they are so in the eyes of their Lord and Saviour. They are his special favourites. They are his crown jewels.

They are all believers, whether they have great faith or little faith. They are not mere repeaters of creeds, but true, hearty believers in the Lord Jesus Christ.

It is only these precious people who are able to see the preciousness of Christ. Faith is indispensable to the enjoyment of Christ. Can a child know how precious is gold before he has been taught its value? Does the beggar in the street appreciate a picture by Raphael, or can the ignorant rightly estimate the value of learning?

Faith is the eyesight of the soul, whereby it discerns spiritual beauty. Faith is the mouth which relishes heavenly sweetness.

God has made faith the mark of his precious people, because it is a grace which greatly exalts God and, at the same time, abases the creature.

Precious are God's people, elect, redeemed, guarded, fed, nurtured, and at last glorified.

## A precious Christ

What need is there for me to enlarge here? We, who believe, know that Christ is precious.

*My Christ is more precious to me than anything that my fellow-creatures have*

1   I see some who live in palaces, sit on thrones, wear crowns, and feast on dainties. I have heard of Alexanders, Napoleons and Caesars; but I envy them not, for *Christ is more precious to me than all earthly dominion.*

2   I see others with great riches; they are afraid of losing what they have, yet they are groaning after more. They have many cares through their wealth, and they must leave it all one day; but Christ is better than all earthly riches. Shall I give up Christ for gold? No, for *Christ is more precious to me than wealth could ever be.*

3   Some people have noble minds; they long for knowledge, they toil that they may measure the earth, survey the heavens, read the lore of the ancients, dissolve minerals, etc., but *Christ is better to me than learning.*

4   Others pant for fame. I shall be forgotten, save by the few whose steps I guided in the path to heaven; but I weep not at that, for *Christ is more precious to me than fame.*

*He is more precious than anything I myself have*

1   If I have a home and a fireside, and feel a comfort in them, yet, if called to suffer banishment, I have a better home. *Christ is better to me than home.*

2   If I have relatives, mother and father, or faithful friends; these I value, and rightly, too. 'Tis a bitter pang to lose them, but *Christ is better than relatives or friends.* He is my Husband, my Brother, my Lover.

3   I have health, and that is a precious jewel. Take it away, and pleasures lose their gloss; but my Jesus is mine still, and *he is better than health; yes, life itself is valueless in comparison with him.*

When I consider the glory of his nature, the excellence of his character, the greatness of his offices, the richness of his gifts, surely he is indeed precious.

## A Precious experience

Merely to say that Christ is precious is nothing; but to know that he is precious, to feel it in truth, is everything. The reality of the experience here spoken of is attested by:

(a)  The self-denials of missionaries
(b)  The sufferings of martyrs
(c)  The deathbeds of saints

Have we felt it? If so, may we once more feel it at his table! Oh, to live ever with the taste of this honey in our mouths, to feast even on the name of our dear Redeemer!

O precious One, help! Help! Help!

# Particular election

'Wherefore the rather, brethren, give diligence to make your calling and election sure: for if ye do these things, ye shall never fall: For so an entrance shall be ministered unto you abundantly into the everlasting kingdom of our Lord and Saviour Jesus Christ' 2 Peter 1:10–11

## Calling

By the word 'calling' in Scripture, we understand two things – one, the *general call*, which in the preaching of the gospel is given to every creature under heaven; the second call (that which is here intended) is the *special call* – which we call the effectual call, whereby God secretly, in the use of means, by the irresistible power of his Holy Spirit, calls out of mankind a certain number, whom he himself has before elected, calling them from their sins to become righteous. The two callings differ very much.

## Make your calling and election sure

(a) Get out of an idle state
(b) Be diligent in your faith
(c) Get godliness
(d) Seek the Holy Spirit's patience

## Why you should make your calling and election sure

(a) It will make you so happy
(b) 'Ye will never fall'
(c) So you can have 'an abundant entrance into Christ's kingdom'

# Fellowship with the Father and the Son

'And truly our fellowship is with the Father, and with his Son Jesus Christ' 1 John 1:3

**What is this fellowship with the Father and the Son, which the apostles enjoyed and which they wished us to share with them?**

    (a)  Mutual communication
    (b)  Reconciled to God by the death of his Son
    (c)  Appreciation of the work they are doing
    (d)  Participation in the work they are doing
    (e)  Being mocked as Christ was mocked

**How may fellowship with the Father and with the Son be enjoyed in the celebration of the Lord's Supper?**

    (a)  By knowing that Christ's sacrifice was an absolute necessity
    (b)  So think about Christ's sufferings that you enter into his mind while he was suffering for you
    (c)  Glorify God concerning the death of Christ while we are at his table

# 'He cometh with clouds'

'Behold, he cometh with clouds; and every eye shall see him, and they also which pierced him: and all kindreds of the earth shall wail because of him. Even so, Amen' Revelation 1:7

**Our Lord Jesus comes**

    (a)  This coming is to be vividly realised

(b) This coming is to be zealously proclaimed

(c) This coming is to be unquestionably asserted

(d) This coming is to be taught as demanding our immediate attention

(e) He is already on the way

(f) His coming will be attended by a peculiar sign
'With clouds.' Clouds signify Jesus Christ's majesty, his might and the terror of his coming for the ungodly.

### Our Lord's coming will be seen by all

'Every eye shall see him, and they also which pierced him.'

(a) It will be a literal appearing

(b) He will be seen by all kinds of living men

(c) He will be especially seen by those who have pierced him.

### His coming will cause great sorrow

(a) This sorrow will be very general

(b) This sorrow will be very great

(c) Men will not be universally converted when Christ comes

(d) Men will not be expecting great things of Christ

(e) They must give an account of their unforgiven state

# To the church in Ephesus

'Nevertheless I have somewhat against thee, because thou hast left thy first love. Remember therefore from whence thou art fallen, and repent, and do the first works; or else I will come unto thee quickly, and will remove thy candlestick out of his place, except thou repent' Revelation 2:4–5

*Revelation 2:4–5*

## Introduction

It was the work of the priest to go into the holy place and to trim the seven-branched lamp of gold: see how our High Priest walks in the middle of the seven golden candlesticks: his work is not occasional, but constant. Wearing robes which are at once royal and priestly, he is seen lighting the holy lamps, pouring in the sacred oil, and removing impurities which would dim the light.

## Christ perceives

First, then, we notice that he perceives. Our Lord sorrowfully perceives the faults of his Church – 'Nevertheless I have somewhat against thee'; but he does not so look at these faults to miss what is admirable in the Church. For he begins his letter with commendations. 'I know thy works, and thy labour, and thy patience, and how thou canst not bear them which are evil.' Do not think, my brethren, that our Beloved is blind to the beauties of his Church. On the contrary, he delights to observe them. He can see the beauties where she herself cannot see them. Where we observe much to deplore, his loving eyes see much to admire. The graces which he himself creates he can always perceive. When we overlook them in the earnestness of self-examination, and write bitter things against ourselves, the Lord Jesus sees even in those bitter self-condemnations a life and earnestness and sincerity which he loves. Our Lord has a keen eye for all that is good. When he searches our hearts he never passes by the faintest longing, or desire, or faith, or love, of any of his people. He says, 'I know thy works.'

But this is our point at this time, that while Jesus can see all that is good, yet in staying faithful he sees all that is evil. His love is not blind. He does not say, 'As many as I love I commend'; but, 'As many as I love, I rebuke and chasten.' It is more important for us that we should discover our faults than that we should dwell on our virtues. So notice in this text that Christ perceives the flaw in this church, even in the middle of her earnest service. The church at Ephesus was full of work. 'I know thy works and thy labour, and for my name's sake thou hast laboured, and hast not fainted.' It was such a hard-working church that it pushed on and on with diligent perseverance, and never seemed to flag in its divine mission. Oh that we could say as much about all our churches! I have lived to see many brilliant projects started and left half-finished. I have heard about schemes which were to illuminate the world, but not a spark remains. Holy perseverance is greatly to be desired. During these past thirty-three years we thank God that he has enabled us to labour and not to faint. There has been a continuance of everything attempted, and no drawing back from anything. 'This is the work, this is the labour', to hold out even to the end.

Oh how I have dreaded lest we should have to give up any holy enterprise or cut short any gracious effort. Hitherto has the Lord helped us. With people and means, liberality and zeal, he has supplied us. In this case the angel of the church has been very little of an angel from heaven, but very much a human angel; for in the weakness of my flesh and in the heaviness of my spirit have I pursued my calling; but I have pursued it. By God's help I continue to this day, and this church with equal footsteps is at my side; for which the whole praise is due to the Lord, who does not grow tired or become weary. Having put my hand to the plough I have not looked back, but have steadily pressed forward, making straight furrows; but it has been by the grace of God alone.

Alas! Under all the labouring the Lord Jesus perceived that the Ephesians had left their first love; and this was a very serious fault. So it may be in this church; every wheel may continue to revolve, and the whole machinery of ministry may be kept going at its normal rate, and yet there may be a great secret evil which Jesus perceives, and this may be marring everything.

But this church at Ephesus was not only hard-working, it was patient in suffering and underwent great persecution. Christ says of it, 'I know thy works and thy labour, and thy patience, and how thou . . . hast borne, and hast patience . . . and hast not fainted.' Persecution upon persecution visited the faithful, but they bore it all with holy courage and constancy, and continued still confessing their Lord. This was good, and the Lord highly approved it, but yet underneath it he saw the tokens of decline; they had left their first love. So there may seem to be all the patient endurance and dauntless courage that there should be, and yet as a fair apple may have a worm at its core, so may it be with the Church when it looks best to the eye of friends.

The Ephesian church excelled in something else, namely, its discipline, its soundness in the faith and faithfulness towards heretics; for the Lord says of it, 'How thou canst not bear them which are evil'. They would not have it: they would not tolerate false doctrine, they would not put up with unclean living. They fought against evil, not only in the common people, but in prominent individuals. 'Thou hast tried them which say they are apostles, and are not, and hast found them liars.' They had dealt with the great ones; they had not flinched from the unmasking of falsehood. Those who seemed to be apostles they had dragged to the light and discovered to be deceivers.

This church was not honeycombed with doubt; it laid no claim to breadth of thought and liberality of view; it was honest to its Lord. He says of it, 'This thou hast, that thou hatest the deeds of the Nicolaitans, which I also hate.' This was to their credit, as it showed a backbone of truth. I wish some of the churches of this age had a little of this holy decision about them; for nowadays, if a person is clever, he may preach the vilest lie that was ever vomited from the mouth of hell, and it will go down with some. He may assail every doctrine of the gospel, he may blaspheme the Holy Trinity, he may trample on the blood of the Son of God, and yet nothing is said about it if he is held in high esteem as a man of advanced thinking and liberal ideas. The church at Ephesus was not of this mind. She was strong in her convictions; she could not yield the faith, nor play the traitor to her Lord. For this her Lord commended her: and yet he says, 'I have somewhat against thee, because thou hast left thy first love.' When love dies orthodox doctrine becomes a corpse, a powerless formalism. Adhesion to the truth sours into bigotry when the sweetness and light of love to Jesus depart. Love Jesus, and then it is well to hate the deeds of the Nicolaitans; but mere hatred of evil will tend towards evil if love of Jesus is not there to sanctify it. I need not make a personal application; but what is spoken to Ephesus may be spoken at this hour to ourselves. As we hope that we may appropriate the commendation, so let us see whether the expostulation may not also apply to us. 'I have somewhat against thee, because thou hast left thy first love.' Thus I have shown you that Jesus sees the evil beneath all the good: he does not ignore the good, but he will not pass over the ill.

So, next, this evil was a very serious one. It was love in decline: 'thou hast left thy first love'. 'Is that serious?' asks someone. It is the most serious illness of all; for the Church is the bride of Christ, and for a bride to fail in love is to fail in all things. It is idle for the wife to say that she is obedient, and so forth; if love for her husband has evaporated, her wifely duty cannot be fulfilled, she has lost the very life and soul of the marriage state. So, my brethen, this is a most important matter, our love for Christ, because it touches the very heart of the communion with him which is the crown and essence of our spiritual life. As a church we must love Jesus, or else we have lost our reason for existence. A church has not reason for being a church when she has no love within her heart, or when that love grows cold. Have I not reminded you that almost any disease may be hopefully endured except the disease of the heart? So when our sickness is heart disease, it is full of danger; and it was so in this case. 'Thou hast left thy first love.' It is a disease of the heart, a central, fatal disease, unless the great Physician intervenes and delivers us from it. Oh, in any man, in any woman, in any child of God here, let alone in the Church as a whole, if there is a leaving of the first love, it is a woeful thing! Lord have mercy upon us: Christ have mercy upon us: this should be our solemn litany at once. No peril can be greater that this. Lose love, lose all. Leave our first love, and we have left strength, and peace, and joy, and holiness.

I call your attention, however, to this point, that it was Christ who found it out. 'I have somewhat against thee, because thou hast left thy first love.' Jesus himself found it out! I do not know how it strikes you; but as I thought it over, this fact brought tears to my eyes. When I begin to stop loving Christ, or love him less than I should, I would like to find it out myself; and if I did so, there would soon be a cure for it. But for him to find it out, oh, it seems so hard, so sad a thing! That we should keep on growing cold, and cold, and cold, and never care about it until the Beloved points it out to us. Why even the angel of the church did not find it out; the minister did not know it; but he saw it, who loves us so well that he delights in our love, and pines when it begins to fail. To him we are unutterably dear; he loved us up out of the pit into his heart, loved us up from the dunghill among beggars to sit at his right hand upon his throne; and it is sorrowful that he should have to complain about our cooling love while we are utterly indifferent to the matter. Does Jesus care more about our love than we do? He loves us better than we love ourselves. How good of him to care one jot about our love! This is no complaint of an enemy, but of a dear wounded friend.

I notice that Jesus found it out with great pain. I can hardly conceive a greater grief to him as the husband of his Church than to look her in the face and say, 'Thou hast left thy first love.' What can she give him but love? Will she deny him this? A poor thing is the Church left to herself: her Lord married her when she was a beggar; and if she does not give him love, what has she to give him? If she begins to be unfaithful in heart to him, what is she worth? Why, an unloving wife is a foul fountain of discomfort and dishonour to her husband. O beloved, shall it be so with thee? Will you grieve Emmanuel? Will you wound your Well-beloved? Church of God, will you grieve him whose heart was pierced for your redemption? Brother, sister, can you and I let Jesus find out that our love is departing, that we are ceasing to be zealous for his name? Can we wound him so? Is not this to crucify the Lord afresh? Might he not hold up his hands this morning with fresh blood on them, and say, 'These are the wounds which I received in the house of my friends. It was nothing that I died for them, but is it not terrible that, after having died for them, they have failed to give me their hearts?' Jesus is not so sick of our sin as of our lukewarmness. It is a sad business to my heart; I hope it will be sad to all whom it concerns, that our

295

Lord should be the first to spy out our declines in love.

The Saviour, having thus seen this with pain, now points it out! As I read this passage over to myself, I noticed that the Saviour had nothing to say about the sins of the heathen among whom the Ephesians lived. They are alluded to because it must have been the heathen who persecuted the church, and caused it to endure and exhibit patience. The Saviour, however, has nothing to say against the heathen; and he does not say much more than a word about those who are evil. These had been thrown out, and he merely says: 'Thou canst not bear them which are evil.' He denounced no judgment upon the Nicolaitans, except that he hated them; and even the apostles who were found to be liars, the Master dismisses with that word. He leaves the ungodly in their own condemnation. But what he has to say is against his own beloved: 'I have somewhat to say against thee.' It seems as if the Master might pass over sin in a thousand others, but he cannot wink at failure of love in his own married one. 'The Lord thy God is a jealous God.' The Saviour loves, so that his love is cruel as the grave against cold-heartedness. He said of the church of Laodicea, 'I will spue thee out of my mouth.' This was one of his own churches, too, and yet she made him sick with her lukewarmness. God grant that we may not be guilty of such a crime as that!

The Saviour pointed out the failure of love; and when he pointed it out he called it by a lamentable name. 'Remember therefore from whence thou art fallen.' He calls it a fall to leave our first love. Brothers, sisters, this church had not been licentious, it had not gone over to false doctrines, it had not become idle, it had not been cowardly in the hour of persecution; but this one sin summed up the whole – she did not love Christ as she once loved him, and he calls this a fall. A fall indeed it is. 'Oh, I thought,' someone says, 'that if a member of the church gets drunk that would be a worse fall.' That is wrong. But it is a fall if we become intoxicated with the world and lose the freshness of our devotion to Jesus. It is a fall from a high estate of fellowship to the dust of worldliness. 'Thou art fallen.' The word sounds very harsh in my ears – no, not harsh, for his love speaks it. But it thunders deep down in my soul. I cannot bear it. It is so sadly true. 'Thou art fallen.' 'Remember from whence thou art fallen.' Indeed, O Lord, we have fallen when we have left our first love for thee.

The Master evidently counts this decline of love to be a personal wrong done to himself. 'I have somewhat against thee.' It is not an offence against the king, nor against the judge, but against the Lord Jesus as the husband of the Church: an offence against the very heart of Christ himself. 'I have somewhat against thee.' He does not say, 'Thy neighbour has something against thee, thy God has something against thee,' but 'I, I thy hope, thy joy, thy delight, thy Saviour, I have this against thee.' The word 'somewhat' is an intruder here. Our translators put it in italics, and well they might, for it is a bad word, since it seems to make a small thing of a very grave charge. The Lord has this against us, and it is no mere 'somewhat'. Come, brothers and sisters, if we have not broken any law, nor offended in any way in grieving another person, this is sorrow enough, if our love has grown in the least degree chill towards Christ; for we have done a terrible wrong to our best friend. This is the bitterness of our offence: Against thee, thee only, have I sinned and done this evil in thy sight, that I have left my first love. The Saviour tells us this most lovingly. I wish I knew how to speak as tenderly as he does; and yet I feel at this moment that I can and must be tender in this matter, for I am speaking about myself as much as about anybody else. I am grieving, grieving over some who are present this morning, grieving for all of us, but grieving most of all for myself, that our Well-beloved should have reason to say, 'I have somewhat against thee, because thou hast left thy first love.'

So much for what our Lord perceives. Holy Spirit, bless it to us!

### Christ prescribes

And now, second, let us note what the Saviour prescribes. The Saviour's prescription is couched in these three words: 'Remember', 'Repent', 'Return'.

297

*Remember* 'Thou hast left thy first love.' Remember, then, what thy first love was, and compare your present condition with it. At first nothing diverted you from your Lord. He was your life, your love, your joy. Now you look for recreation somewhere else, and other charms and other beauties win your heart. Are you not ashamed of this? Once you were never tired with hearing about Christ and his gospel: many sermons, many prayer-meetings, many Bible readings, and yet none too many. Now sermons are long, and services are dull, and you must have your jaded appetite excited with novelties. How is this? Once you were never displeased with Jesus whatever he did with you. If you had been sick, or poor, or dying, you would still have loved and blessed his name for all things. He remembers this fondness, and regrets its departure. He says to you today, 'I remember you, the kindness of your youth, your love when you searched after me in the wilderness.' You would have gone anywhere after your Lord in those days: across the sea or through the fire you would have pursued him; nothing would have been too hot or too heavy for you then. Is it so now? Remember! Remember from what you have fallen. Remember the vows, the tears, the communions, the happy days; remember and compare them with your present state.

Remember and consider that, when you were in your first love, that love was not so warm. Even then, when you did live to Christ, and for Christ, and with Christ, you were not so holy, not so consecrated, not so zealous. If you were not so advanced then, think about how you are now – now that you have come down even from that poor attainment? Remember the past with sad forebodings of the future. If you had come down from where you were, who is to tell you where you will end up falling to? He who has sunk so far may fall much further. Is it not so? Though you say in your heart, like Hazael, 'Is thy servant a dog?' you may turn out worse than a dog. You may prove to be a wolf! Who knows? You may even now be a devil! You may turn out to be a Judas, a son of perdition, and deny your Master, selling him for thirty pieces of silver. When a stone begins to fall it falls with an ever-increasing rate; and when a soul begins to leave its first love, it quits it more and more, and more and more, until at last it falls terribly. Remember!

*Repent* The next word in the prescription is 'Repent'. Repent as you did at first. The word so appropriate to sinners is appropriate for you, for you have grievously sinned. Repent of the wrong you have done your Lord by leaving your first love for him. If you could lead the life of a seraph, only breathing Christ's love, only existing for him, you would have done little enough. But to leave your first love, how grievously you have wronged him. That love was well-deserved, was it not? Why, then, have you left it? Is Jesus less fair than he was? Does he love thee less than he did? Has he been less kind and tender to you than he used to be? Say, have you outgrown him? Can you do without him? Have you a hope of salvation apart from him? I challenge you, repent of this evil towards One who has greater claim on your love than he ever had. He ought to be loved today more than you ever loved him at your best. O my heart, is not all this most certainly true? How badly you are behaving! How ungrateful you are. Repent! Repent!

Repent of much good which you have left undone through lack of love. Oh, if you had always loved your Lord at your best, what you might have known about him by now. What good deeds you might have done through the power of his love. How many hearts you might have won for your Lord if your own heart had been fuller of love, if your own soul had been more on fire! You have lived the life of a poor beggar because you have allowed such a poverty of love to take you over.

Repent! Repent! To my mind, as I thought over the text, the call for repentance grew louder and louder, because of the occasion of its utterance. Here is the gracious Lord, coming to his church and speaking to her angel in tones of tender kindness. He condescends to visit his people in all his majesty and glory, intending nothing but to manifest himself in love to his own elect as he does not to the world. And yet he is compelled even then to give a chiding, and to say, 'I have this against thee, because thou hast left thy first love.' Here is a love-visit clouded with a telling-off – a necessary telling-off. What a mischief sin has done. It is a dreadful thing that when Jesus comes to his own dear bride he should have to speak in grief, and not in joy. Must holy communion, which is the wine of heaven, be embittered with the tonic of expostulation? I see the upper springs of close fellowship, where the waters of life leap from their first source in the heart of God. Are not these streams most pure and precious? If a person drinks from this he will live for ever. Shall it be that even at the fountain-head they will be dashed with bitterness? Even when Christ communes personally with us must he say, 'I have somewhat against thee'? Break, my heart, that it should be so! Well may we repent with a deep repentance when our greatest joys are flavoured with the bitter herbs of regret, that our best Beloved should have something against us.

*Return* But then he says in effect, 'Return'. The third word is this – 'Repent, and do the first works.' Notice that he does not say, 'Repent, and get back thy first love.' This seems rather strange. But then love is the chief of the first deeds, and, moreover, the first deeds can only come from the first love. There must be in every declining Christian a practical repentance. Do not be satisfied with regrets and resolves. Do the first deeds; do not strain after the first emotions, but do the first deeds. No renewal is so valuable as the practical cleansing of our way. If the life is made right, it will prove that the love is so. In doing the first deeds you will prove that you have come back to your first love.

The prescription is complete, because the doing of the first works is meant to include the feeling of the first feelings, the sighing of the first sighs, the enjoying of the first joys: these are all supposed to accompany returning obedience and activity.

We are to return to these first deeds at once. Most people come to Christ with a leap; and I have observed that many who come back to him usually do so at a bound. The slow revival of one's love is almost an impossibility; as well expect the dead to be risen by degrees. Love for Christ is often love at first sight! We see him, and are conquered by him. If we grow cold the best thing we can do is to fix our eyes on him until we cry, 'My soul melted while my Beloved spake.' It is a happy circumstance if I can cry, 'Or ever I was aware, my soul made me like the chariots of Amminadab.' How sweet for the Lord to put us back again at once into the old place, back again in a moment! My prayer is that it may be so this morning with any declining person. May you so repent as not merely to feel the old feelings, but instantly to do the first deeds, and be once more as eager, as zealous, as generous, as prayerful, as you used to be. If we should again see you breaking the alabaster box, we should know that the old love had returned. May the good Master help us to do as well as ever, yes, much better than before!

Notice, however, that this will require a great deal of effort and warfare; for the promise which is made is 'to him that overcometh'. Overcoming implies conflict. Depend on it, if you conquer a wandering heart, you will have to fight for it. 'To him that overcometh,' he says, 'will I give to eat of the tree of life.' You must fight your way back to the garden of the Lord. You will have to fight against lethargy, against an evil heart of unbelief, against the numbing influence of the world. In the name and power of him who bids you repent, you must wrestle and struggle until you achieve the mastery over self, and yield your whole nature to your Lord.

So I have shown you how Christ prescribes. Now I wish to dwell with earnestness on the last part. I have no desire to say a word by which I should show myself off as an orator, but I long to speak a word by which I may prove myself a true brother pleading with you in deep sympathy, because in all the ill which I rebuke I mourn my own personal share. Bless us, O Spirit of the Lord!

## Christ persuades

Now see, brethren, Christ persuades. This is the third point: the Lord Jesus persuades his erring one to repent.

First, he persuades with a warning, 'I will come unto thee'; 'quickly' is not in the original, the Revised Version has left it out. Our Lord is generally very slow at the work of judgment: 'I will come unto thee, and will remove thy candlestick out of his place, except thou repent.' This he must do: he cannot allow his light to be apart from his love, and if the first love is left, the church shall be left in darkness. The truth must always shine, but not always in the same place. The place must be made fit by love, or the light will be removed.

Our Lord means, first, I will take away the comfort of the Word. He raises up certain ministers, and makes them burning and shining lights in the middle of his Church, and when the people gather together they are cheered and enlightened by their shining. A ministry blessed by the Lord is a singular comfort to God's Church. The Lord can easily take away that light which has brought comfort to so many: he can remove the good man to another sphere, or he can call him home to his rest. Death can put out the candle which now gladdens the house. The church which has lost a ministry by which the Lord's glory has shone forth has lost a good deal; and if this loss has been sent in chastisement for decline of love it is all the harder to bear. I can point you to places where once there was a man of God, and all went well; but the people grew cold, and the Lord took away their leader, and the place is now a desolation: those who now attend those courts and listen to a modern ministry cry out because of the famine of the Word of the Lord. O friends, let us value the light while we have it, and prove that we do so by benefiting from it; but how can we profit if we leave our first love? The Lord may take away our comfort as a church if our first zeal dies down.

But the candlestick also symbolises usefulness: it is that by which a church shines. The use of a church is to preserve the truth, wherewith to illuminate the neighbourhood, to illuminate the world. God can soon cut short our usefulness, and he will do so if we cut short our love. If the Lord is withdrawn, we can go on with our work as we used to do, but nothing will come of it: we can go on with Sunday schools, mission stations, branch churches, and yet accomplish nothing. Brethren, we can go on with the orphanage, the college, the colportage, the evangelistic society, the book fund and everything else, and yet nothing will be effected if the arm of the Lord is not made bare.

He can, if he wills, take away from the church her very existence as a church. Ephesus is gone: nothing but ruins can be found. The Lord can soon take away our candlesticks out of their places if the church uses her light for her own glory, and is not filled with his love. God forbid that we should fall under this condemnation. Of thy mercy, O Lord, forbid it! Let it not so happen to any of us. Yet this may occur to us as individuals. You, dear brother or sister, if you lose your first love, may soon lose your joy, your peace, your usefulness. You, who are now so bright, may grow dull. You, who are now so useful, may become useless. You were once an instructor of the foolish, and a teacher of babes; but if the Lord is withdrawn you will instruct nobody, you will be in the dark yourself. Alas, you may come to lose the very name of Christians, as some have done who once seemed to be burning and shining lights. They were foolish virgins, and before long they were heard to cry, 'Our lamps are gone out!' The Lord can and will take away the candlestick out of its place if we put him out of his place by a failure in our love for him.

How can I persuade you, then, better than with the warning words of my Master? My beloved, I persuade you from my very soul not to encounter these dangers, not to run these terrible risks; for as you would not wish to see either the church or your own self without God's light, to pine in darkness, it is necessary that you abide in Christ, and go on to love him more and more.

The Saviour holds out a promise as his other way of persuading. It seems a very wonderful promise to me: 'To him that overcometh will I give to eat of the tree of life, which is in the midst of the paradise of God.' Observe, those who lose their first love fall, but those who abide in love are made to stand. In contrast with the fall which took place in God's paradise, we have man eating from the tree of life, and so living for ever. If we, through grace, overcome the common tendency to decline in love, then we will be confirmed and settled in the Lord's favour. By eating from the tree of knowledge of good and evil we fell; by eating from the fruit of a better tree we live and stand fast for ever. Life proved true by love shall be nourished on the best of food; it shall be sustained by the fruit from the garden of the Lord himself, gathered by the Saviour's own hand.

Note again, those who lose their first love wander far, they depart from God. 'But,' says the Lord, 'if you keep your first love you shall not wander, but you shall come into closer fellowship. I will bring you nearer to the centre. I will bring you to eat from the tree of life which is in the middle of God's paradise.' The inner ring is for those who grow in love; the centre of all joy is only to be reached by much love. We know God as we love God. We enter into his paradise as we abide in his love. What joy is here! What a reward love has!

Then notice the mystical blessing which lies here, waiting for your meditation. Do you know how we fell? The woman took the fruit from the forbidden tree, and gave it to Adam, and Adam ate and fell. The reverse is the case in the promise in front of us: the Second Adam takes the divine fruit from the tree of promise, and hands it to his wife; she eats and lives for ever. He who is the Father of the age of grace hands down to us immortal joys, which he has plucked from an undying tree. The reward of love is to eat the fruit of life. 'We are getting into mysteries,' someone says. Yes, I am intentionally lifting a corner of the veil, and no more. I only mean to give you a glimpse at the promised boon. Into his innermost joys our Lord will bring us if we keep up our first love, and go from strength to strength therein. Marvellous things are locked up in the caskets whereof love holds the key. Sin set the angel with a flaming sword between us and the tree of life in the middle of the garden; but love has quenched that sword, and now the angel beckons us to come into the innermost secrets of paradise. We shall know as we are known when we love as we are loved. We shall live the life of God when we are wholly taken up with the love of God. The love of Jesus answered by our love for Jesus makes the sweetest music the heart can know. No joy on earth is equal to the bliss of being completely taken up with loving Christ. If I had my choice of all the lives that I could live, I certainly would not choose to be an emperor, nor a millionaire, nor a philosopher; for power and wealth and knowledge bring with them sorrow and travail; but I would choose to have nothing to do but to love my Lord Jesus – nothing, I mean, but to do all things for his sake, and out of love for him. Then I know that I should be in paradise, yes, in the middle of the paradise of God, and I should have meat to eat which is all unknown to the people of the world.

Heaven on earth is abounding love towards Jesus. This is

the first and last of true delight – to love him who is the first and the last. To love Jesus is another name for paradise. Lord, let me know this by continual experience. 'You are soaring aloft,' cries one. Yes, I own it. Oh, that I could allure you to a heavenward flight upon the wings of love! There is a bitterness in declining love: it is a very consumption of the soul, and makes us weak and faint and low. But true love is the foretaste of glory. See the heights, the glittering heights, the glorious heights, the everlasting hills to which the Lord of life will conduct all those who are faithful to him through the power of his Holy Spirit. See, O love, thine ultimate abode. I pray that what I have said may be blessed by the Holy Spirit so we all are brought closer to the Bridegroom of our souls. Amen.

# The need for purity in order to enter heaven

'And there shall in no wise enter into it any thing that defileth, neither whatsoever worketh abomination, or maketh a lie; but they which are written in the Lamb's book of life' Revelation 21:27

### The strictness of the law . . . 'any thing that defileth'

Satan cannot. Sin cannot. What a matter of rejoicing for Christians!

How can a person enter?

Not by ceremonies. Not by the law. Not by sincere obedience in part.

The heart must be purified.

All past sin forgiven. How? By free grace.

All present sin crucified. How? By the Holy Spirit.

All future sin avoided. How? By the Spirit's help.

**The impossibility of entrance . . . 'in no wise'**

God has said so. He will not allow it; nor will the angels; nor the redeemed. A wicked man would not be happy in heaven.

No prayers, cries, groans, strife, can get a dead, unholy sinner into heaven.

If a person is not in, he is out for ever, no coming in, no change.

Call to enter in by faith in Jesus Christ.

# Index

# *Index*

**NIV Bible Commentary**

*Edited by Alister McGrath*

*The highly acclaimed one-volume guide to God's Word*

A one-volume commentary written in a clear, accessible style with the minimum of theological jargon. Ideal for those just starting out on serious Bible study and wanting to gain a firmly established understanding of Scripture. Clearly introduces leading Bible themes, offering succint and informative comment for everyday reading of the Bible. Based on the New International Version but can also be used with other translations. Features maps and charts throughout.

*"An astonishing achievement and an invaluable resource ..."*
Nicky Gumbel

*"Probably the best one-volume commentary on the market – a sensible investment."*
Christian Herald

*"This commentary is informative, easy to read, and conveys much of the author's sense of wonder and delight in the Word of God."*
The Baptist Times

Paperback   ISBN 0 340 66142 9

**The NIV Study Bible**
*General Editor: Kenneth L. Barker*

The world's bestselling study Bible based on the NIV is ten year's old in 1997 and still as popular with Bible readers around the world.

This remarkable Bible includes:

*the acclaimed New International Version* the world's most popular modern English Bible translation
*20,000 study notes* which appear on the page to which they apply explaining words and concepts, interpreting difficult verses, and giving textual and historical background
*introductions and outlines* to every book in the Bible
*100,000 cross references* in a convenient central column
*100 maps and charts* placed throughout the test, including a colour map section with index at the back
*five essays* giving additional information on specific subjects
*subject index* to enable full use of the study notes
*comprehensive short concordance* with 35,000 entries

Cased   ISBN 0 340 41052 3

## NIV Thematic Study Bible
### General Editor: Alister McGrath

*The best commentary on Scripture is Scripture itself:*

*"I am an enthusiast for the NIV Thematic Study Bible ... because its maxim of letting Scripture explain Scripture is so completely right-minded ..."*

J I Packer

Using the *NIV Thematic Study Bible*, readers can:
*identify and explore the leading themes of Scripture
*see how themes interweave and develop through the Bible
*come into direct contact with and rapidly access the relevant Scriptures with the minimum of subjective comment

The *NIV Thematic Study Bible* has many unique features:
*over 120,000 theme references appear, over half of them in the margins of the Bible pages. These indicate the key themes of the Bible text and refer the reader to the Thematic Section of the Bible for detailed study

*over 2,000 themes appear in the Thematic Section. These include:
an explanation of each theme
key Bible references on the theme
cross references to related themes

*Themes are arranged in a nine-fold clasification system based on Scripture:

| | | |
|---|---|---|
| God | Creation | God's people |
| Jesus Christ | Humanity | The life of the believer |
| Holy Spirit | Sin and salvation | Last things |

*introductions to each book of the Bible, emphasising each book's themes
*almost 200 panels giving more detailed descriptions of key themes
*an alphabetical index of themes, panels and book introductions
*colour maps

Cased, blue    ISBN 0 340 56708 2
Calfskin, black   ISBN 0 340 65660 3

## The New International Version

First published in 1979, the NEW INTERNATIONAL VERSION has become the world's most popular modern English Bible translation.

More than 100 scholars from diverse denominational backgrounds worked for 15 years to complete this distinctive translation. Their principal concern was to be faithful to the original texts, and to reflect the literary and stylistic diversity within the Bible.

The result is a Bible eminently suitable both for private study and public reading.

All Popular editions feature:
*topical headings which enhance ease of reading and understanding
*poetic passages printed as poetry
*table of weights and measures
*explanations of original names, measures and phrases in the
*footnotes
*clear, readable print
*Bible Guide containing
  The Bible at a glance
  The land and people of the Bible
  Well-known events in the life of Jesus
  Plan of the Bible
  Key events in the Bible
  Bible maps

A large range of Bibles is available in the NIV, for more details contact your local bookshop or the publisher.